RENEWALS 458-4574

WITHDRAWN
UTSA LIBRARIES

When I Married My Mother

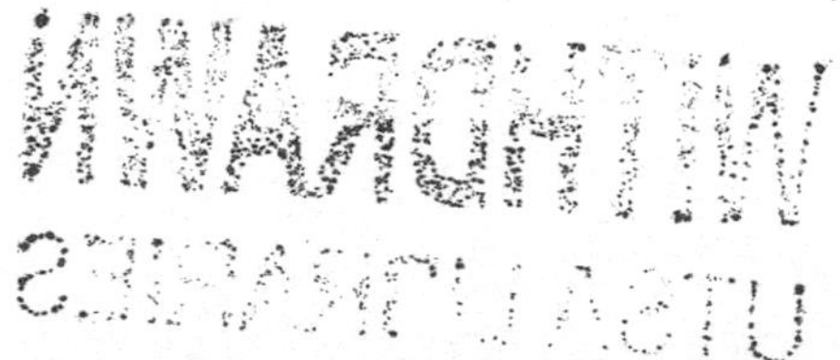

Library
University of Texas
at San Antonio

When I Married My Mother

A Daughter's Search
for What Really Matters —
and How She Found It
Caring for Mama Jo

JO MAEDER

DA CAPO PRESS
A Member of the Perseus Books Group

Library
University of Texas
at San Antonio

Copyright © 2009 by Jo Maeder

The lyrics from "Tight Connection to My Heart (Has Anybody Seen My Love)" by Bob Dylan are reprinted by permission: Copyright © 1985 Special Rider Music. All rights reserved. International copyright secured. Reprinted by permission.

All photos courtesy of the author; the author gratefully acknowledges the following for use of additional photos:

Chapter 24, page 227, Bill Stone Photography
Chapter 27, page 253, © Trina D. Olson
Chapter 31, page 289, Portrait Innovations

All rights reserved. No part of this publication may be reproduced, stored in a retrieval system, or transmitted, in any form or by any means, electronic, mechanical, photocopying, recording, or otherwise, without the prior written permission of the publisher. Printed in the United States of America. For information, address Da Capo Press, 11 Cambridge Center, Cambridge, MA 02142.

Designed by Trish Wilkinson
Set in 10.75 point Goudy by The Perseus Books Group

Cataloging-in-Publication data for this book is available from the Library of Congress.
ISBN: 978-0-3068-1795-3

Published by Da Capo Press
A Member of the Perseus Books Group
www.dacapopress.com

Da Capo Press books are available at special discounts for bulk purchases in the U.S. by corporations, institutions, and other organizations. For more information, please contact the Special Markets Department at the Perseus Books Group, 2300 Chestnut Street, Suite 200, Philadelphia, PA 19103, or call (800) 810-4145, ext. 5000, or e-mail special.markets@perseusbooks.com.

10 9 8 7 6 5 4 3 2 1

To all the mothers in my life,
past and present:
Julie, Charlotte, and, of course, Mama Jo

Before we begin . . .

Memoirists face an impossible task: to write a story that captivates strangers without alienating those we know, and often love, who are in the story. By changing a few identifying characteristics, and blending some events and conversations for continuity, it is my hope that I have achieved this delicate balance between disclosure and discretion. My tree man, however, really is named Forrest. I couldn't possibly come up with something better than that. Or "something butter," as he would say.

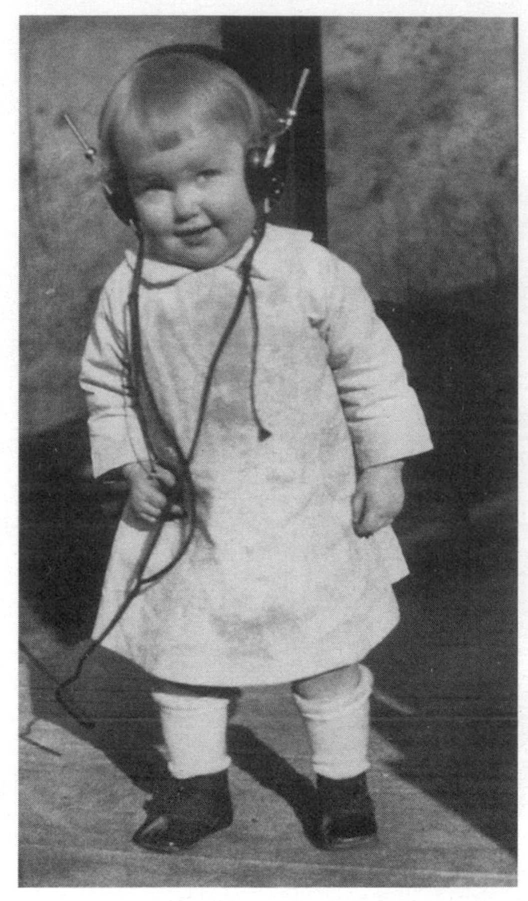

Mama Jo, early 1920s. My DJ DNA begins.

"Britney Spears" Spells "Presbyterians"

"Shoutin' out to the Bronx, Brooklyn, and Bayonne," I said with a smile in my voice to my radio audience of millions. "Here's the new Destiny's Child . . ." I paused to give their song just the right verbal frame and purred with all the naughtiness it deserved, "*Bootylicious.*"

I'd been a DJ since the decadent Miami disco days back in the late 1970s. At the time, I was the age of many of my current listeners. Now at forty-five, in another millennium, I wasn't sure if I was to be applauded or pitied for still being able to pull off this act. I reasoned I only appeared on Z100 on the weekends, so I wasn't hooked anymore. Kind of like someone who only smokes cigarettes they've bummed and says with total conviction that they've kicked the habit. During the week I was a proper, anonymous TV announcer.

I sang along with Beyoncé while I scanned MTV's Web site looking for something I could say over Missy Elliott's "Get Ur Freak On." I counted the minutes until I could blast J-Lo's "Let's Get Loud." After all these years, I still couldn't believe I was paid to do this. Being on the mighty "flame-throwing from the top of the Empire State Building" Z100 was not only fun, but it also gave me cachet with the successful set I hobnobbed with. Or, at least, with their kids, who listened to the station.

My days of living in an expensive Manhattan high-rise "kennel" were finally over. I now resided in a spacious, charming estate cottage in northern Westchester. I played softball at the home of a media mogul who had his own baseball diamond. I kept myself toned and full of the latest gossip at a pricey Pilates studio/torture chamber that was patronized by Bedford's best. I happily embraced the illusion that I was wealthy, too.

My personal life was never boring. I loved men and they loved me. It just never seemed to happen at the same time. But I was living in the land of endless sparkling possibilities. All would soon change. All would soon change.

As my last set of ads aired on Z100 that Saturday afternoon, my cell phone vibrated: Arthur, my only full sibling. He lived down South in a place called Green-Something and had become born-again. About all we had in common now was exasperation over what to do about our challenging mother.

I tried to hide my wariness when I answered, "Wassup!"

He sounded equally upbeat. "I'm calling to invite you to my wedding!"

I knew he had a special someone and that this was bound to happen, but it meant that I would not only have to endure an event I found as loathsome as lyrical, I'd also have to trek to Green-Something. The only time I'd been there was two years before to, reluctantly, witness Arthur's total-immersion baptism.

In my perky DJ voice, I commented, "That was fast."

"I picked my first wife. The Lord picked my second. You should try putting your faith in Him, too, Jo."

I answered through my teeth, "Yes, Arthur." I could not get used to hearing him talk like this.

"I know how hard it is to crowbar you out of there," he said, as I detected even more southern honeyness in his once-northern voice. "But it's in five months, which gives you plenty of time to work it into your busy schedule." He knew my usual excuses so well. "It'd shore mean a lot to me if you could make it."

My eyes darted around as I tried to process what he was saying, survey several computer screens and digital clocks, and formulate in my head what I was going to say next on the radio and to him. "Where do I fly into again?"

He chuckled. "Greensboro only has one airport. It's not like New York."

Right—Greensboro! I recalled from my one visit there that the airport was so small, it only cost Arthur a quarter to park in a space that was just a few steps from the terminal. Meanwhile, I'd paid fifty bucks to keep my car at the New York airport for two days and had to use a shuttle bus in the process as well. Did he ever gloat over that. But he had to live in Green-Something. So there.

Trying to sound enthusiastic, I said, "I promise I'll be there." For one day.

"Great!" He cleared his throat, which put me on alert. "Ah, do you think you could pick up Mama Jo?"

Suddenly, I was no longer on the Z100 airwaves or aware of his voice. I gripped the phone and let out the Mama Jo Groan—a guttural, agonizing sound only she could provoke in us. It was similar to the one you make when you've locked your keys in the car or computer gremlins have devoured an important file. I'd have to fly into Richmond, Virginia, then drive to Greensboro, North Carolina, four hours away, then back to Virginia, then fly home to New York. That wasn't even the hard part. It was prying my mother out of her junk-filled house, getting to the wedding on time, and getting back to Richmond to catch my flight.

Mama Jo wasn't just messy; she was a world-class hoarder. And doll collector. Many of her life-sized ones were sprawled on top of piles of boxes, eyes staring at the ceiling, limbs stiff, like earthquake victims. I pictured myself sitting in her dark, depressing house, waiting for hours, breathing in musty air, while she locked herself in her bathroom and refused to budge, as she had done regularly since I was a child. She was ten times worse now. So was I in my ability to deal with someone who refused to get help, or accept it.

"Arthur," I whined, "please, not that. Anything but that."

"Come on," he said encouragingly. "You're the straphanger." His word for a New Yorker. "The daughter of a marine."

And not just any marine. Our father had dropped out of high school to enlist at age sixteen, fought in the Banana Wars and

World War II (including the brutal battles of Peleliu and Iwo Jima). He received two Purple Hearts. He'd earned his diploma through night school and rose to the rank of lieutenant colonel, just two grades below brigadier general, without any formal training as an officer. He now rested in Arlington National Cemetery. He wasn't able to manage our mother either. They eventually divorced.

"Can't someone else pick her up?" I asked. "Like your daughter?"

"She just totaled her car. I don't think soooo."

It struck me that the pressures of my go-go New York life were nothing compared to being the father of a defiant teen with a newly minted driver's license.

"Neither you nor Mama Jo made my first wedding," Arthur said petulantly.

In retrospect, my not taking time off from college to be there for him, and Mama Jo not making it because her second husband got drunk while she dillydallied, was pathetic. Our family ties were like wisps of a cotton puff that couldn't hold a single thing together. As far as I was concerned, the less we saw of each other, the better.

"What about the train?" I asked. "That's how she made it to your baptism."

"With Mike's help," he pointed out, referring to Mama Jo's saint of a neighbor. "She's almost eighty. You know she'll never get there without him."

How could I possibly be old enough to have a mother that old? And it was her own fault that Mike wasn't her good friend (wink, wink) anymore. Why did I have to deal with this?

"Janet's family will all be there." Arthur was getting emotional now, another sign my brother had really changed since getting that old-time religion. I envisioned him standing in his kitchen with a beer in one hand and his ample belly pushing out a T-shirt that paid homage to the Redskins (he hadn't severed all of his ties with our D.C. roots, nor those with his favorite beverage—though his consumption wasn't nearly what it used to be).

"Shit!" I yelled, forgetting I wasn't supposed to swear in his presence anymore. I threw the phone down, grabbed my headphones, and said on the air just as "Oops! . . . I Did It Again" started, "Did you know if you rearrange the letters in 'Britney Spears' it spells 'Presbyterians'?" Britney moaned right at that moment. Yes! It still felt great to hit the "post" in a song's intro. I turned up the inner juice and said, "Dave Stevens is next with your 'N Sync tickets on Z . . . one . . . hundred!"

I zipped the microphone fader down and high-fived the fresh-faced Dave, who had just walked in. Only another DJ truly understands the thrill of a song's vocal starting the microsecond you stop talking, but Dave didn't look in high spirits. I clutched my cell to my chest and asked him what was wrong.

He grumbled, "I'm not the youngest ZJ anymore."

"Sure, Dave." I took off the reading glasses that were hanging from a chain around my neck. "You're barely in your twenties."

"They just hired someone for weekends who's nineteen."

The stinging realization that I'd stayed at this party way too long burned into me harder than a saline injection for spider veins. But I'd rather not DJ at all than work at the kind of "age-appropriate" station you hear while getting your teeth cleaned. Nor could I go back to my last on-air incarnation: the miniskirted, wild wig–wearing "Rock and Roll Madame" on the classic rock station. I'd left that job after five years because I was bored out of my gourd. Most of the artists were either disbanded or dead. What would I talk about now if I resurrected that persona—how much Pink Floyd memorabilia was going for on eBay?

I folded my reading glasses and vowed never to be seen wearing them on the premises again. Slinging my large black leather purse that doubled as a portable office over my shoulder, I went back to my phone call. In a faraway voice I said to my brother, "Sorry about that."

"You sure know all the cool trivia, don't you?"

"What do you mean?"

"'Britney Spears' spells 'Presbyterians.'"

"Oh, yeah, that. Well, it stuck in my head because that's how we were raised."

Mama Jo was none too pleased when her son became a Baptist, which confounded me. I'd asked her, "Wouldn't you rather he embrace some form of Christianity than none?" She had just shaken her head. I wasn't sure if her disapproval was directed at him for leaving the fold or at me for not comprehending the gravity of what he had done. Probably both.

Personally, I didn't reject religion. I just refused to align with a particular faith in the same way I refused to align with a particular political party. I was registered as "Unaffiliated." Even "Independent" was too much of a commitment.

"So tell me more about the wedding," I said to my brother as I scribbled my illegible signature on the engineering log and briskly left the studio with a fake happy wave to the young buck Dave, whom I still wanted to punch in the nose for telling me about the even younger new-kid-on-the-mike.

Arthur, like a lawyer building a case, said firmly, "Janet's waited forty-three years for this day, and we're going all out. There'll be about three hundred guests."

Instead of leaving the station, I plopped down on the couch where famous guests were afforded a spectacular view of Manhattan before appearing on the Z100 airwaves. "Three hundred?" The wedding being Janet's first was also a surprise. My notion of the South was that people got hitched the day they got out of high school.

I found myself privately scheming. If I shuttled Mama Jo through two states for this, I'd be set in the family-obligations department for at least another five years. "Arthur, I'll do it. Even if it takes TNT to blast her out of that house."

"Thank you." His relief was unmistakable. "I prayed with all my heart that you'd take this on. If cost is an issue, let me know. I'll be glad to help." My brother was a notorious tightwad. What was next, divinity school?

"No," I said, "that won't be a problem."

"Just make sure you get there the day before," he commanded. "Don't leave Richmond the day of the wedding." His voice rose a full register when he said, "You know how she is."

I was glad he found it amusing when I said, "You sound just like Poddy."

Poddy was a name for our father that Arthur came up with as a cross between "Poppa," what we called him, and "Daddy," what our friends called their own fathers. Arthur had said, "Poppa sounds so old." I couldn't believe our dad went along with it, but he was in his fifties then and often mistaken as my grandfather. He must have preferred being called Poddy to being called old.

My brother and I ended our call, and I filled out a vacation request form before it slipped right out of my middle-aged mind. Afterward, I stayed uncharacteristically motionless as I stared out at the massive skyline before me and thought, Damn! Within three years of ending a marriage that had lasted the same length as our parents' (twenty years), Arthur had managed to find what I'd spent a decade and a small fortune in therapy looking for after my divorce: a new permanent mate. Could it really be as simple as becoming born-again? I didn't buy it. My aunt Julie on my father's side and her lifelong partner, Charlotte, weren't deeply religious, and they were my role models for couplehood and just plain living in general. And I knew plenty of (okay a few) happy heterosexual couples who weren't "Bible thumpers," as our father would have called his own son now, were he alive.

My ex-husband had said after we formally parted, "We had a good five years together, didn't we, Peaches?" Yes, we did—until he turned into my mother. She collected dolls; he collected comic books. He would take forever to pay bills (unless they pertained to buying comic books); she would take forever to get ready to go anywhere. They were both loners and, I suspected, depressed. Yet I hadn't seen their similarities initially. I now recoiled from anyone who collected anything that took up physical space. The only obsession I condoned was my own: I was an insatiable, stockpiling Story Junkie. Start telling me a good tale, and I turn into a salivating dog that's caught the scent of sirloin.

I'd recently said to my therapist, "I don't get it. The first chance I had to break away from Mama Jo, I took it. Yet I keep being attracted to men like her." Men who were there but not there, who said they loved me but had too many problems of their own to make me feel it. Almost all of them had one thing in common with Mama Jo: they had lost their fathers when they were young (literally or figuratively), they had no brothers, and their mothers never remarried—or at least not while the sons still lived at home. They became the man of the house way before they were ready, and they both loved it and resented it. Hello, chronic flaky behavior. This was also a mirror image of my own life if the genders were switched. I'm the first to admit I can easily implode when too much is expected of me.

"You haven't resolved your abandonment issues," my therapist had said.

Everyone I knew in therapy (which was pretty much everyone I knew) was talking about abandonment issues. I was sick of hearing about it. Plus, I felt my family had abandoned Mama Jo, not the other way around.

Aunt Julie had disagreed with me on that point. "Your mother didn't even fight for you in the divorce. What mother doesn't fight for her children?" A depressed one who knew her children would rather be with their father, that's who.

"I have guilt issues!" I had insisted to my therapist.

"And you may have an unresolved Oedipal complex," she had said. "You were at the critical age of fourteen when you won your father from your mother in their divorce. That's why men who are stable and always there for you—as your father was—don't appeal to you. You aren't supposed to be attracted to Daddy."

So, in other words, I was doomed.

Twilight was now beginning to settle over the city, and a fascinating reverse image of what I saw in the daytime was beginning to emerge as countless lights turned on. Dave Stevens played back a silly call from a listener. I saw my reflection in the window as I happily listened along with the phone bit. Though I still wore a size 6 and sported a hip, mostly black and animal print wardrobe, I could have been Dave Stevens's mother. What could I do to not look it? Get tattoos and body piercings? Date men half my age?

As I left the premises, a new Aerosmith song filled the hallways that were covered with platinum records. I sang along and felt the familiar rush of arrested adolescence. Was I any different from an aging rock group still crankin' out albums and touring? Or doll nuts and comic book fans forever clinging to their youth?

Radio had been my first true, irrational, giddy love that blossomed when I was a child, when I believed that there were actually little people inside the radio singing. It was consummated at my college radio station the first time I spoke into a microphone. Like any long-term romance, it just wasn't the same now.

I mentally fast-forwarded and tried to see myself as an octogenarian. Would I end up as eccentric, unhappy, and alone as my mother? I was starting to feel the edges of my sanity fray as my usual optimism about the future quietly did a "cold fade," like the final E-major chord of the Beatles' "A Day in the Life," which lasts for more than a minute. What could I do now to make sure that this Big Apple woman fell as far as possible from the twisted tree that was her mother? I felt such pity for her. And anger. And sorrow. I felt put upon, yet I hadn't done a thing. It was becoming increasingly clear that she was slipping into She Can't Live Alone Anymore Land. What could I do? I had to be in New York for my work . . . I had to be here for Julie and Charlotte, the ones who had really been there for me since I was a teenager . . . My mother wouldn't accept help even if it was offered . . . I had to think of my own future.

T minus five months and counting to Arthur's wedding and getting my mother there. All I could think of was one of our father's favorite sayings: "I smell f#&k up."

Me, in Alaska, 1960, playing with my favorite toy

The Return of the Six-Armed Man

As the day of my departure for Richmond drew closer, long-forgotten memories burbled up. Many of them I wanted to erase and record over like an embarrassing videotape. I even remembered a nightmare I kept having when I was in the first grade.

The Federal Aviation Administration, my father's employer after his long stint in the marines, had transferred him to Anchorage, Alaska, in 1959, the year it became the forty-ninth state. It was seen as the equivalent of combat duty for the government; he'd pay his dues for two years and then come back to a better job if he proved himself.

I was only five the summer we left Alaska to go back to the D.C. suburbs, but I somehow knew the good times were over. I pressed my face and hands against the cold window of our droning prop airplane as we rose above perpetually snow-covered mountains and glistening glaciers and felt for the first time the sensation of my heart being pulled out of my chest, as though it had a mind of its own. I blubbered through my tears, "I'll be back 'Laska. I'll be back."

I looked down and thought of the mountain streams where we had panned for gold, the greenhouse in our backyard with its intense earthy smells, and a large moose antler we had discovered when the snow melted. I spent hours and hours sitting in it with my friends and pretending it was a boat, a car, or a magic carpet. My mother called it "a place to dream in the sun." Some other kid would enjoy it now. I missed my friends, too. I stayed plastered to the airplane window that day, focusing on Alaska until it completely receded from my sight, as if by staring at it I could keep it from disappearing.

Once in Virginia, we settled into a house by a major road with a lot of traffic. I hated it until I saw that there were woods behind it. I fearlessly explored them and was instantly transported back to Alaska. I would hunt for box turtles and interesting rocks. I'd sit quietly and study the birds in the trees. I'd fill my lungs with the lush air.

My happiness would subside when I came back inside. My father asked me, "What happened to my queen of the Yukon?" I flatly replied, "She's still in the Yukon."

By the time my first day of first grade rolled around, I had just turned six and was in better spirits. I was going to "real" school in a brand-new outfit. Then I got on the bus to take me there. In Alaska, my mother had walked me to my small kindergarten class. Now I had to ride in this big, loud, raucous thing. Worse, my brother, age ten, acted like he didn't know me and sat far away. I was a pip-squeak first grader and instantly felt my inferiority.

The elementary school had a student body that numbered more than a thousand. There was a long line of school buses in front, a crush of strange kids everywhere. The bathroom smelled of ammonia. The ringing of bells reminded me of boxing matches I'd seen on TV. I sat at my desk and cried for two weeks straight.

I was allowed to bring in a doll from home but kept crying because the kids teased me about it. Then I was put with a more experienced teacher. I don't know what she did, but she stopped the tears. It may have been as simple as my being put with a new group of kids who didn't know what a crybaby I was. It was my first taste of the power of starting anew.

Then the Six-Armed Man appeared.

I kept dreaming that a man with six arms was terrorizing the area where we lived. Despite my parents' assurances that there was no such menace, I was certain I'd be his next victim. Overnight I went from innocently playing in the woods behind our house to hiding in my room with the door locked.

This went on for weeks until one night I dreamed that a TV news anchor told viewers how to escape the Six-Armed Man. If you were attacked, just ask the creature, "What's that scar on your arm?" While he looked at each of his arms to figure out what you were talking about, you could safely escape. Just like that, I wasn't afraid of him anymore.

If only I could vanquish my middle-aged fears as easily, I thought, almost forty years later.

To take my mind off the impending doom that I kept feeling, I wondered what I was crying about back then. What did the Six-Armed Man represent? Was it the general upheaval of leaving Alaska and the loss of control over my life? Was it school? Did I miss my quirky older half-brother, George, and his funny faces that always made me laugh? He had gone off to college and left us. Was it from my father being gone most of the time now? Working in D.C. meant he had a long commute and a more demanding job. Each weekday morning, he'd stand outside our bedroom doors in his suit and tie while holding his briefcase and shout, "Up and at 'em! Up and at 'em! Up, up, up, up, up! Up, up, up, up, up!"

I'd hear his car door shut and the engine start, and through my bedroom window watch him leave. Then I'd make my way to the kitchen to turn on "The Joy Boys of Radio" on WRC. Arthur and I would plop Pop Tarts into the toaster and make ourselves glasses of orange-flavored Tang from a powder, the drink of the astronauts. At some point Mama Jo would appear. We were used to the fact that our mother didn't move at the same speed as the rest of the world.

My father would return in the evening, read the newspaper, and then watch Walter Cronkite's newscast, shushing anyone who tried to speak during it. We rarely ate together as a family, and when we did, we were allowed to get up whenever we finished as long as we followed the "wash and put" routine to rinse our dishes and place them in the dishwasher. I retreated to my make-believe world of books and TV shows filled with happy families that bore no resemblance to mine.

My mother retreated, too. She made a lot of trips to see her mother, Florence, who lived about thirty minutes away. Granny, my great-grandmother who had lived with Florence for thirty years, had died when we were in Alaska. Was losing her grandmother why Mama Jo seemed so unhappy, too? And why couldn't she get anywhere on time? She was always that way, but now it was worse. She had signed me up for dancing, modeling, and horseback riding classes to help me get over my "shyness." It was humiliating to arrive late, and terrifying on the way there. She'd drive like a maniac because she was running behind. We'd been in one car accident together, and she'd totaled another car when she was alone.

To distinguish me from my mother when I was a kid, I was called Jody. As to why I was named after my mother—her first and middle names—Mama Jo explained, "It was either that or Gertrude, after your father's mother." I grew up feeling like I was meant to be her clone. As I entered adolescence, it was obvious I was anything but that.

I slunk even further into my own world, a cynical hippie, blasting rock and soul music in my bedroom. Mama Jo, a long-standing member of the DAR, wanted me to join the CAR (Children of the American Revolution). No way. She wanted me to go to doll club meetings with her and my grandmother Florence. Absolutely no way. I loved dolls as a kid, but I'd grown out of that fixation like *normal* people should, especially when my teenage body looked nothing like my Barbie doll's. I also had terrible eyesight, and my teeth resembled a mako shark's.

Mama Jo would go through a painstaking ritual any time she bought a new doll. "The lips are better on this one," she'd say, after comparing it to one that looked exactly the same to me. She'd also examine its eyes, fingernails, and clothes, and would inspect it for any scratches or marks. What did she think of her far-from-perfect daughter?

I gave in to her request to join the Job's Daughters, the younger version of the Eastern Star that she and Florence belonged to, which was the female version of the Masons. I wanted it to make my mother happy, to let her win at least one battle. I was also curious to see why it was so secretive. I wasn't allowed to talk about what went on in a Job's Daughters meeting. I couldn't remember anything anyway other than having to wear white hose, white shoes, and a long white satin robe with a purple cord that crisscrossed my chest, march and turn corners in a certain way, and utter some mumbo jumbo. It reminded me of Fred Flintstone's Loyal Order of Water Buffaloes.

My father began having medical issues. He had pains in his legs that had something to do with his heart, and he'd begun shooting himself with insulin injections for his diabetes. One shelf in our refrigerator was filled with small glass vials. He said to me, "I'm not going to be around much longer." I was more worried about him than my mother seemed to be.

There were a couple of angry outbursts between my parents. It was so unusual to hear my mother raise her voice that it was funny and scary to me. One day my father sat us all down and announced, "I'm retiring and moving to Miami. I'm supposed to walk every day, and I'll be able to do it year-round there. Who wants to come?"

Are you kidding? No snow! Palm trees! And according to the announcer on the Jackie Gleason TV show that was taped there, "The Sun and Fun Capital of the World!" I immediately signed on. Arthur wasn't as easy to convince. He was graduating from high school and wanted to stay near his friends. Poddy promised him a new car if he went to college down there. While he publicly supported the Vietnam War, he didn't want his son to be killed in it. He also thought Arthur and I should stay together after Mama Jo said, "I'm staying here. I was almost swept up in a tornado when I was a kid, and I'm afraid of hurricanes."

I halfheartedly said, "You can prepare for a hurricane." That was the extent of my trying to change her mind.

I knew my parents weren't happy together. I'd never seen one sign of physical affection between them (or between any of us) my entire life. They hadn't slept in the same bedroom for several years. They said it was because of his snoring, but her hoarding had begun. Her bedroom was now filled with boxes and miscellaneous stuff. I suspected when she came in late at night that she had a boyfriend. It wasn't the first time I'd felt that.

Despite my optimism over moving to Miami, I was still a serious misfit. I vowed that I would never get married, never have children, never rely on a man to pay my bills after seeing my mother's postdivorce reversal of fortune, and I would kill myself when I turned thirty. Everyone over that age seemed miserable.

Aunt Julie and Charlotte changed my mind on the last one. They also, eventually, got me over my fear of crowds and urban madness by taking me into Manhattan to soak up art and theater. I hate to think how my life would have turned out had I not gotten to know these two cool ladies who lived in the woods and loved me as much as I loved them.

Arthur lasted about two years in Miami. He moved back to Virginia, to Richmond, to finish college. We were cordial, but never that close again.

Looking back to that time, I realize I was at the age when kids naturally pull away from their parents and siblings. It's part of becoming your own person. But I really pulled away from Mama Jo. And I was still annoyed at her for not being the mother I wanted her to be. I was sure that was never going to change.

3

Rescuer Syndrome

Mama Jo with her father, circa 1923

The day before Arthur's wedding, a familiar dread rose within me as I eyed Mama Jo's modest 1950s brick house in a sleepy suburb of the state capital of Virginia. She had moved here in the 1980s, after her second husband died, to be near Arthur and his new family. He looked after her and her house. Then his job took him to another city.

Now her grass needed to be cut. Overgrown bushes hid windows shaded with tightly closed venetian blinds. I braced myself for the gloomy world that awaited me.

Adding to my angst was that my mother had indignantly insisted that her eleven-year-old Ford Escort wagon ran just fine and I didn't need to rent a car. In New York I drove a sporty new Saab convertible. I guess I wanted to prove I didn't think I was better than she was, and that I still had faith she could take care of her life. I didn't rent a car. Her neighbor Mike gave me a lift from the Richmond airport.

I'd risen at four thirty that morning in order to fly down and pick her up. The plan would have stayed on course had my flight not been canceled right before I reached the airport. It was now late afternoon. I knocked and waited. Called out. Waited. At last I heard her inside fiddling with several locks and muttering, "Dammit . . . Dammit."

Once the door was open, I could tell she had aged in the two years since I had last seen her. A black cane supported her hunched-over frame. Her hair was flat and in need of a perm. Baggy jeans and a loose dark shirt hid her body, but I could tell from her face that she had lost weight. It was when we embraced and her head sank into my chest that I knew she was in steep decline. We had always been the same height. Now her back was so round, her ribs so bony; it was like putting my arms around a fragile birdcage.

As I kept hugging her, I saw her in my mind as she had once been—a voluptuous woman in a yellow dress that was tight at the waist and flowed out in pleats. Her wavy auburn hair was set with hairspray. Her full lips were coated in Avon's Crimson Beauty lipstick. That Mama Jo was long gone.

Patting her rounded back a couple of times, I cautiously asked, "Ready to go?"

"I thought we were going tomorrow."

I stopped patting and stiffened.

She snapped, "You said your flight was canceled and we'd go tomorrow."

"No, I didn't," I said, trying not to snap back. "I said I'd be late and to be ready when I got here so we could leave right away."

In my regulation New York uniform that consisted of black couture French pants, a black designer top, and black pointy-toed boots, I strode down Mama Jo's crowded corridor and stuck my head into her messy bedroom. At least she had an open suitcase on top of her bed in the little sliver of space left where she slept. It was a start. "You're almost packed!" I said approvingly.

"That's from my last trip. I haven't emptied it out yet."

Out came the Mama Jo Groan from deep within my throat. We were hours away from leaving. A lifetime of irritation over this chronic issue made every muscle in my neck tense and my shoulders rise.

"I can't find my lipstick," she said as though that explained everything.

She still couldn't go anywhere without her lipstick. Just like me. "Use mine," I curtly offered. "I have two shades."

"I want my own."

"They're Chanel," I said temptingly.

"I want my own."

My voice turned ugly again. "Maybe if you didn't have six different purses that all looked the same you might be able to find it. You only need one." As if she could ever part with any of them.

I surveyed the mess in her room: piles of boxes with dolls, teddy bears, and clothes strewn over them. A narrow pathway led from the door to the bed. This used to be the guest room. Her master bedroom and a second guest room were now so filled with who-knew-what that the doors wouldn't even open.

My gait slowed as I shuffled back down the dark hallway to the kitchen that still had a two-foot-high stack of empty single-serving cereal boxes in one corner and every surface covered with jars and cans and miscellaneous junk. In her refrigerator I found food that should have been thrown out long ago next to fresh milk, cream cheese, and English muffins. She was still able to drive and shop for herself, but her diet was obviously limited.

A formerly gaping hole where her stove used to sit was now filled with boxes, bags, and pots and pans. I had heard various reasons from others as to why she disposed of this major appliance: she saw a mouse in it, she was afraid of a gas leak, or she was mad at my brother, Arthur, for picking it out without consulting her. All she would tell me was, "I didn't like it, so I got rid of it." Now her hot meals were either delivered or heated up in a microwave.

Back in her bedroom, I said, "Okay, Mama Jo, I'm going out to get some coffee while you get packed. Do you want anything? Orange juice? How about bananas? You told me once you're supposed to eat one every day for the potassium."

"That sounds good," she said in a friendlier tone. "Let me give you some money."

"No, I've got it. I just need your car keys."

When she said, "I have to find them," I held in a groan. A sharp pain appeared in my temples.

While she looked, I simmered on a small area on her sofa that was the only place left to sit in her entire house. I scanned the scores of yellow plastic bags scattered about, filled with untouched newspapers. Atop a mountain of stuff across from me was a large doll—an old, overweight, buxom lady wearing roller skates and squeezed into a sequined tube top and hot pants. She kept eyeing me. I asked her, "What are you staring at, Grandma?" *You're talking to a doll, Jo.*

I turned my gaze to the left and saw mail, coupons, and flyers heaped on her small teak dining table and on the matching chairs. Behind me on a ledge stood a muscle-bound Arnold Schwarzenegger action figure about a foot tall with one bulging arm raised, palm open, as if he were blessing the wreckage before him.

My mother's hoarding tendencies had dramatically increased since her uncle Sid, slightly older than she, died three years before. Mama Jo and Uncle Sid had had a long-standing prickly relationship, yet they had politely surmounted their differences merely because there was no one left in the family from their generation and they lived so close to each other. Now that he was gone, she had only her friend Ginny, a woman in her fifties who collected dolls. Unfortunately, Ginny had her hands full with her own life and children. They didn't see each other that much. My mother just kept buying more stuff to fill the void within her.

Our present unproductive pattern continued as the clock ticked away. I'd pluck a newspaper out of a yellow plastic bag, do a crossword puzzle several months old, then offer to help my mother, then insist that I help her. "Dammits" would spit out of her mouth like little bullets. I'd do another puzzle and try to calm down.

I started coughing. If I became sick from breathing the bad air here, I was really going to be "p.o.'ed," as my mother would have said. My voice paid my exorbitant New York bills. No voice, no work.

I walked to the closed bathroom door and through it again asked Mama Jo where the car keys might be. "I've been up since 4:00 a.m., and we have a four-hour drive ahead of us. I need coffee!"

"I'll be out in a minute, dammit!"

Her dawdling was inflicted on everyone. One of her friends from long ago had informed me, "I once called her in the morning and invited her to lunch. We agreed she'd come to my place at noon. When three o'clock came and went, I called and asked, 'Are we having lunch in this lifetime or the next?'" She relayed the story to me as though she thought it was funny, but I wasn't surprised they weren't in touch anymore.

Sitting there amidst my mother's clutter, thinking about her sad existence and my beloved aunt Julie, who had suffered a massive stroke that left her mind scrambled and body crippled, I dissolved into tears. If only there was something I could do.

Mama Jo eventually came out of the bathroom, and I called from the sofa, "Did you find the keys?"

She stormed into the living room, picked up a stuffed black gorilla, hit a button on it, and stormed back out. I sat there with my mouth open while it played "Wild Thing." Yeah, Mama Jo, you make everything groovy. If only I could put batteries in *her* and push a button to get her going.

"You may have Rescuer Syndrome, Jo," my therapist had said in a recent discussion about my mother. "She can't be rescued. You need to look after yourself."

"But she's my mother," I had responded, on the verge of hysteria. "I have to help!"

She had warned, "I'm afraid the more you try to do for her, the more frustrated you'll become."

Like the last time I visited her. I filled twenty garbage bags with junk and dragged them to the curb. Her neighbor Mike e-mailed me later with the news that she'd dragged them all back in after I left. It was no wonder they weren't an item anymore. If only she'd gone on an antidepressant when Uncle Sid died. Or when my therapist had suggested it to her—after I brought her into a session saying it was to help me, not her. "She never followed through," my therapist said. "You can't change who she is."

I slumped back into my mother's cluttered sofa and softly moaned.

Finally she produced the keys to her car. I rushed out the door, into the front seat, and turned the ignition.

Nothing. Not a sound.

Grabbing the steering wheel, I shook it and screamed. Then I cursed—more at myself for not following my instinct and renting a car in the first place.

I trudged over to Mike's. He was around seventy, and his wife had died from Alzheimer's several years back. In his grief, and my mother's loneliness, they found each other and even visited me once in New York. I was thrilled that she had a companion—until Mike had a change of heart with, apparently, no explanation. My mother did not take it well, and having him right next door only made it worse. I was certain it was her chronic lateness and that messy house that sabotaged the relationship.

Or maybe Mike was just too laid back to even try to get her to change. He had a folksy, never-agitated voice and overall gentleness that must have made Mama Jo feel as though everything would be fine. He opened his door with a friendly smile, and I told him what was going on.

"She probably left the overhead light on again and the battery's dead," he said lightly. "Oh, boy."

I went into New York mode. "Is there someplace close where I can rent a car?"

We hopped into his near-vintage Cadillac Deville, his only possession that was remotely ostentatious. He wore simple, no-iron clothes, and sent me e-mails that covered what chores he did that day and descriptions of the food served at the Bull Roast at the Elks Lodge. I didn't tell my mother about these exchanges for fear she'd be jealous.

I rubbed the red leather seat and said, "There's nothing like an old-school Caddy."

"Yep. Put in a new transmission at two hundred thousand miles, but other than that, gosh, it's been great. I'm almost at three hundred now."

As we safely cruised along at the speed limit, I glowed from the feeling of floating on a cushion of air—even if we were creeping along, by my standards. I wanted to talk to him about what happened between him and my mom, but feared if I pushed it in my usual forthright manner, I might alienate him completely. I couldn't do that. I needed him to help with Mama Jo if her situation worsened. Rather, when it did.

And when it did, it wasn't a load I could share with my brother. He'd become the primary focus of our mother's fury. When she couldn't find something, which was often, she was sure he'd taken it. I tried to reason with her. "He doesn't live anywhere near you." Or, "Why would he steal a shoehorn? I'm sure he can buy one of his own." It made no difference. She didn't want rational explanations.

I called the groom-to-be to tell him the latest development. Arthur let out the Mama Jo Groan. "Come tomorrow," he wearily suggested. "You've had a long day."

"No," I insisted. "We'll will be there tonight."

I felt bad for Arthur. What was causing our mother's passive-aggressive antics this time? Did she not want to go to her son's wedding because she was still angry about his moving away from Richmond for a better job? Or was it the table and mirror she wanted that he had disposed of as executor of Uncle Sid's estate? She was still incensed about that. Arthur was right—there was no room for them in her house. She should be getting rid of junk, not adding to it. I explained to her that he was going through a lot himself at the time—a divorce, his company being sold and uncertainty over his job, trying to clean out and fix up Sid's house for it to be sold, and dealing with endless paperwork while living four hours away. Couldn't she show her son a little empathy? Nope.

It hit me as Mike and I made small talk on the way to the car rental office that the wedding could be reminding her that she hadn't married Mike, or wasn't attending it with him. The whole situation could be stirring up all kinds of blackness in her heart. I could very well be going to Greensboro on my own.

I rented a minivan and then realized that the seat would be too high for Mama Jo to negotiate. I wasn't used to thinking about another person's needs.

It was well after five when I pulled up to her house in a gold Monte Carlo. Not even a power nap and a gallon of coffee could give me the energy I needed to maneuver my mother out the door and drive for four hours. I dragged myself back over to Mike's.

"Could I stay in your guest room tonight?" I asked, clearly annoyed that we weren't taking off as planned.

"Sure!"

"First, though, I need dinner."

The last thing I wanted to do was go to a chain restaurant, but that was pretty much all the area offered. I'd spent time in the South of France over the summer and knew it was a long shot but asked anyway, "Do you know of any French restaurants around here?"

"Hmmm." He gave it some thought. "Actually, there's one that's supposed to be pretty darn good not even a mile away."

"Excellent. Would you like to join us? My treat."

He politely declined, and I headed off to prod my mother to get ready.

"Come on, Mama Jo!" I said to her brightly. "We'll pack later and leave early tomorrow."

"French? What kind of food is that?"

"Wonderful. You'll see. And you can wear one of your berets!" I made it sound like we were having a playdate. Won't it be fun!

Then I waited. And waited. And finally dozed off.

I knew the moment we walked into La Petite France that we were underdressed. The decor radiated class. The hostess was wearing a chic navy pantsuit and matching scarf swirled around her shoulders, in the way that only French women know how to do. With a delightful accent she welcomed us as if we were royalty and discreetly chose to focus on my mother's red beret instead of her stained pants and old sneakers.

I said to Mama Jo, "I don't care what this meal costs. We're livin' it up." She smiled in agreement. It was a great big smile that filled up the entire bottom half of her face and one I rarely saw. It caused me to respond in kind.

As the bubbly flowed, so did the cheer. We clinked our champagne flutes often. "To Arthur and Janet!" "To France!" "To Mama Jo!" "To Jo Junior!" When I added, "To Mike!" there was wistfulness in her response: "The best neighbor I ever had."

Not a barbarous remark was exchanged as we were doted on by the waiters and chatted up by the chef and greedily scarfed down seared foie gras and grilled fresh fruit, truffle-dusted wild boar carpaccio with tender arugula and dandelion, fresh Dover sole with almond effilées, and pan-roasted duck with fresh ginger and cherry-brandy peppercorn sauce. Mama Jo ate so much I wondered when she'd last had a good meal. When would be the next one after I left? This dinner was a Band-Aid on a situation that needed a body cast.

Family tradition added to my shame. Mama Jo had cared for her mother, and her mother had, in turn, cared for hers. I was Ms. Independent from a new generation. I lived far away. I had New York talent agents representing me, dah-ling. And my mother drove me nuts. I could never *ever* live with her, or leave New York.

"Mama Jo," I said earnestly as I leaned into the table covered with a crisp white linen cloth, "Julie's worse. She's lost a lot of weight. She can't do anything for herself." Even though my aunt was my surrogate mother for most of my life, Mama Jo never seemed to mind. She now looked genuinely concerned.

"I've been thinking about her," she said. "How's Charlotte doing?"

"Considering her age and what she's dealing with, great. But she asked me to look into nursing homes in case something happened to her and Julie had to be put somewhere."

I didn't tell my mother that I thought the places I saw were awful. There was, however, an old friend of Julie and Charlotte's who was in assisted living and loved it. "I think what Charlotte's doing for Julie is crazy," she'd said to me, full of energy, even with oxygen tubing in her nose. "No one should have to look after someone like that! It's just guilt." Since moving into her new home (or rather, room), she had discovered a talent for painting. Her walls were covered with her bright Fauvist-like pieces. I left her that day thinking maybe she was right. Assisted living wasn't that bad. A month later, a flu virus spread through her facility and she was dead.

Nevertheless, I had to have some kind of plan of action in place for Mama Jo. I looked at my mother across the table and put on my Public Service Announcer voice, the one a director might coax out of me with "Give me concerned, but not treacly." I said, "Maybe we should look at some places here just in case something happens to you. I worry about you constantly."

Her brow knitted, and she looked like she was going to choke. "I'm fine."

There'd been a story in the news recently about an elderly woman shooting and killing her daughter because she was threatening to put her in a home. Then I heard of another dauthter socking her aging mother in the jaw and knocking her out in order to extract her from her house. I wanted neither to hurt my mother nor to have her hurt me.

"What if you fall down like your aunt Gladys did? They didn't find her for three days." My stomach flip-flopped as I recalled that incident. Gladys had immediately been taken to a facility. When I visited her she was shrunken and lethargic, barely smiling through glazed eyes. She didn't live much longer. "If someone had been checking on her every day . . . Maybe someone should look in on you?"

"Like who?"

"There are people who do this for a living."

"I don't want any strangers in my house."

The truth was, neither did I. I'd heard plenty of stories of elder abuse or embezzlement by caregivers. A more immediate concern was where this person would sit if they were hired.

Breaking the somber mood, the waiter appeared with our bananas Foster and set the dessert aflame before us. As startled as Mama Jo was, she didn't miss another waiter slipping around her other side to remove her bread plate that still had a piece of baguette on it. Her bony hand clamped down on his. "I'm not done." He apologized and left.

I moaned with pleasure as I dug into our dessert. I wanted to lighten the moment and signal to her "Forget what we were just talking about. It's too depressing."

Catering to my mother, another basket of soft, warm baguette slices soon arrived, to her delight. I nodded toward her plate. "Out of everything you ate tonight, what did you like the best?"

She answered without hesitation. "The bread and butter."

I tried to block out what the night's tab would be as she slathered a whipped light-yellow spread onto a piece from the basket and popped it into her mouth with a big grin.

Another unsettling thought cropped up. When she and Mike had visited me in New York, we had plowed through a bottle of wine, and, not used to drinking, she became ill. Now we had just downed champagne, wine, and peach muscat. Plus, she had uncommonly gorged herself. She would surely be sick again. We'd never make the wedding!

Even worse was the thought that this dinner might give her a coronary. Me and my wanton New York yuppie ways. What was I thinking?

I gave her two Tums before she went to bed and crossed my fingers.

Trying to fall asleep in Mike's guest room that night was hard. I lay awake obsessing. Was letting my mother retain control over her life, no matter how bad it was, the right thing to do? Maybe it wasn't that bad to her. It was her home, filled with her possessions, possessions that would never leave her, or hurt her. Meanwhile, I was watching her deteriorate, doing nothing, and feeling like a horrible human being.

My brother was about to start a new life with a great woman, judging from the few phone conversations we'd had. I didn't think I'd ever be envious of my brother, but I was. Add to that my frustration over what to do concerning Mama Jo, and that I was undoubtedly the one who would have to deal with it, whatever "it" was.

I just wanted to wake up back in New York, far away from all of this.

Not the Roses-and-Chocolate Type

Family portrait, 1967, two years before we split away from my mother

With exactly one minute to spare, Mama Jo and I made it to the church. Gasping for breath, we spied Janet in the foyer about to walk down the aisle. Upon seeing us, her mouth dropped. "I was so worried yew weren't going to make it! Arthur's been a wreck!"

I was too taken by her appearance to respond with a weak apology. I hadn't seen a photo of Janet and didn't know what to expect. She had a heart-shaped, pixielike face, twinkling, playful eyes, short reddish hair, and an hourglass figure that was poured into a gorgeous white wedding gown with a train that rivaled Princess Diana's.

She looked at my long blue dress and asked, "Did I tell yew the bridesmaids were wearing cornflower blew?"

"Uh, no." Had I made a blunder wearing the same color?

"I just said that to everyone because I've got a surprise for Arthur. They're really maroon, the color of his favorite football team, the Redskins!" She turned to my mother in a long burgundy skirt and matching top and beamed, "Mama Jo, your outfit matches perfect. I should have made yew a bridesmaid!"

My mother broke into a wide smile as she held onto my hand for balance. Janet's considerable warmth melted all the tension that had been building just getting there. I was astounded I hadn't been nailed for speeding during the three-hour ride that should have taken four.

Arthur was waiting at the altar with a frozen expression, until he saw us and visibly relaxed. My heart went out to him. My admiration, too. It takes a lot of guts to make this kind of commitment to someone. But I was still mad at Mama Jo. We should have arrived in time to give Arthur a hug of reassurance, tell him how good he looked in his black tux, and fiddle with his bow tie.

Musicians began playing Pachelbel's baroque classic Canon in D Major as sixteen bridesmaids and groomsmen fanned out on the platform, smiling like beauty pageant contestants. Behind them were hundreds of lit candles that formed a heart with wings. I inconspicuously checked out the men sitting around me. They had a clean, all-American look, a soft kindness and politeness about them. And every one of them was probably married to a woman he'd met in high school.

I studied Arthur to see if the Redskins ruse hit its mark, but his face had gone back to its serious state. My cute young nephew, James, was onstage in a black tuxedo with tails that matched his father's and the other groomsmen's. My tomboy niece, Chris, ten years older than James, sat next to me dressed in dark pants and a black shirt. It was the first time in years that I'd seen her without a baseball cap on backward. She'd refused to be in the wedding party if she had to wear a dress. It was going to be very interesting to watch this family become "blended."

Arthur and Janet were pronounced husband and wife, and I teared up from seeing how happy they were. The crowd filed out and into a cavernous room nearby that I instantly recognized as where Mama Jo and I had been obliged to attend a lecture on "666 and the Antichrist" after my brother's total-immersion baptism.

I made a mad dash for the beverage table. Did I ever need a glass of wine. After hearing my request, the man serving said with surprise, "Ma'am, there's no alcohol here. This is a church."

There was also no dancing, another letdown. But there was entertainment: a religious play about married life put on by members of the church. The New Yorker in me came raging forth as I duly noted all of this to dine out on when I returned home.

Arthur and Mama Jo shared an embrace that showed how thrilled he was to have her there. I couldn't see her face because it was buried in his pillowlike stomach. In general, she seemed to be enjoying the attention she was getting as his mother. Janet's mother, Wanda Lou, was also in high spirits, and it wasn't just because her other daughter finally made it down the aisle. She seemed to be a naturally exuberant person. The contrast between her and Mama Jo was inescapable.

"Why, Mama Jo," Wanda Lou said, "it's so nice to meet yew! I just love your son."

My mother's pleased countenance changed as she archly responded, "I guess he does the best he can."

I could see Wanda Lou wasn't expecting that. She stayed charming, said, "Thank yew for coming all this way," and kept moving. Would Mama Jo ever forgive Arthur?

I tended to my mother like I was her handmaiden, bringing her food and drinks and reminding her of her new daughter-in-law's name. I saw the pity in people's eyes when they viewed her hunched-over shape. They had to lean in close to hear her soft voice and tended to yell at her, as though she couldn't hear. I could tell it bothered her because she'd pull away as they spoke. They also didn't wait long enough for her to answer and jumped in with another question or comment. It seemed to be taking my mother longer to process a response.

I also saw their surprise when they found out that this Yankee blonde with a lilac pashmina shawl draped over her arms was the groom's sister. One of his buddies joked, "Was Arthur adopted?"

Even strangers could see that, as a family, we were worlds apart from each other. As the reception wore on, my crossed leg impatiently bobbed up and down as I counted the minutes until I could leave. Like I did at every wedding I had attended since my divorce, I thought back to my own spectacle in 1985.

The slogan of the New York radio station I was on at the time was "I Do 92" (it was located at 92.3 on the FM dial). When management heard that I was engaged and planned to marry quietly on Valentine's Day with no formal wedding (it wasn't in our budget), they thought it would be simply wild if we actually said "I do" on 92. They promised a catered event and a nice location, and they'd cover the cost of everything else: wedding gown, bridesmaids' gowns, honeymoon suite at a ritzy hotel, a cruise to Bermuda, and airfare for my parents to fly in. "Cover" most likely meant bartered. With reservations, but not many at that point, my fiancé and I agreed. The whole media circus was planned in four weeks. I was a Bridezilla for 3.98 of them.

The blessed day ended with my husband of a few hours screaming "F#&K OFF AND DIE!" to the producer of the Dr. Ruth Westheimer sex-and-relationship TV show just as we were about to go on as guests. What caused this shocking outburst was an enormous amount of alcohol consumption on his part to defray his above-average wedding jitters, and the producer telling us we'd have to introduce ourselves because Dr. Ruth "couldn't pronounce your names anyway."

My husband's face was flushed with anger. So was mine, but from embarrassment. I had one second to decide if I should slap some sense into him and be a "show must go on" trooper, or stand by my man, who was standing up for me, and leave.

Now, really. This was a nationally televised TV show. They could at least put our names up as a screen credit if she couldn't pronounce them! The whole point of our being there was to get publicity for myself and my radio station. We'd hung around all day in our wedding attire for this. Okay, we'd hung around drinking all day in our wedding attire for this. With my husband blotto, and me past tipsy, it wouldn't go well anyway. We indignantly stormed off with my job in jeopardy and me thinking, *what* have I married?

Despite that episode, I never regretted that day for one reason: when my father walked me down the aisle, I had the distinct feeling I was never going to see him again. There was something shaky and weak about him. When he begged off dinner that night because he wasn't up to it, I expressed my fears to my husband. He said I was overreacting (this was before the Dr. Ruth explosion). "That tough marine will live forever."

My father died two weeks later of a heart attack.

His health had not been good for a long time. Bud did the impact of "losing" me that day, and of seeing Mama Jo one last time, hasten his departure?

She had made it to my wedding alone (her second husband had died of cirrhosis the year before). My father's new wife did not come. She felt it should just be my parents. Her absence allowed Mama Jo to look after my father when he wasn't feeling well that night. I don't know what they discussed. I was glad they had that time alone to talk things through and sweep away whatever ashes remained from the ruins of their marriage. It would have never happened had I not gone along with that crazy on-air wedding.

Someone gushing, "You're Arthur's sister? Why, it's so nice to meet yew!" brought me back to where I was: a megachurch in the Bible Belt. I shook the woman's hand and plastered on a smile. As she tried to chat up my mother, a bad feeling suddenly seized me. I might never see Mama Jo again after this wedding.

The next day, we drove back to Richmond as Arthur and Janet jetted off to a Caribbean honeymoon. This time I was going the speed limit and noticed the hand-painted roadside signs that said JESUS SAVES . . . ABORTION IS MURDER . . . REPENT. How could my brother live in a place like this, much less love it?

I turned on the radio and searched for something to listen to, stopping when I heard a Led Zeppelin favorite. I started bouncing up and down and singing along. "Can I blast it, Mama Jo?" With a smile, she nodded yes, but when I really cranked it, she winced and I dropped it back down.

"Not exactly my cup of tea," she said.

I let it go a few more seconds before hitting the power button. "Let's just enjoy the silence," I said.

As we passed through sparse, flat countryside, she soon fell asleep, head leaning to the left. I thought about our dismal relationship. At least by not having a child I avoided a similar letdown. Was I smart or a coward?

The Monte Carlo zipped across the Virginia state line, and I turned to a more pleasant thought: the expression of contentment on my brother's newlywed face and the genuine happiness I felt for him. Had our parents ever been in love like that? They had to have felt something.

When Mama Jo finally woke up, I asked her, "How did Poddy propose to you?"

Her eyes were a startling blue when light reflected on them. I could see her mentally shift to somewhere on her inner horizon. "He sat down with a pen and paper and calculated how much cheaper it would be if we lived together."

"How romantic."

"He wasn't the roses-and-chocolate type."

He sure wasn't. When we lived in Virginia, I once spied in a Sears catalog, of all places, a gorgeous turquoise evening gown that looked like something a Grecian goddess would wear. I thought it would be perfect for Mama Jo's many dressy Eastern Star events. I urged my father to get it for her as a birthday present. She was taken aback when presented with it, and touched, but I thought at the time, "Why doesn't he ever do anything like that on his own? Why do I have to be the one to suggest it?"

I asked my mother now, "What was your wedding like?" I had a vague memory that it took place in New York City.

"We were married in someone's office at a Presbyterian church in Greenwich Village. Your father had taken me to New York to meet his sister, and we did it while we were there."

"What about Florence and Granny?" She shook her head. Her own mother and grandmother weren't there? "So you never had a wedding?" She didn't answer my question. I had learned as an interviewer that silences were golden. Something interesting almost always comes out of them. I kept glancing in her direction.

She finally said, "I just wanted a friend who would take care of me, but he was like a shell. I could never get inside him." After a longer silence she said, "He'd look at the clock by our bed and time himself to see how fast he could do it."

Whoa! As I tried to get that image out of my mind, I wondered if my father had a "stamina" issue and put it in that context to cover it. But that was too much information. Instead, I asked, "Do you think he ever cheated on you?

"I found lipstick on his collar. Smelled perfume. You be the judge."

"Shit!" I exclaimed, as I glimpsed a flashing light in my rearview mirror. I'd been so distracted by what my mother was telling me that I hadn't realized I was flying along. I was unable to talk myself out of a $150 speeding ticket and spit out a "Dammit" after the officer walked away that sounded just like one of Mama Jo's.

That's what I get for being so damn curious about the past, I reasoned, and vowed not to go there anymore for the rest of the trip. Probably wouldn't be a bad idea if I didn't ever go there again.

On Long Island Sound with my half-brother, George, 1959

5

A Certain Air of Inefficiency

I saw prayer as meditation with an agenda: a stilling of my heart, an opening of communication with myself that guided me as to what I needed to do, so I was, in a way, praying to God—but a God within.

I prayed often for a solution to the Mama Jo situation. The answer I received was a gradual Downward Spiral.

First, I lost my long-term, high-paying voice-over contract with a prominent television channel that represented most of my income. Then Z100 decided to use celebrities as ZJs during the weekend and relegated me to "on-call" status. Although part of me was relieved, it would most likely mean I wouldn't make enough to continue getting medical insurance through AFTRA, my union.

Prestroke, Aunt Julie used to say about my frenetic life, "You're like Alice in Wonderland, running as fast as she can just to stay where she is."

If only I were staying in place. Now I was running even faster, but backward.

She'd also said that she saw me with a doctor someday. The only doctor I knew at the time was the funky singer Dr. John. I always kept her prediction in the back of my head and when I was fixed up with a sexy neurosurgeon, I thought, "This is the one." We didn't get too far down the road to romance, though. He fell for one of my best friends. Soon the only kind of guys I was attracting were struggling young musicians who held firmly to the misconception that I could help their careers.

When I got fed up with my own drama, I'd call my mother and listen to hers.

"I can't find my damn yardstick," she hissed. "I know Arthur took it."

"Stop! Stop! Stop! He didn't take it or anything else!" I hung up. From then on I made sure I called her only when I had a glass of wine in hand.

During one of our calmer conversations, I heard the duty-bound daughter in me say, "I wish I could be there for you, Mama Jo, but my work is here." I was commuting into the city almost every day for voice-over auditions that usually went nowhere and the occasional booking when they did. I knew I should put out feelers for a full-time DJ job, but I didn't have the necessary indestructible spunk at the moment to do that. I prayed for another great VO gig to materialize.

In another tense phone call with my mother, she bitterly said, "Sometimes I just want to take a match to all this stuff."

In my now well-honed Public Service Announcer voice, I said, "Don't overwhelm yourself. Just do a little at a time. If there's anything I can do, let me know." Sure. Just hand me my magic wand.

All was calm for a few weeks. Too calm. Then came a call from Mike. He informed me that some teenagers Mama Jo thought she knew well, and trusted, had asked her if she'd like her car washed. Instead they took it joyriding and got it stuck in a field of muck. Mike helped get it back. "Oh, boy," he said. "I'm glad it all worked out."

For now. Who would take advantage of her next?

Though Mike made it sound like helping my mother wasn't that big a deal, I knew relying on him all the time had to stop. She wasn't his problem. And he couldn't watch her every moment, even if he wanted to.

When I suggested to her that it might be time to stop driving, she barked, "How am I supposed to get around? Fly?" and slammed the phone down.

Fretful calls and e-mails among Arthur, Mike, and Mama Jo's best friend, Ginny, increased. When Mike wrote, *I fear she'll soon be with*

God, I had a complete under-the-covers-in-a-fetal-position bawling breakdown. I felt gutted. Why was this affecting me on such a cellular level? I had never been that close to my mother.

My therapist prescribed the antianxiety drug Ativan for me to take on an as-needed basis. I asked her if I should be on an antidepressant. She said, "Losing a parent is hard, Jo. Grief is natural. But you're very resilient. If this doesn't help, let me know."

Friends became scarce as I went on about my mother. I couldn't blame them. What could they say or do? One suggested I get her a fax machine, like he had done for his mom in Colorado. "Every day I fax her and she faxes back, so I know she's okay."

When I shot his suggestion down with, "There's no room for a fax at my mother's, plus she doesn't have touch-tone service and refuses to get it. Even if she did, she'd never remember how to use the damn thing," he replied, "You really do have a problem."

I began having a recurring vision of reaching into my car for something. Suddenly, a truck appears out of nowhere and smashes into me.

It alternated with another: the moment I almost drowned in a Miami swimming pool the summer of 1969.

My father, brother, and I had stayed at a motel until our townhouse was finished being built. The ladder in the deep end of the motel pool was pulled out from the side, allowing me to swim between the ladder and the wall. I pretended I was a dolphin and showed off to two girls who were hanging around the pool, each time making my trick of swimming through the rungs more difficult. They tried to stop me. "You're going to get stuck," they said.

I was determined to prove them wrong and swam through the bottom rung, toward the wall, and down, blowing out my air to prevent the water from going up my nose.

I got stuck.

I could see the girls watching me, reaching for me, screaming at me. They were just inches away, but I was trapped. I blacked out. I didn't see a tunnel of white light, like many people say they've seen when they almost died. I saw mice dressed as musketeers in a triangular formation walking toward me. Then I heard, "She opened her eyes!" I was on my stomach. Someone was pushing on my back. I was gasping for air. I was put on a stretcher and into an ambulance. I kept gasping for an hour.

At the hospital, my father told me the girls pounded on our door. He plunged into the pool, somehow got me untangled without breaking my legs, but I was a dead weight. He couldn't lift me out. The girls tried to help between their screams. Two college guys who lived at the motel heard them and came to the rescue. My father made me laugh which he said, "I can't believe I remembered to take my cigarettes out of my shirt pocket before I jumped in."

A doctor said to me, "When someone is drowning, the stomach fills first; then the water goes to the lungs, and you die." According to your X-rays," he took a beat before adding, "your stomach was full."

When I heard this, I felt kind of blasé in that emotionally cut-off way teenagers have down pat. I knew I wasn't supposed to die yet. My father and mother must have had the scare of their lives—especially my mother, who was so far away from me then.

Now I saw her in that swimming pool where I had been. I could see her submerged, trapped, and giving up. I couldn't save her. Not by myself.

I arranged for Meals on Wheels to deliver food to Mama Jo and offered to pay Mike and Ginny to check on her. Mike refused to take any money. "I'll be glad to do what I can," he said. I knew he worked full-time, had several children and grandchildren, and had more than enough on his plate. Ginny also refused to accept payment and added, "I'd love to help, but I live on the other side of town, work day and night, and there's no such thing as a short visit to your mother's."

Mama Jo's phone was cut off. She swore she never saw the bill. Mike made sure her phone was turned back on. Ginny reported that collection notices were piling up. Mama Jo would not let her mail be forwarded to me so I could take care of her bills.

She didn't acknowledge my birthday that year. She usually sent me a card with a small check long after the fact. When I sent her a gift basket for hers she never called to thank me, which she had always done in the past. When I phoned to make sure she received it, she said she had tried to call and my number was disconnected. I went over the phone number with her. She was forgetting to dial "1" first.

The folders I had been stuffing with elder-care information were growing so thick I had to make subfolders. What I could not make was a decision.

The final block in my shaky foundation was pulled out when I was asked to leave my charming, hard-to-come-by estate cottage in Bedford so that the landlord's daughter could move in with her new family. "I've been kicked out of my home!" I wailed to friends. "I'm too old for this crap!" Through my Pilates Mafia I found another cottage, but I didn't want to hang anything on the walls. I had a feeling I wouldn't be there long. I simply couldn't afford to live in New York anymore.

These were the things I prayed for every day, though I knew there was no chance any of them would happen:

1. A house no one could kick me out of except the bank holding my mortgage. (I was now living off of the money I'd been saving for a down payment.)
2. An adopted child. (Right. I needed someone to adopt me.)
3. A roommate whose income didn't fluctuate, whom I could count on to stick around, and who could contribute more than a couple hundred dollars for a small room (which was all I could offer and all it was worth).
4. A solution to the Mama Jo problem.

I spoke to a social services woman in Richmond who was experienced with situations similar to my mother's. She tried to say in an understanding tone, "We can always go in and forcibly remove her if she's an endangerment to herself and then put her in a nursing home." Tears filled my eyes as she added, "Hoarders cross all socioeconomic backgrounds and are, basically, incurable. Nothing works. Not therapy, not drugs, not even cleaning up their environment. In fact, that could be the worst thing you could do. They can turn violently angry if put in a new, clean place and want all of their things back." She attempted to end the call on a positive note: "At least she isn't the worst case I've heard of—a woman who lived on top of five feet of stuff in her house. Can you imagine?"

Janet, my new sister-in-law, was a woman of deep compassion who came from a close-knit family. She suggested to Arthur that they add on to their house and have Mama Jo come live with them. Shocked by the notion, Arthur said, "You have no idea what you're suggesting," but invited my mother to stay with them for two weeks to see how it went before making the offer. As the day approached for them to drive up to Richmond to get her, Mama Jo became increasingly agitated. It dawned on me that she probably feared they'd never bring her back.

I said to Mama Jo, "No one's forcing you to do this. They thought you'd like to get away for a little bit." Her silence prompted me to say, "Would you like me to tell them you don't want to go?"

"Yes." Her voice sounded like that of a little girl.

Arthur and Janet understood and instead decided to visit her, stay at a hotel, and broach the subject while having a meal at a restaurant. It took three hours to get her there, and the whole time she made rude remarks to them and the waitress. When they were finished, Mama Jo didn't think Arthur should pay for the meal because, according to her, the service and food were bad. Even the irrepressible Janet threw up her hands in defeat.

I visualized social services going in and dragging my little mother out of her home kicking and screaming. I could never live with myself after that. Nor could I live with doing nothing.

"That place is a fire hazard," Arthur said, his voice strained with as much frustration as mine. "Not only will it burn down with her in it, but it could burn down other people's homes and kill them, too. I can't do anything because she's still mad at me. I've asked her to forgive me for whatever she thinks I've done wrong, but she won't." He added sadly, "That's not very Christian, if you ask me."

I suggested to Arthur that maybe her anger at him dated back to ten years earlier, when he accepted a work transfer to another state. "She'd relocated to Richmond when your daughter was young to help take care of her. Maybe she feels you deserted her."

He answered, "I ran it by her before I took that job, and she told me she understood completely, that if you don't move when the company asks, you'll never get ahead." Understanding and accepting are not the same.

I explained to Arthur that I'd learned it was quite common for an elderly person slipping into dementia to single out one person as the lightning rod for their paranoia and growing fears about dying. "I'm sorry it's you," I said. Especially since it meant I was the one having to deal with her.

"Me, too, but something has to be done. She can't even drive now."

A few days before, she'd journeyed to a nearby shopping center and became confused as to where she was. She called the police. They left her car in the parking lot and drove her home because her registration, inspection sticker, and insurance had expired. Good old Mike retrieved the car.

As for the other car-related issues, I tried to settle them by phone and was told I needed power of attorney. I convinced Mama Jo to give me the "POA" (broad legal authority to make most important decisions in her life) by saying, "It's just in case something happens to you. If I don't have this, then I'll have to petition the court for guardianship, and who knows what choices will be made while I wait for that to happen?"

By agreeing to do this, she was placing enormous trust in me—and I was taking on an equally large responsibility. Meanwhile, I was watching my savings evaporate as work only trickled in. I had to get my own life back on track.

Mama Jo was Poddy's second wife. Technically, she was his third, but we weren't supposed to know about Betty, the older vaudevillian actress he'd been briefly married to when he was a young stud. My half-brother, George, from the official "first" marriage to a woman named Alice, had lived with us off and on until he graduated from high school in Alaska. He'd resided in England since the 1970s with his British wife. We'd had little communication until e-mail came along. He was flying over to see Aunt Julie and Charlotte and agreed to come with me to Richmond to try to help with the Mama Jo situation.

The fall leaves were gloriously ablaze as George and I drove south in my Saab for the seven-hour drive. His dark brown hair was a muted gray now, but he still possessed a delightfully offbeat sense of humor. I'm sure the latter came in handy in his work with the criminally insane. I hoped his experience, coupled with his status as an insider whom Mama Jo might trust, would aid in dislodging her from her uninhabitable home. "You have to be gentle but firm with her," he counseled. "Gentle but firm."

Easy for him to say.

I asked him his impressions of Mama Jo when he was young.

"Weeeeell." He often started sentences with a drawn-out "Well," "Yeah," or "Ah" as he gathered his thoughts. "There seemed to be a certain air of inefficiency about her."

Laughing, I said, "That's putting it mildly."

"Poddy was always saying, 'Help Mama Jo,' 'How's Mama Jo doing?' 'Is she ready yet?' 'See what's she doing,' 'Help Mama Jo.'"

He relayed a story I'd never heard before about her. When she worked on the same floor as my father, her boss (a friend of my father's) asked her to write up the minutes of a meeting that had just occurred. What should have taken her thirty minutes to complete, in a single page, instead took her hours and went on for many pages. A therapist today might diagnose her as being obsessive-compulsive—or having attention deficit disorder, which, surprisingly, can also manifest itself as having the ability to hyperfocus on something.

"George," I asked, "why would a marine, who lived to give orders and have them followed, marry someone like Mama Jo? Poddy was a 'One-two-three, march!' kind of guy. The only marching she did was to the beat of her own drum."

He quietly gave it some thought. "She was young, very pretty, and nice to me. My father introduced me to her—before he and my mother split—to see what I thought of her. I liked her, but I was only seven and too young to really get what was going on. But I knew something wasn't right about it."

"Wait. He was still married when he started seeing her?"

"Yeeeeeeeah, I stupidly said something about her to my mom. I showed her a photo that my father had, and that was the end of it."

If my father was still married when he was wooing Mama Jo, then her strict mother and grandmother, whom she lived with until she wed, most certainly did not approve. What a way to start a life with someone.

Once George and I arrived in Richmond, he quickly became my heaven-sent Mama Jo "whisperer." She was delighted to see him, and he didn't blow his cool once. His voice was smooth, soft, nonaggressive, nonjudgmental. I suppose if I were walking fresh into the situation, I'd have a lot of patience, too.

I sat on the crowded couch, drumming my fingers or doing crossword puzzles. I could hear George, at the other end of the dark, jammed hall, saying, "We're trying to find your wallet. Where do you usually keep it? When did you see it last?"

I picked through the piles of mail on her dining table and unearthed more collection notices. Stuffed in junk-mail envelopes were family photos going back to my grandmother's childhood, Social Security checks that were never deposited, important tax documents, and two twenty-dollar bills. Every single thing would have to be inspected! What I really wanted to find was her divorce papers. She once claimed she hadn't received a cent from my father when they split. I always wondered if that were true.

I felt the eyes of the Schwarzenegger action figure upon me and wanted to yell at it, "Don't just stand there! Do something!" The other dolls stared me down as well. I was sure they were damning me for being a bad daughter. Or did they want to get the hell out of here, too?

My eyes fell on the gift basket filled with cookies and chocolate that I'd sent for my mom's birthday. It was perched precariously on a pile of junk. I hoped I wasn't seeing what I thought I was seeing. I took a closer look. I was. It was unopened. She was either severely depressed or not physically able to undo the ribbon that enclosed it. If that wouldn't make someone depressed, what would?

It was astonishing she had managed to live alone this long.

I stayed calm and in the background while George took charge. We managed to accomplish several major objectives on that trip. First, we went to a lawyer's office, and Mama Jo granted me power of attorney and signed an advance health directive. I made sure the lawyer was a woman because she'd had a bad experience with a male attorney once. I was taken aback when my mother said before the appointment, "I hope she isn't black." I'd never known her to be racist and feared it was another sign of senile dementia and that she'd soon be spewing expletives like deranged people often do.

We made it to Mama Jo's dentist to replace a front upper tooth that had come out. I had winced every time she stuck her tongue through the gap it left and grinningly said, "I look like a jack-o'-lantern."

I also convinced her to have her mail forwarded to me. I said, "It's just temporary so I can get your bills paid and do your taxes." She swore that she'd filed her returns, but couldn't remember her accountant's name.

Finally, we got her to her general physician. He wouldn't say anything as definitive as "You can't live alone anymore" to my mother. He hadn't seen the way she lived, though Arthur had described the situation to him in great detail in a letter. He did, however, write her a prescription for the drug Paxil that's used for treating depression, obsessive-compulsive disorder, and anxiety. He said, "Let's see how this works."

My thought was, "Let's see if she remembers to take it."

By the time George and I left Richmond to head back to New York, I was thrilled with how much we'd accomplished. "George," I said, "when the day comes to get her out of that house, I'm sending you a first-class ticket to come over."

My heart sank when he said, "Aaahhhhh, I wish I could help, but I used up all my holiday time on this trip."

Just before we reached my home in Westchester County, two cars zoomed around us as we patiently sat at a red light. There was no question I was back in New York, back to another life that was, thankfully, far away from my mother's nightmarish one and crazy enough in its own right to help me block out hers. But for how long?

Mama Jo's signature beret began at an early age

6

"I'll Smile at You If You'll Smile at Me"

I was staggered when I heard my mother's voice after she'd been taking the Paxil for two weeks. "Mama Jo," I said excitedly, "you sound so young and happy! Don't stop taking those pills!"

But of course she did, as I learned when I called a few weeks later and she was mad at Arthur again. Her explanation for stopping the Paxil was, "It made me pee too much."

Two possibilities hit me. First, she was incontinent, and Paxil, most likely, had nothing to do with it. Second, in her now-lucid state, she realized the full extent of what she had to do to improve her life, and that was a far worse frame of mind to be in than a fog of depression. Maybe I was wrong about the first one.

I was also concerned she wasn't taking her Synthroid, a thyroid medication she'd been on for most of her adult life. She couldn't remember if she'd taken it and didn't want to take too much, so she skipped it. Or she couldn't find the vial, which I had had refilled and delivered to her twice. A whacked-out thyroid can cause all kinds of mental issues. "I don't think she has Alzheimer's," I optimistically said to Arthur on the phone. "She just needs to get her medication right. If only I could hire someone to look after that. She won't let me."

He again urged me to petition the Lord. "I keep a prayer journal," he said "Mama Jo is at the top of my list, and many others'. The Lord will give us an answer, Jo. Just watch."

Instead of making me feel better, as though God would handle everything in some magical way, it made me feel worse. "Handle" would invariably mean something terrible happening. The only one of my brother's biblical bromides that did resonate with me, and deeply, was "Man plans. God laughs."

When I was told by my local Social Security office that I couldn't have my mom's monthly checks direct-deposited into her bank account without her physically appearing in their offices to approve it, I confidently said, "I have power of attorney," and began to pull out the paperwork to prove it. The woman brusquely said, "Doesn't matter. If she can't do this herself, you have to have a letter from a doctor stating she's mentally incompetent."

I held it together until I returned to my car. Even if it was true that my mother had lost her marbles, there was something about seeing it in writing that I simply couldn't face.

My brother and I went around and around with the limited choices of actions we could take and why they wouldn't work. Even buying her a gizmo she could wear around her neck with a button she could push in case she fell would be a waste of money because she'd lose it. She needed to see her doctor regularly. There were services that picked up elderly people and took them to their appointments, but no one was going to wait for hours while she pulled herself together.

"If we could get her into assisted living," Arthur said, "just for a short while, at least the house could be cleaned out. That's the hardest part."

"I agree, but you know if a decision is made for her, she'll be furious. And if she isn't happy, no one will be happy." I rubbed my forehead, a habit I'd fallen into over the past year.

"Jo, she'll never just go along with this idea."

I rubbed even harder. "I know, I know. And how could I take off weeks—no, months—to get rid of that mess even if she did? I'm strictly freelance now, which means never knowing when I'm going to work. All it takes is not being available once, and that client will probably never call me again."

I was tired of going nowhere on this topic and changed the subject to Mama Jo's taxes. "I found out from the IRS that she hasn't paid them in three years and a fourth return is due soon."

My brother let out the Mama Jo Groan. "She'll have interest and penalties, too."

"Why me?" I whimpered. "You're the accountant and business manager who makes the trains run on time. You could handle this blindfolded!"

He laughed. "I guess the Lord thinks otherwise, Jo. Why else would Mama Jo only allow you to do it?"

Infuriated at his simplistic view, I said, "Did you ever think maybe it's the devil doing this?"

He calmly replied, "The Lord tests. The devil tempts."

I did the Give Me a Freakin' Break Groan and went back to the matter at hand. "I'm fighting the IRS penalties, claiming she has senile dementia," I told him. "But guess what else I found out? She had a home health care policy that would've paid a hundred dollars a day for someone to help her. It lapsed due to lack of payment."

This time the sound he made was more like he'd dropped a brick on his bare foot.

"So I had a nice chat with a lady at the Bureau of Insurance in Richmond," I continued, "and she said there was now a law that any policy that covers dementia, as this one did, has to have a contact person listed in case a payment is missed. Since Mama Jo bought the policy before that was the case, they could be off the hook." I raged about how a salesperson could sell her the policy without a contact person, law or no law.

"They just wanted her money," Arthur said.

"But they'd have a lot more if she was still paying!"

"Not if they had to start paying out on the policy."

"And I haven't even told you about the more than five grand she owes on a credit card with a 22 percent interest rate."

Now he sounded like he was falling off a tall ladder.

I snapped, "Now multiply that by a hundred, and you know how I feel!" I also told him I'd discovered that she had bought, and just paid off, two burial plots in the family site in Kansas City. "She bought them after Uncle Sid died."

"Why two?" he asked.

"Maybe the other one was for Mike." I let that sorrowful note hang in the air.

He offered, "Maybe she bought it for you."

I cringed at that notion. "No way do I want to be buried there. I have no connection to Kansas City or to that side of my family. Put me in the Buddhist monastery in New York where Julie and Charlotte are going to be one day."

It felt really weird to be talking about this.

Soon I was back in Richmond, armed with my Bliss Pill, Ativan, to take Mama Jo to see assisted-living places nearby. I said, "It's a fact-finding mission. I'm not putting you anywhere. I'm not throwing out anything. But I live so far away and need to have a plan in place should anything happen to you like happened to Julie."

I also convinced her to take a trip with me to Greensboro and visit facilities with Janet and Arthur. "It's just research," I explained. "You might want to be there at first instead of Richmond because you'd have more family around you." I was so surprised she agreed to do this that I feared she'd pull one of her passive-aggressive acts and never get ready to go.

I was also on a mission to find one of her old tax returns. All she could recall about the accounting firm that did her taxes was that it was "a bunch of last names that are all alike." Finally one came to her. I looked in the phone book and found several companies with that name. I picked one and was thrilled it was the right one. The woman who answered said, "She hasn't been in for so long I thought . . ."

"No, she's very much alive."

It would take several thousand dollars to have the returns done and to pay what she owed. The money she inherited from Uncle Sid from the sale of his home was already half gone and at the rate expenses were mounting wouldn't last much longer.

Amazingly, coaxing her out of the house to look at assisted-living places wasn't that hard, though I became deeply concerned when she tried to put on a bra over the one she was already wearing and did the same with a shoe. I prayed she was just uncommonly nervous—which heightened my own apprehension about what we had to do that day.

She wouldn't walk out the front door until she found just the right color beret to wear and cocked it on her head just so. Then she applied her lipstick as her hand shook. I said nothing and looked away, trying not to imagine myself in her place one day. How well I was getting to know the expression "There but for the grace of God go I."

She grasped her black cane with an unusual fancy gold top in one hand, my hand with the other, and we made our way to her old red station wagon. I couldn't afford to rent a car. It hadn't been easy to have the battery replaced and her car brought up to date legally and mechanically from a distance, but I was becoming adept at cajoling people to go out of their way to help me with my mother's various problems. I think it was the borderline insanity in my voice and their thoughts, whatever they were, about their own mothers that greased the wheels.

As we pulled out of the driveway I joked, "And we're off . . . like a herd of turtles."

She smiled so widely that I could see the gaps on the side of her mouth where her recently lost dentures were supposed to go. How was I going to get her to a dentist for new ones? How many thousands of dollars would they cost? (Answer: $2,920.) Would she lose them as well? Yet she had to get them so she could eat solid food.

The assisted-living facility in Richmond felt like a cross between a dormitory and a hospital, except everyone had gray hair. The more upbeat the director was, and the more little old ladies grinned at my mother from their walkers, the more I could tell she didn't like it there, though she clasped her cane and made polite comments like, "I suppose it's good to be somewhere so if I fall I'll be found right away."

Back in the car, I asked her what she really thought of the place.

She gave me a skeptical look over her wire-rimmed glasses and tightly said, "I'll smile at you if you'll smile at me. No, thank you."

Her comment cracked me up.

We headed on to Greensboro with her head falling to the left each time she nodded off. She woke up from one brief nap, caught me yawning, and said, "I'm going to get my license renewed so I can drive again."

That would be an unmitigated disaster, but I'd let the DMV break the news to her—assuming they would. I said, "Let's see what we find in Greensboro. Maybe you won't have to drive." I knew as soon as the words left my mouth and she turned her red beret–covered head toward her window that I shouldn't have said that.

She was probably heartsick at the thought of losing her independence, her stuff, and leaving Mike and Ginny. She might not have many friends, but the two she had were the gold standard. Ginny had lost her mom not long before she met Mama Jo in a doll store. They instantly bonded. And it may not have worked out the way my mother wanted with Mike, but he obviously still cared about her, and she for him.

As we drove on, I had to keep telling Mama Jo what state we were in, where we were going, why we were going there, and who her son had married.

"Janet, Janet," she said. "I like her. Why'd she ever marry Art?"

"Maybe Arthur's more of a catch than you realize."

"I sure wish he'd give me back the shoehorn he took."

"We'll look for it when we're there, okay?"

"I'm sure he's hidden it—and the yardsticks, too."

She had once said—with such conviction that I almost believed her—that he had come into her house one day and taken an album of family photos when he thought she was asleep. On another occasion, she had stunned Janet when she called one night screaming, "I want my pink doll stove back! I know Arthur took it!"

My sister-in-law told me, "I've seen Arthur break down and cry over the things Mama Jo says to him. It's awful. Just awful. I don't know what to do."

As upsetting as it was to hear that, it was also comforting to know that I wasn't the only one shedding tears over this impossible situation. It didn't make it any less of a problem to deal with. If only my mother and brother could somehow mend their relationship.

Mama Jo and I received a warm southern welcome at Arthur's. I felt better every time I walked into that house due to Janet's loving presence. She gave us both a big hug and gushed over how nice it was to see us.

We hopped in their red Durango that roared like a Harley and saw two more assisted-living places. The first one was predictably depressing. The second was brand-new and looked like a fancy hotel, but even the biggest room was minuscule compared to my mother's house.

"Look, Mama Jo," said Janet. "They have buttons you push if you need any help."

"We'll have someone give you your pills every day," said our tour guide, "for an extra charge."

As the tour wore on, my mother and I became quieter. I felt like I was inside her skin, feeling what she was feeling. I was starting to lean over like her, as though my heart, as well, was waterlogged with decades of sadness, and the weight of it was pulling my chest down.

"Group hug!" Janet sang out in the parking lot when it was all over. The four of us formed a huddle as she prayed.

"Dear Lord, please help guide us. We love Mama Jo so much and want what's best for her, but we want her to be happy, too. Please show us how we can do Your work."

We were quiet for several moments before my brother said, "Amen."

Okay, I thought, if ever I needed a sign from above, it was now.

We went out for dinner, and I immediately went to work on a glass of wine as I frowned at the fat- and sodium-laced menu (they even offered fried ice cream). Janet began to talk about a recent mission trip she'd taken to Appalachia with members of her church.

"I was talkin' to these two lumberjacks in the local diner," she said in her adorable North Carolina accent, "and I commented on how I hadn't seen any black folks around. And this one says real proud, 'That's right. We run 'em off.' And the other says, 'We had one family come here 'bout a year ago. They lasted a week.' Well, I couldn't believe what I was hearing! So I said real sweetlike, 'Gee, that's too bad because my husband's black.'"

Arthur and I howled with laughter. What a stitch she was! I looked at Mama Jo to check her reaction. I was glad to see it was the same, though when she laughed she just flashed all of her teeth and shook. No sound. A lot like the way my ex-husband laughed, come to think of it.

There was still more to Janet's outrageous tale. "Then I found a book on Africa in the boxes we'd brought up, and I left it at the diner inscribed to the lumberjacks. I wrote, 'I thought you'd like to know more about my husband's culture in case we come back to live.'"

I had always liked Janet, but now I loved her. Somehow she made all of our differences disappear.

Back at their house, Arthur and Janet insisted we stay in their bedroom because the bed was bigger and more comfortable than the one in the guest room. When it was time to go to sleep, it wasn't easy for Mama Jo to make it up the stairs to the second floor. I stood behind her, my hands on her hips. "I'm right here," I said. "Just take it slow. There's no rush." She had to stop every few steps and catch her breath. This was not good.

We quietly undressed for bed, and I felt a little odd sleeping with her, but the second glass of wine I'd had with dinner helped to put me at ease. Then Mama Jo took off her shoes. A stench like roadkill filled the room. I covered my mouth and involuntarily retched. "I'm sorry," I gasped, "but I can't sleep in here." She looked at me inquisitively. Fanning the air, I said, "I can't breathe." Naturally, she was hurt. I left quickly. Her condition was so much worse than I had thought.

I softly knocked on the guest room door and explained to Arthur and Janet what was going on. They gave me blankets and pillows so I could sleep on the sofa downstairs. I threw them on the couch and felt worse. I couldn't leave Mama Jo up there. I went back. She wouldn't look at me as she attempted to change her socks. I tried to hold my breath.

"I'm sorry," I said.

"Gee, don't let me *contaminate* you."

"Would you like me to help you take a bath?"

"No. I don't want you to get sick again."

"Let me wash your feet. Then everything will be okay."

"No."

"Please."

"*No*."

I went into the bathroom and began running the water in the large bathtub, hoping she'd change her mind. Finally she hobbled in, and I helped her sit on the edge of it. I gently soaped up her feet, carefully rubbing off the black crust that had caked between her toes. Her toenails were gnarled, almost reptilian. Mine, meanwhile, were nicely pedicured and painted a bright coral. I could feel my face grow warm from the shame and sorrow I felt.

"Mama Jo, why don't you see a podiatrist?"

"A what?"

"A foot doctor. You need to have your toenails cut regularly." As soon as I said it I thought, How will she get there?

I couldn't believe the next words that came out of my mouth. "How would you feel if I moved down here and we lived together?"

She looked as if she didn't understand.

"Here in Greensboro. Not you and everything in your house," I said gently but firmly. "You have to promise me you'll let go of most of it. Keep the dolls, of course, but most of it has to go. I'll build a recording studio and do announcing work from home. I won't make as much, but it's not as expensive down here, and if we pool our resources, we should be okay. The whole family will be together again and—" I felt a sharp contraction in my chest, and my businesslike tone evaporated, "I can take care of you."

Her mouth dropped, and her eyes lit up. "Really?" Unable to speak, I nodded yes. She asked, "What's wrong?"

I couldn't put it into words. I felt as much joy as pain. Between deep sobs I got out, "I'm so sorry it took me this long to say that."

"It's okay, it's okay." She patted my arm. "You had to live your life."

No, it wasn't okay. My life? Acting like a teenager on the radio and spending obscene amounts of money to live in a part of the world I couldn't afford? How could I have let things get this bad? I ran the back of my hand across my wet cheek. "I love you so much, Mama Jo." When was the last time I said that to her and really meant it?

Her soft reply was, "Not as much as I love you."

I reached around her little birdcage back that would never be straight again and with the other hand brought her head gently to my pounding heart.

Was I dreaming? Was I drunk? She would never get rid of anything. She would never get better. She was only going to get worse.

Arthur would say that the Lord was leading me on this path. I also heard my therapist's voice telling me I had Rescuer Syndrome. Who was right? All I knew at that moment was that I felt like we were rescuing each other.

We slept together that night for the first time in perhaps our entire lives, mirror images, backs to each other, curled up into little balls with our boundaries still in place, though not quite as firmly as before.

A family vacation to Nags Head, North Carolina, after we left Alaska, 1962

7

A Nonrelationship

The announcement of my Brilliant Idea resulted in a swift and stern intervention from my friends. "The road to hell is paved with good intentions . . . How will you date if you're living with your mother? . . . How could you ever live in the Bible Belt? . . . What if you start talking with a southern accent? It'll hurt your work . . . You can't leave us! We love you! . . . What about the damn dolls? . . . Family. The other F word."

And those were the nicer comments. Once they had a few drinks in them, they were more blunt. "You're out of your freakin' mind . . . This is twenty times worse than getting mixed up with struggling musicians . . . This is just your Babyitis flaring up again . . . You don't even like your mother! Why would you do this to yourself? Why?"

I lightheartedly replied, "I'll just pretend I'm in a John Waters movie. It'll be fine."

"John Waters? It'll be more like Stephen King, or one those Chucky evil-doll movies!"

I crossed my arms and said forcefully, "If it doesn't work, at least we've downsized that horrible house. And maybe if I deal with my Mother Issues directly with her, I'll stop dating men who are like her." I added philosophically, "Or I'll accept that this is my fate."

"Would someone please talk this woman down from the ledge?" cried one. But another said, "Okay, give it a try. You'll be back in a month."

On the surface, it indeed had disaster written all over it. I would have to take money out of my Sacred Retirement Nest Egg to buy a house. I couldn't use the proceeds from the sale of my mother's house for two reasons. First, in order to sell it, it had to be empty. The real estate broker said, "Most houses you want to show with furnishings. It makes them look homier. Not your mother's." Second, buying the North Carolina house with my money kept it out of reach of a nursing home should Mama Jo need to be admitted to one in the next five years, known by Medicaid as the "look-back period"—the time they could attach themselves to any assets that were my mother's, even after they had passed into someone else's hands.

Oh, for the days when I didn't even know the difference between Medicare and Medicaid.

Also in the minus column of Operation Mama Jo was that I would have to leave New York, my home since the 1980s, filled with dear friends and countless business contacts. I was now forty-seven and sure that the slim chance I had left to make a life with a man, maybe adopt a child, would soon be gone. Who would I find in Greensboro? A guy who loved NASCAR and turkey shoots, had a name like Billy Bob, and pronounced "beer" as "burr"?

I might be able to handle one turkey shoot.

I called my friend Michele, whom I'd met in Miami that rough summer of 1969 when my family broke apart. Our friendship had endured longer than any other. "How would you describe my relationship with my mother?" I asked.

"When I first met you," she said, "I didn't even think you had a mother. You never talked about her. When you finally did, it was with annoyance. Her always being late, the dolls, that group she made you join—"

"The Job's Daughters."

"—that you never went to in Miami. Remember when you cut off that white robe with the purple cord, turned it into a minidress, and wore it to a school dance?"

"Don't ever repeat I did that!"

She wrapped up my query with: "I'd say you have a nonrelationship with your mother. Yeah, that's what it is: a nonrelationship. Aunt Julie was more your mother."

I told her my Brilliant Idea.

"WHAAAAAAAT?! You're going to *live* with her? Near *Arthur?*" But after discussing it thoroughly, and hearing how determined I was, she said, "Maybe it isn't that crazy. You'll have given it your best shot. In the end, that's all we can do."

Leaving Julie and Charlotte was the hardest part of this plan. Charlotte, too, was skeptical about it's success. "I don't think you'll last two minutes," she said. "You're just not a Greensboro kind of person." Or Greensboring, as I had learned the locals call it.

Even Arthur and Janet were shocked by my plan. "Are you sure you know what you're taking on?" they asked. When they saw I wasn't going to change my mind, they first praised the Lord for finally answering our prayers. I was firmly in the "the jury is still out" camp on that one.

Arthur also made it clear that they could make no guarantees as to how much they could do. Janet's new cleaning business was a full-time job; Arthur worked long hours. His teenage daughter was a source of constant concern, and his young son was a rising basketball star who needed to be shuttled to games several nights a week. There was the married couple's "Honey Do" list that never grew shorter. Like all Southern Baptists, the church was central to their lives, and they had many commitments with theirs. I knew that saying to my brother "What could be more Godly than to care for your mother?" would go over about as well as asking Mama Jo to sell some dolls. It would also entail Mama Jo forgiving Arthur and allowing him to help her, which had yet to occur and might never.

Did I feel resentment? Some, but I was the one in a better position to care for our mother. I knew they'd help to some degree, which was better than no help at all. And a son giving his mother a bath or "toileting" her makes both parties uncomfortable. It's just the way it is.

At least Mama Jo could contribute toward paying the bills—as long as she didn't have to go into a nursing home. My business model was as shaky as a dot-com start-up, but I had to forge on and hope for the best. I could always tap into my IRA some more, though I'd rather drink cyanide. More likely, I'd sell the damn dolls.

I resolutely stated to Arthur, "Something just tells me this move south is what I have to do."

"In that case," he said, "if the Lord led you to it, He'll lead you through it."

He gave me one more piece of advice that he had learned since moving to Greensboro: "When you call someone on the phone, you can't just get right to what you want to talk about. You have to shoot the breeze a bit."

That sounded as hard as what Julie had suggested when I'd asked her, "How do you help someone so that they don't resent it?" Even in my aunt's debilitated poststroke state she had moments of lucidity. She answered in her now monotone voice, "Don't use the word 'help.' Say, 'What would you like me to do?' Pride cometh before the fall."

It was unbearable to leave her, but I had to.

Then what even I admitted was a miracle occurred, though it hardly seemed like one at first. Arthur lost his job. He was in his early fifties and had been with the same company since his mid-twenties. "A new boss came in, and we just didn't see eye-to-eye," he said.

I suspected it was a classic case of "trimming the gray" from the employee base to keep the cost of benefits and salaries down, the usual reason people over fifty get eased out.

He was given a nice severance package and didn't need to find a job that instant.

He said, "There's always a blessing, Jo, no matter what happens. Now I can help you find a house and move Mama Jo. If that's not the Lord's work, I don't know what is."

"I'll believe it when she lets us do what we have to do without making a big stink."

"I'm putting it in my prayer journal right now."

Soon I was making many trips to North Carolina and clomping around in dangerous ice storms while Arthur videotaped each real estate contender.

"Okay, this one has vinyl siding," he said as though it were a positive attribute.

I responded, "Eck. Vinyl?"

"Maintenance-free, Jo! Trust me, that's what you want."

He would also swoon over a house with no crawl space. "You don't want to go wriggling around in some dark, dank place checking on the furnace," he stated.

My response was, "How often does anyone need to do that?" I'd never owned a home before. If there was ever a problem with a dwelling I was living in, I called the super or caretaker. Arthur just shook his head.

My main concerns while house hunting were: enough living space downstairs for Mama Jo and her dolls, a big kitchen, plenty of space for myself on another floor for total privacy, and QUIET so I wouldn't have to spend thousands of dollars on soundproofing. In other words, no crowded developments, like my brother's. I didn't want to drag out this decision, nor did I want to make it too hastily. This was where I was going to be—with my mother—almost every hour of every day.

As I rejected houses, Mama Jo's panic was rising back in Richmond. "I don't know what to throw out!" she would say. "I have too much stuff!"

I'd try to calm her down by saying, "You don't have to get rid of anything yet. As soon as I'm moved in, you'll come down to North Carolina to live, and we'll go up to Richmond on weekends to work on your house." A plan that would take forever to complete. "Just let me buy *our* house first." I didn't want it to seem like she was moving in with me, but that we were both starting over in a new place.

When I finally had the house I thought would work best, I described it to her over the phone, snapped photos, and mailed them to her to make sure it met with her approval. The winner was ten minutes from my brother in a sleepy, bucolic area that reminded me of the horse-country part of Westchester that I was leaving. I was drawn to the house for its layout, ample land, surrounding woods, and feeling of serenity. The owners were high school sweethearts who had built it and raised their kids in it. It had good emotional energy. It was, however, in its late-teen years, the age when I'd heard things start to go wrong with a house and kids. But it couldn't all happen at the same time, could it?

I blocked out that it had vinyl siding and a crawl space and was in a development.

While packing, Mama Jo's friend Ginny called and said, "She's opening boxes and throwing the contents on the floor. She just can't handle this."

I called her right away. "Just hang on, Mama Jo! As soon as I get settled and put in your walk-in shower, I'll be there. Otherwise, you'll have to stay on the second floor until it's done, and you might fall down the stairs. The same is true at Arthur's."

In a small voice she said, "Okay."

I was beginning to wonder if she would survive until I was able to do everything that needed to be done.

My going-away party was a little sad, but mostly fun. There were bagpipers, a belly dancer, nearly a hundred people from all walks of life, and a lot of gifts, including a six-hundred-dollar Home Depot certificate that I naively assumed would carry me along for quite some time.

Some of my gal pals were still mad at me for leaving. "Don't be proud," one said. "We all make mistakes."

Arthur began getting estimates from contractors on various jobs that needed to be done and laid them out for me on an Excel spreadsheet. He even gave directions to his house the same way. I wondered if his will was written in Excel, too. He advised me to always get three estimates for any work I needed done, "And pick the one in the middle."

Leaving New York wasn't easy, but by then I'd met a few people who had gone through living with, and taking care of, an elderly loved one. They all said the same thing: "You'll never regret it." I wasn't convinced. Their parents weren't doll-collecting, depressed hoarders who historically got on their last nerve.

Just before I pushed off for North Carolina, I happened to watch Werner Herzog's cinematic masterpiece *Fitzcarraldo*. I was spellbound as Klaus Kinsksi's mad character goaded the Peruvian natives into hauling a steamship over a mountain for some insane, greedy reason. The actors and crew actually did this, not a special-effects computer program, and many were nearly homicidal or suicidal by the end. I couldn't help but think that cleaning out my mother's house might bring my sanity to the same brink.

I got a second cell phone with a North Carolina number so that I wouldn't lose my New York number. I still needed to maintain the illusion to others—and myself even more—that I hadn't left. I was sure I'd return when this situation with my mother was resolved. It could very well be sooner rather than later.

On the morning of April 15, Lupe, my cat; my girlfriend Tara; and I wedged ourselves into my packed Saab and hit the road. Tara's height, in her words, is "five feet twelve inches." We felt like Thelma and Louise going off to college. Or rehab.

Tara owned several properties and had long chastised me for being a renter. She had to see with her own eyes that I now owned a house. She was also there for moral support should I have serious second thoughts about this relocation.

We finally arrived at my new country-style home, which looked so warm and inviting from the outside, with its front porch and many trees sprouting new leaves. Tara gushed over how pretty it was, and I felt good. I noticed a paneled truck in the driveway. "Must be the painter who's removing the hideous '80s wallpaper. He's charging me three grand."

"Jo," she said, "that's a deal. Marriages have been ruined over removing wallpaper. It's a nasty job."

I stayed happy until I saw my painter standing in my kitchen surrounded by buckets. He looked at me with a pained expression. "Um, I accidentally did something when I was removing the wallpaper in the bathroom above," he said. "The toilet sprung a leak, causing water to pour through the recessed lighting here." He said he would replace the toilet, fix everything, and air it all out with fans to keep mold from growing.

Mold?! I'd heard all kinds of horror stories about mold. I turned to Tara, the expert. She shrugged. "Of all the problems I've dealt with, I've never had this one."

While he handled that, Tara needed to hop on her computer to do some work. She was a speechwriter, and some bigwig somewhere was eagerly awaiting her words to make him sound even smarter. She could work with a dial-up—if the phone service had been turned on, as it was supposed to have been.

I was in the midst of sorting out that when the movers appeared. At least my things were here . . . safe and sound . . . I hoped.

Just as the moving van pulled out of my driveway and I was staring at the furniture and mountain of boxes left behind, Mike called. He got right to the point. "Your mother dialed 911 saying she was dizzy. The ambulance came and took her to the hospital. Oh, gosh, I'm worried."

The emergency room nurse I spoke to said, "She's disoriented and only weighs eighty-six pounds. The fire inspector declared her house a health hazard, and she can't go back there. You need to come get her now."

Each sentence was like a sock in my gut. "But I'm four hours away, getting the house ready for her to come live with me!" It was decided she'd go into assisted living until I could come get her.

When Mama Jo was put on the line to talk to me, she was livid. "Get me out of here," she said roughly. "I want to go home." I tried to tell her she was going somewhere temporarily where she would be safe and well fed. I don't think she believed me.

When I reported this new development to Arthur, his initial shock turned to awe. "It's the Lord doing his work again, Jo! We had no idea how we were going to get her out of the way so we could clean out her place!"

I added, "And she can't blame us because she called 911." I had to admit, it was pretty amazing. And I was overjoyed that he was still saying "we" when referring to clearing her mess.

The good vibes between us momentarily vanished when he informed me that my cat, Lupe, my constant companion for the past ten years, couldn't stay with Janet while we were in Richmond. "She's not a cat person, and neither am I," he said. There are no words more insulting to someone who is a cat person than those. He softened his decree with, "And with all the kids coming and going here, she might get out and get gone."

I was frantic. There was no way I could take her with me to that junkyard of a house. I hired a professional pet-sitting company with a name I could trust—Spoil Me Rotten—and prayed the workers in my home didn't let Lupe out by accident to "get gone."

There was a knock on my front door. "Hi there!" said a good-looking man about my age with blond hair and a huge smile. "I'm your next-door neighbor, Van. Just wanted to introduce myself. If you need anything, let me or my wife, Gina, know."

I let out a sinister Cruella de Vil laugh. Where should I begin with the answer to that? I gave him a brief overview of my situation while taking down his number. After he left, Tara whispered, "I think he's a swinger, Jo."

"What? Come on . . ."

"No, there's definitely something a little, I don't know. He was just too happy. Too nice."

I would later find out that both he and his wife were ministers.

Before I took off for Richmond, I needed to quickly set up my computer-driven recording studio to make sure everything was working. I'd landed contracts with a few radio stations around the country as their "imaging voice." That's the nameless person you hear between songs, and in and out of commercials, who repeats the station's slogans, like "More music, less talk!" They didn't pay much individually, but I could do the work from home. If I racked up enough of them, I'd be fine. They e-mailed me the copy; I recorded it and sent it back. A quick turnaround was essential.

To my horror I discovered my PC was DOA. Wouldn't even boot up. I had no techie person here to turn to. I was hysterical. Tara had allotted three days for her visit south, and they were about up. She had to get back to her daughter and well-functioning office. It wasn't until I saw her off at the airport that I felt truly alone.

I returned home to find a thick packet from the assisted-living facility. It was all paperwork I had to fill out immediately and send back. I had the sensation of pins being stuck in my eyeballs. When I had to write out a four-figure check to them, I became a living voodoo doll with pins sticking in me all over. How was I going to pay for a new computer as well?

Not paying off my credit card balances for the first time in my life actually worked in my favor. I was inundated with offers in the mail for cards with 0 percent interest, even on cash advances. The catch was that it lasted for only a year, and then the interest rate went sky high. I procured two cards, maxed them out to the tune of twenty thousand dollars, and vowed to use only what I needed while making a little interest on the cash sitting in the bank. I'd pay it all back as soon as my mom's house was sold. I was sure there was no way I'd use it all.

Somewhere a Greek chorus was trilling, "Man plans. God laughs."

Mama Jo meets with Shirley Temple's approval before heading out to an Eastern Star event, 1940s

The Reinvention Express

Four months after I conceived of the Brilliant Idea, and four days after Mama Jo went into assisted living, Arthur and I were on our way to Richmond to face the biggest mess we had ever laid eyes on.

The weather had turned gray, wet, and chilly. The windshield wipers chunk-chunk-chunked through a steady drizzle. I warmed my hands with a cup of bitter convenience-store coffee that I'd attempted to make palatable by adding hazelnut-flavored nondairy creamer. We were dressed in work clothes: jeans, sneakers, and sweatshirts. My top was emblazoned with COLUMBIA, my alma mater. Arthur's stated, GOD'S XXL PROPERTY.

We said nothing as we drove through desolate parts of North Carolina and Virginia. Finally I broke the silence. "The only way to get through this is to pretend she's not our mother."

My comment jolted him out of his own mental meanderings. "What do you mean?"

"If we tell ourselves we're doing this for someone who's just very sick, we won't get so angry."

The wipers chunked back and forth a few more times. He answered, "You're right."

On a more upbeat note, I said, "Did I tell you the broker's reaction when I first asked her about selling Mama Jo's house?" She had handled the sale of Uncle Sid's home after he died and had paid a visit to my mom at that time. I put on her sweet southern accent:

"Oh, you mean the woman with the little baby dolls that she treated like people?"

He made an unpleasant face. "Like the big stuffed bear she kept in the passenger seat of her car so she'd have someone to talk to."

I justified her action by adding, "It was also so she wouldn't seem like she was alone when she was driving at night." We exchanged a knowing glance as only two war buddies can do. There was no denying that an unexpected bond was re-forming between my brother and me.

We vented about being raised by someone who was chronically late. Not surprisingly, we grew up to be punctual people with little tolerance for those who weren't.

I searched my memory banks for the last time Arthur and I took a road trip together. "Wasn't it 1969? When you, me, and Poddy moved to Miami?"

"In the '66 Chevy Impala station wagon," he said.

"I remember the eight-track tapes we listened to," I said excitedly, the DJ in me springing to life. "The Beatles' *Yesterday and Today*; Cream, *Disraeli Gears*; Led Zeppelin's first album; and Jimi Hendrix, *Are You Experienced?*"

Thirty-four years later, I could still see my father sitting behind the steering wheel of that tank of a car in his khaki pants, his belly pressing against the steering wheel, a thick gray mustache that contrasted with his thinning gray hair, and prominent bags under his eyes that I hoped I wouldn't inherit. When he really wanted to rub it in how bad our music was to him, he'd roll his eyes back in his head and drone a line from Jimi Hendrix's "Manic Depression."

It was a tense and tumultuous summer, even without our move to Miami sans Mama Jo. The Manson murders were so gory and incomprehensible I couldn't watch the media coverage of them. The Stonewall riots in Greenwich Village that officially started the gay rights movement had me worried about Julie and Charlotte. A quick visit to see them before we packed up and headed south had proved illuminating when I learned that Aunt Charlotte wasn't a "real" aunt and that she and Julie slept in the same bed. I found them even more fascinating, and at the same time too different for me to relate to. Our deep bond would begin to form over the next year due to Julie's efforts.

America had been embroiled in the Vietnam War for some time. If I saw one more dead cow on the nightly news lying on its back with its legs pointing straight up in the air, or heard venerable anchorman Walter Cronkite enumerate how many more soldiers were killed that day, I was going to throw up my Swanson TV dinner.

Our father and Arthur, a high school senior then, continually butted heads—and occasionally traded blows—over my brother's antics, like drinking or being involved in leaving a huge dead sea turtle on the front doorstep of an elderly couple. I thought my brother was an ass. He wasn't too crazy about me either, because I never got into trouble, did well in school, and made him look even worse.

Our golden retriever and yellow Labrador mix, Sandy, took off repeatedly. As our departure date for Miami approached, we received numerous phone calls from strangers and law enforcement officials saying they'd found him miles from our home.

The week Mama Jo quietly moved out of our home that overlooked the Potomac and into a small, dreary apartment with a view of a shopping plaza, the rest of the world was glued to a TV for the spine-tingling moment when man finally walked on the moon. It was easy not to notice my mother was gone.

The night before the three of us were to pile into our stuffed car and head to our new home with our dog and cat, I snuck out of the house to see some friends one last time, really hoping to see a guy I had a crush on. I thought I'd closed the door tight enough so the dog wouldn't get out, but not too tight to make a noise when I returned.

When I crept back home a few hours later, the door was wide open and Sandy was long gone. My self-hatred knew no bounds. I loved that dog. The guy I was hoping would finally show me some attention barely noticed I was there. Why did I even bother? I was leaving!

As we cruised the neighborhood the next morning looking for Sandy, I never admitted I was responsible for his final jailbreak. I was supposed to be "Little Miss Perfect," according to my brother.

"We were supposed to leave at six sharp!" my father bellowed. "We're not going to spend all day looking for that damn dog!"

Tears streamed down my face as I wailed, "We have to! We have to!"

"The way that dog roams, he could be miles away by now!"

We finally gave up, and I felt nauseous as we passed, for the last time, the houses, roads, and shopping plazas of suburban northern Virginia that I knew so well. When I imagined my dog returning to our house and finding us gone, I'd cry harder.

Arthur and Poddy were getting fed up with me. "Face it," Arthur said. "He kept running off. He wanted to be free!"

Like Mama Jo.

Like me, too.

Free to start a new life. Free of being my mother's "living doll," as my father would say. Free of having to be perfect. Free of having to be a Job's Daughter and fit in with the "right" crowd in my mother's eyes that felt all wrong to me.

The first day of our trip south grew worse when we stopped to have lunch in a restaurant. We couldn't leave our cat, Tiger Sam, in a locked hot car with the windows up, and we had to roll them up tight because so much stuff was in there. We were towing an eighteen-foot boat and placed Tiger Sam in the boat on a leash while we went inside to eat. When we returned after lunch, Tiger Sam was gone. Only his leash and collar remained.

I was again despondent as we searched and searched. How far could our cat have gone? We inspected the field next to the parking lot. We called out. We looked. We called out some more. Did someone see him and take him? Did he escape on his own? If that were the case, then we were so toxic that not even our pets wanted to be with us.

We were all on the Reinvention Express.

Sitting in Arthur's Durango now, heading for Richmond for Phase 2 of Operation Mama Jo, I said to him, "I still wonder how Tiger Sam got away. How could he have wriggled out of his collar? Maybe he jumped and was being strangled, and someone ran over and freed him?"

Arthur said with conviction, "I think Poddy snuck out of the restaurant while we were eating and let the cat go because he didn't want to deal with him." I was shocked he would think that. He was shocked that I was shocked. "Of course he'd do such a thing." I refused to believe it . . . at first.

"We should have had a carrying case for the cat," I said in my all-knowing schoolteacher voice. "It's dangerous to drive with an animal loose in the car. We also could have taken him into the restaurant if we'd had one."

"I wonder how the dog got out of the house," he said. "I bet Poddy let him go, too." I still couldn't admit I was responsible for that happening. Then again, maybe my father did open the door for the dog after I snuck out, and I was feeling guilty all these years for nothing.

We were quiet for a long time while we listened to a classic rock station. The lady DJ talked about an appearance she was making at a car dealership that weekend. I was relieved those days were over for me. I was even losing touch with pop culture. When I passed through the checkout line at the supermarket, faces that I no longer recognized stared back at me from the covers of tabloids. I didn't mind at all.

As we drew closer to Richmond, I said to Arthur, "I asked the broker how long she thought it would take for us to clean out the place."

"I can't wait to hear," he said flatly.

"She said, 'At first you'll be traipsin' down memory lane. You know, oh, look at this! Oh, look at that! Then you'll go into Bitch Mode and really get it done.'" Arthur slapped his thigh and laughed. I added, "She also said it could be worse."

"You're kidding."

"She said, 'At least it doesn't smell like cat piss or have dead animals in it.'"

"I guess that's one way to look at it."

In a pained voice, I asked him, "Could we really have done anything sooner?"

"I don't think so. And let's stay focused on the future."

I wondered how well we would succeed at shutting out the past as we sifted through not just our mother's stuff but also that of her late husband, mother, grandmother, and uncle, and things of ours that she'd kept. Mama Jo had turned her garage into a storage area, enclosed a patio, and used that as a dumping ground. The basement laundry room was also jammed with junk. There were people who could be hired to do this, but how would they know what to throw out and what to keep?

"We should go see her first, don't you think?" I asked.

"I guess."

"I'm just afraid she's going to demand we take her back home and then watch us like a hawk as we clean it out."

"Particularly with me there," he said. "We'll get nothing done."

Except a lot of screaming at each other, I thought. "But it'll put off facing . . ."

"We have to face it, Jo."

"We have to face her, too." I suggested we take Mama Jo to lunch. "If she wants to come back with us, we'll tell her it's not safe. Don't use the word 'condemned'! But we have to be sure to include her, ask her what she wants us to save. We can't act like Attila the Hun."

"Only if she brings it up," he said sternly. "Don't put ideas in her head!"

My cell phone rang. It was my voice-over agent bearing bad news. "Your Philly station is changing formats," he said. "They'll continue to pay until your contract is up in two months."

After I got off the phone, I yelled, "Shit! That was my biggest client."

"There's no need to swear, now."

"I have to make more money." I rubbed my forehead. "Oh, well, I guess it's one less client to worry about since I have no time to work anyway." I became agitated, waving my arms, bouncing around in my seat. "How does anyone working full-time deal with something like this? Or someone who's married with kids? And she isn't even living with me yet!" I went back to rubbing my forehead.

Driving into the assisted-living parking lot, I saw a line of empty rocking chairs on the front porch. I could already feel the decaying lives inside.

My eyes fell first on Mama Jo's roommate, who looked younger than the other faded, crumpled residents we passed in the lobby. Then I saw my mother's small frame lying on a twin bed, on top of the covers, eyes closed. When we spoke her name, she lit up, and we all happily embraced.

We shook hands with our mother's roommate, whose eyes seemed a bit glassy. She was apparently starved for company and began to chat us up. Mama Jo remained quiet as Arthur and I went into that chipper voice people put on when they visit someone in the hospital, that you're-really-in-bad-shape-but-we're-all-pretending-you're-fine one.

I blurted out to the roommate, "You seem so young to be here," hoping she'd take the reference to her youthfulness as a compliment.

"Well," she said without inflection, "my husband died, then my mother, then my father, then my dog. One right after the other. I became depressed and couldn't take care of myself, so my brother put me here. I don't have any children."

I gulped. Was I looking at myself in the not too distant future? All I could say was, "I'm sorry to hear that."

The room was dark and reeked of a cheap deodorizer that was plugged into an outlet next to the roommate's bed. I think it was supposed to be vanilla. I was soon trying to suppress dry coughs. How did they stand it? When I learned that the small bathroom was shared with two other women who entered from the other side, I concluded it was probably better to have the deodorizer than not.

"Would you like to go to lunch, Mama Jo?" Arthur asked.

"No," she said. "I'm not hungry."

"She just ate," her medicated roommate offered.

When I asked my mother what she'd had, she couldn't remember. I'd have to try to stop asking her questions that taxed her memory. It would be a hard habit to break.

Mike had brought over a few things for her, but she needed more: a comb, toothbrush, underwear. "And my cane," she said. "They've got me using that contraption." She nodded at a metal walker with wheels. "Don't bring the one that was Granny's, the black one with the gold top. Someone will take it. Look for an old wooden cane." I recalled that the director of the facility said I should put my mother's name on everything I brought over, just like Mama Jo had done for me when I went away to camp.

"Would you like to have dinner later?" I asked.

"No, thanks."

"Sure?"

"If you have time, but I'll be fine if you don't."

She said nothing about her home, nothing about getting her out of that dismal place. When Arthur and I walked out of hearing range, he said, "Wow, that was easy."

"Too easy," I replied. When we reached the car I dashed back to her room.

She looked at me with surprise. "Did you forget something? Sit down and count to ten. That's what Granny always said to do."

I sat down, but I didn't count to ten. I whispered in her ear what I'd wanted to say before, but couldn't in front of her roommate, who was never leaving. "I promise I'll get you out of here as soon as I can."

She held onto my arm, pulled me closer, and whispered, "I need my girdle." I thought that was odd. Who was she going to impress with a flat tummy and tight butt here? "And some maxi pads." When I didn't say anything because I was putting the two together, she said, "Sometimes I have a little accident."

"I understand."

She said softly, "I know I left you with a big mess. Just save the dolls and the family things. That's all I care about."

Thrilled as I was to hear her say that, I was also alarmed. Did this letting go of her possessions mean she was ready to die? When I told Arthur what she'd said, his eyes widened. "That's the Lord working, Jo. That's the Lord!"

I wanted to believe him, but the cynical New Yorker in me also thought, Where the Lord goes, the devil follows.

Mama Jo, sweet sixteen, 1938. The yearbook caption read: "Mischievous imp of gaiety."

9

"Is There Something You've Never Told Me?"

We bought the largest plastic garbage bags we could find plus paper towels, latex gloves, and disinfectant cleaner. I also bought medical masks to keep any stirred-up airborne gunk from entering my larynx or lungs and affecting my voice.

When we pulled into Mama Jo's driveway, I was pumped with caffeine and my DJ energy. "Let's go!" I cried. "I can't wait to start throwing out shhh—crap."

He laughed. "Remember when you used to jump all over Poddy for his swearing?"

I drew a blank. "No, I don't."

Arthur reached into the back of his SUV and lifted out two electric air purifiers. "You said, 'Why do you swear so much?' and he said, 'I don't swear.' And you said, 'Yes, you do!' Then he said, 'I haven't said a damn swear word in the last five minutes.'" Still laughing, he said, "And you also used to say to him, 'You're not always right, but you're never wrong!'"

I remembered that one fondly. I was the only one who could stand up to him and get away with it. "And how about when Mama Jo would say to him when he was bossing us around, 'This is a family, not a *platoon*'?"

Arthur imitated him giving us advice before we went out on a date: "No friggin' in the riggin'!"

In my father's deep, growling voice I added to that last topic, "And don't get glandular!"

We agreed we could use those marine go get 'em genes now to get this job done. However, the first thing I did was pure Mama Jo. I put the stuffed gorilla in a handy place to sing us "Wild Thing" when we needed a moment of levity.

We set up the air purifiers, opened all the windows, and formed a systematic approach. Anything broken, stained, moth-eaten, or smelly would be tossed. Exceptions were items doll-related, or that appeared to have been in the family a long time. We tried to designate an area for things going to North Carolina, but there was no available space. It was like trying to organize the contents of five houses crammed into one.

An estate liquidator with a refined air showed up to assess the situation. He looked around in a daze and said, "Where did she live?" Spying a plastic horse on its side in a pile of junk, he inspected it. "Do you have any more?"

"Those things?" I said. "I had about fifty when I was a kid. Every color in every pose. I got rid of them a long time ago."

"They're Breyers and worth about thirty dollars each."

He singled out a few more items and said, "Call me when you've gone through it all."

After he left, I turned to Arthur. "If only we could find someone to sell this stuff on eBay. I have no time or patience to do it."

"Neither do I."

April showers bring May flowers, they say. With all the rain in the forecast, a yard sale was out, too.

Help soon arrived in the form of Ronnie, an African American in his thirties who lived in the neighborhood, saw the activity going on, and came by to see what was up. He said he'd done yard work for our mother.

"You couldn't get nothin' past her," he said passionately. "She stood out on the front steps and stared me down while I worked. Watched my every move."

We hired him on the spot, and he assured us, "I got your back."

I worked on turning the basement into a holding bin for things that were to be kept. Arthur tackled her bedroom so he'd have a place to sleep since I was staying at Mike's. Ronnie helped with the heavier objects and loading up the U-Haul with stuff to go to Goodwill and the Salvation Army.

Within no time my surgical mask was history. It was scratchy and only made more sweat drip down my face than was already there.

Next to Mama Jo's washer and dryer were several folding tables piled high with dirty clothes. Behind them were stacks of carrying cases for the Persian cats Mama Jo and her late husband used to breed in what I thought were disgusting and cruel conditions. I hoped I wouldn't come across evidence of their brief fling with marmoset monkeys.

As I tossed case after case into the backyard, I recalled what my mother had said when her last cat died and she decided she wasn't going to get another one because she was afraid of tripping over it and breaking her hip: "I miss Jellybean so much. Have you ever had a cat lick a tear off your face?"

And she still wouldn't see a doctor for an antidepressant.

I earmarked the pet items for the real estate broker who was also active with the local animal shelter. She'd told me her parents had died when she was young and added, "When I see what people go through later in life caring for theirs, like you're doing, I think it might have been a blessing."

Now here I was, clearing out my mother's house as though she had died, but she hadn't. It made it harder because I didn't know what things she would want in the future. Ginny, her good friend, had said in one of our many phone calls that her mother's Alzheimer's had taught her that she tended to remember objects that had been in her line of sight, not things in closets, drawers, or packed away. I wasn't convinced Alzheimer's was my mother's problem, and I also suspected she had an encyclopedic knowledge of her possessions, like my ex-husband did with his comic books.

I took a break to check on Arthur's progress. Taped across the door of Mama Jo's former bedroom, next to where he was working, was a yellow plastic strip she must have found at a construction site. It said: DISASTER AREA. I could only push the door open about a foot due to whatever was piled high beyond it, blocking the way. I snarled, "How the hell are we ever going to get in here?"

After an hour I was able to push the door open another foot. Then I started kicking it in frustration.

Ronnie summed up Mama Jo perfectly. "Man, your mama is wide open, and I mean wiiiide. Some of these dolls make my hair stand on end—what little I have." Taking in the endless mess, he said, "I can't wait to see the look on the mover's face. He's gonna shit twenty bricks."

"Oh, no, he won't," I said. "Most of this is not coming with her."

"I'll believe that when I see it" was Arthur's take after already hearing me say "Don't get rid of that!" many times.

When our spirits were flagging, Ronnie would reassure us with, "It's a journey, man. It's a journey."

Just like the broker predicted, our labors were often punctuated by "Oh, my God!" and "Look at this!" Occasionally, there'd be a shriek of disgust, such as when Arthur found a bag of human hair. Anytime a female in the family had a significant haircut, my mother saved what was snipped off for Aunt Gladys, a doll maker, to create a doll wig out of it. We ultimately found dozens of bags of human hair, which I donated to Locks of Love to be made into wigs for cancer patients, if they were still usable.

There was a box labeled "Hill's Horse Meat" that had dolls in it. A trunk that said "Human Blood" on the side was stuffed with doll clothes. But my most memorable scream came when I saw a glue trap that had been set down to collect insects. At first I thought it was empty. When I picked it up, I realized it was jam-packed with roaches, crickets, and spiders.

Shocking in a subtler way were the hundreds of to-do lists I found in which my mother's handwriting changed from neat to chicken scratch.

There were moments that gave me goose bumps in a good way, like when I found a piece of paper attached to the back of a very simple, small, well-used wooden corner shelving unit. It was a note in someone's handwriting I didn't recognize that said: "Made before the Revolutionary War by a colored slave for the wife of McIntosh that fought in the War. See D.A.R. ancestry." Had that note not been there, this remarkable antique would have been given away or thrown out.

Ginny called periodically to check in, or I called her to ask questions. "I found a bag filled with dozens of little white plastic disks with three prongs sticking out of each one. Any idea what they are?"

"Those are the things they put in pizzas when they deliver them to keep the top of the box from falling onto the pie."

"But why would she save them?"

"She thought they looked like doll tables for a dollhouse." I thought of how many pizzas this represented. It turned my stomach that this was what she was living on while I was eating my fancy dinners in New York. She added, "If you find a bag of toothpaste caps they're supposed to be doll cups." How sad it was that my mother kept thinking she was going to get around to putting up one dollhouse, much less many, when she couldn't even manage her own home.

As slogged on, waves of nostalgia or sadness washed over me. Sometimes I'd let out a loud belly laugh over a silly thing, like finding my pink Corinne's Dance Studio case and inside the itty-bitty purple tutu I wore in a tap-dancing recital when I was three and we lived briefly in Massapequa, Long Island. The shoes my mother had painstakingly painted gold were tucked in there, too. When I found the lyrics she had typed out that went to the song I danced to—"Ain't She Sweet"—and a photo she took of me in action, I wept.

I'd put things like that aside and take them with me when I visited Mama Jo, just to see her light up. I also suspected I'd never find them again. My valiant attempts to keep straight the stuff coming south met with mixed results at best.

She looked at the photo of me dancing and pointed to me in the middle. I was the smallest of the group of seven girls. "You know how I know that's you?" she asked.

"You're my mother. Of course you recognize me."

"You're the one they're looking at because you were the best."

Well, a couple of the girls were watching me. But it hit me how extremely supportive of me my mother had been when I was a child. Even when I was a misanthropic teenager, I couldn't remember her nagging me or outright putting me down. Would I have had the guts to become a Top 40 DJ when I'd never heard a female one before if I'd been raised otherwise? It was as though I could do no wrong in her eyes.

She could do no right in mine.

I vowed not to look at anything too closely or I'd never finish. Over and over, I failed.

In one of my successful zombie states, I started tossing things like a can of men's shaving cream, a pair of men's sneakers, and pills that had been carefully placed in a daily dispenser. They were probably her late husband's from twenty years before. The dispenser might come in handy, so I dumped the contents and set it aside. Then it hit me.

"Uh, Arthur," I said sheepishly as he wiped sweat off his brow, "is this one of your blood pressure pills?" I held it up for him to see.

"Yeah." He saw my look of remorse. "Why?"

"I forgot you were staying here! I was in the Purge Zone and threw them out!"

"WHAT?!"

We started picking the pills out of the garbage, which, fortunately, was just a bunch of papers. In no time we were laughing about it.

The next day I found her typewriter. I wondered if it still worked and went in search of a power outlet.

Arthur irascibly called out, "What do you want that for? You use a computer now."

"Mama Jo doesn't, and she's been saying for years she's going to write a story about the family, particularly Granny."

He made that dropped-a-brick-on-his-foot sound. "She's never going to do that!"

I plugged it in. It started to hum. I had a beautiful vision of her sitting at a table in North Carolina with no clutter around her, no bills to pay, no meals to prepare or order, and finally writing her book. "I'm taking it. You never know."

Like a true parent, he scolded, "Your house is going to turn into Mama Jo's if you're not careful." As if that terror hadn't passed through my brain ten thousand times. Rubbing his sore lower back, he said, "Now where's that Ronnie?"

Our helper was becoming increasingly unreliable, and when he did show up, he was too entertaining to be useful. One time he got on the subject of cellulite on a woman's body. "A little is okay, but when you got a whole cornfield goin' on—turn off the lights! I mean, all the way off." It was easy to stop working in his presence and just laugh.

I said, "It's a journey, Arthur. It's a journey."

"It's bullshit, if you ask me," he retorted. "And don't tell Janet I said that."

I moved into another room and started tossing. After a while I spied something in the bottom of a teacup and called out, "I just found a bolo tie with what looks like a pick ax and some gold in it."

I heard a box drop as he came running. "I've been looking for that for forty years!" It was funny to see him gush over it. His wife had said to me, "He can't stand any kind of knickknack whatsoever. But after seeing Mama Jo's house, I understand why."

And speaking of Janet, the lovey-dovey phone calls between her and Arthur were highly amusing. I'd never seen this side of him before. I also knew he couldn't wait to get back to her, even though he'd said, "The road to a lasting marriage is full of potholes, and some are pretty deep. But we know the Lord wants us to be together, and that gets us through them."

It reminded me to say to him, "Keep your eyes out for our parents' divorce papers."

"Why?"

"She once told me she received nothing. I found it hard to believe after they were together for so long. And she didn't work through most of the marriage."

He stood there, absorbed what I was saying, and replied, "If she had gotten alimony, she would have just spent it on more junk." He went back to what he was sorting. Would she have? I wondered. Feeling utterly jettisoned by her own family surely contributed to her hoarding.

I took a Diet Coke break, sat on the front porch, eyed the mailbox that was hanging precariously from the brick exterior, and for the hundredth time swore I was going to fix it or get someone else to. To my right was a third Dumpster already full of junk.

There were some other papers I was sure were buried in my mother's house that I didn't want Arthur to find. I considered whether I should tell him about them in advance in case he did. I was sure they'd prove quite a shock, especially given his deeply religious outlook on life now. I decided to stick to the military credo: Information should be given on a need-to-know basis.

Where would I begin my explanation anyway?

My father was an exceptional storyteller. No wonder I was a Story Junkie. In a low and masculine voice, and with a deadpan delivery, he'd take his time telling you a yarn, stringing you along until you believed every word he was saying, only to find out he was setting you up for a joke. But one time, when I was sixteen, he wasn't.

He was sitting in his favorite living room chair in our Miami townhouse. It was round and orange, and it swiveled. "There's something I want to tell you," he said as he leisurely sipped some artificially sweetened black coffee.

I flopped on our bright multicolored sofa and waited patiently. It was probably something having to do with my trip the next day to New York to see Aunt Julie and Charlotte for the summer, followed by a week with Mama Jo and her new husband.

"Before you were born," he said, "I was coming back from a business trip. Your mother was supposed to pick me up at the airport. I'd called ahead. She was all nice and sweet and said she'd be there. She wasn't. I figured she was running late as usual. I waited and waited. Called home. No answer. Waited some more, figuring she was on her way." He took a slow puff on his Kent cigarette. "After waiting for over an hour, I took a cab. No one was at the house. There was no note. Nothing. I started unpacking, opened the closet door, and saw that her side was empty. Then I got it. She'd taken Art and gone to her mother's." He took another drag. "That's how she was. Furtive."

"And a lot more," I joked. "Pod, you don't have to justify anything. I totally get why you didn't want to live with her." He seemed to want to tell me more. "Is that it?"

"Yeah."

"So why'd you stay together if she wanted to leave you?"

He paused. "She wanted to have you."

I was too immature, and detached from my mother, to be touched by this statement. In fact, its sappiness bothered me. I was already convinced I wasn't going to have children. People who just had to have a kid and felt that was the whole purpose of life were morons in my adolescent eyes.

But why had my father brought it up? Did he think he was going to kick the bucket while I was away, and he wanted me to know that? I shook my finger at him and said, "If you die, I'll kill you!"

Unlike Mama Jo, he made a sound when he laughed; a staccato hissing.

I spent that summer with Julie and Charlotte in their artsy bohemian home in the woods ninety miles from Manhattan, exploring Eastern religions and meditation with Julie. Their home felt like my true home.

After that blissful time, my week with my mother and her husband ranged from awkward to excruciating. Mama Jo had quickly remarried to a man who shared her impressive powers to accumulate material objects. Things never got as bad as my mother's present house, but they even had a big antique printing press crammed into a spare bedroom that they occasionally printed Eastern Star material on. He was ten years younger than she, had never been married, had no children, and adored her and me.

I did not return the affection. He smoked like a chimney and continually drank. He wasn't a mean drunk, just a garrulous one, rambling on for hours, sipping one glass of vodka after another. Mama Jo covered for him by saying, "He was in a motorcycle accident when he was your age and had to have a steel plate put in his leg that still hurts. That's why he limps and why he drinks." What-ev-eeer.

The day before I was to leave, Mama Jo sat on her guest room bed while I picked through a closet crammed with women's clothes, some dating back to what looked like Granny's day. I was searching for something funky I might want to wear. A lot of my wardrobe came from thrift stores. I spotted something beige and tight at the waist that was practically see-through. "What's this?" I asked. "A dress or a slip?"

"That's the dress I wore, with a slip under it, when your father persuaded me to stay with him."

My head whipped around. She was grinning. So was I.

She turned serious when she said, "I tried to leave him before you were born. He took me to dinner and, well, you were conceived that night."

I still wasn't overwhelmingly moved. I mean, if I had never been born, I would never have known I hadn't been born. It was one of those existential concepts I easily embraced. I did want that dress, though. I appreciated the story behind it. She happily gave it to me. Given the sexy, diaphanous nature of it, I would say she didn't need too much convincing to stay with my father.

At the airport, as I was leaving to go back to Poddy in Miami, the dress packed neatly away in my suitcase, she gave me that crooked smile of hers that meant she wanted to say something and was having a hard time saying it. "I want you to know that you were very much a child of love."

Huh?

As I cruised through the clouds that day, I was in a daze. Was she saying she fell back in love with my father or that she was in love with another man? I was completely shaken by this possibility and over the years gently tried a couple of times to get her to open up about it, but she wouldn't. I didn't dare ask my father. I wasn't really sure I wanted to know. The older I got, though, the more it ate at me. I just never saw the right opportunity to bring it up again.

The year I turned forty, I invited Mama Jo to visit me in the first house I lived in when I moved out of Manhattan. We were sitting silently on the sofa in my living room as I tried to conjure up more activities to fill the time we had left together. The sound of a neighbor's dog barking prompted her to say, "Sid finally told me what happened to Little Fella."

Sid was her uncle. "Who's Little Fella?"

"A little white dog I had when I was a kid in Kansas City. He was the cutest, smartest thing." I could see her bright blue eyes dull a bit. "One day I came home from school, and he was gone. I looked and looked and looked. Granny tried to convince me he ran off, that dogs just did that sometimes. I didn't believe her. I knew he wouldn't do such a thing. Then Sid finally told me last year that Little Fella had been hit by a car, and no one had the heart to tell me because it was so soon after my father had died."

I gasped in shock. What they'd said was far worse, in my book, than just telling her he'd been killed, yet typical for my family, especially my mother's side. Anything unpleasant was swept under the rug, never to be spoken of again. But I saw my opening.

"Is there something you've never told me?" I asked.

She looked up, surprised. "Like what?"

I resettled myself on the sofa, moved in closer, and rested my arm on the back of the couch, almost touching her back. "Like my father isn't my real father."

A silence followed as she looked everywhere but at me. Then it finally came out: "It could have been ——." She told me the name of our pediatrician in Virginia. My entire body tingled in a searing, bright moment of clarity. I could easily picture him: tall, blond, sharp featured. She kept taking me back to see him, even after we'd moved away from the area. At thirteen I'd begged her to let me get my ears pierced, she insisted he do it, a doctor, not someone in a mall. My impression was that he'd never done such a thing and was nervous, which made me even more nervous. That was right before the move to Miami. I never saw him again.

No wonder there was so much tension between my parents. My father must have known or suspected. My God, how did that affect his feelings toward me? I always felt he loved me very much, and I loved him. Did I do my best to please him so he wouldn't reject me? Was I compensating for my mother's rejection of him?

She turned to me. "I couldn't believe it when you asked us why you didn't look like the rest of the family."

"I did? I said that? When?"

"Several times when you were a little girl."

"How did Poddy . . ." I stopped and just thought, Oh, no. Oh, no.

Mama Jo said she thought the doctor's nurse was in love with him. "She made it very hard to see him and didn't want to put my calls through." A knowing smile spread across her face. "My code name was Mrs. Vermilion."

It was a word I hadn't heard in so long I wasn't sure what it meant.

"An orange-red," she said. "Kind of like cinnamon but brighter." Kind of like *The Scarlet Letter*, I thought. I was impressed by her cleverness, a quality I had never associated with her before. "He thought of you as his," she said. "He only had sons."

Well, Ms. Need-to-Know needed to know the truth. I asked Aunt Julie, my father's only sibling, if she'd submit to a DNA test. If I was related to her, I'd have my answer.

I was. I sent a copy of the results to Mama Jo. I was sure she never threw it out.

I saw my mother differently, and more compassionately, after that. I'd been in a far-from-perfect marriage, too. Fortunately, we didn't have children to complicate things. I even tried to locate the philandering pediatrician for my mother so she could have some closure. He was deceased.

Now, as I sifted through my mother's belongings with my brother (an act that felt part archaeological dig and part exhumation of a grave), I wondered if I was still hanging on to the anger and shame I'd felt when I'd first had suspicions that my mother was having affairs. Or was it just a matter of my mother being stuck at age eight when she lost her father and me being stuck at fourteen when I lost her? When do those age groups ever get along?

Mama Jo in one of the camera stores that developed hundreds of her photos

10

Bitch Mode

At the end of another day of throwing out junk, plus having the rear door of my mother's station wagon bang down on my head every time I opened it because a strut was broken, I stiffly lowered my aching body into a chair at Mike's kitchen table. I wanted to look him straight in the eye and say, "It was the house, wasn't it? That's why you broke it off with my mother." I also wanted to ask, "Why haven't you gone to see her?" I didn't because he'd already done more than enough. I just thought it would lift her spirits. Or would it? Maybe she'd be embarrassed, and he knew it.

Mike was eating a heated frozen dinner and asked me, "How's it going?"

I growled as I poured myself a much-needed beer, "I wish I knew if this was the darkest hour before the dawn or if it's only going to get darker."

He relayed a story about a couple that used to live down the block. Her mother died, and they discovered a dresser stuffed with savings bonds that were worth two million dollars. "They retired the next day," he said.

That reminded me of a tale I'd heard about a man who inherited his uncle's house and all that was in it. The second floor was filled with clocks that he sold for six hundred thousand dollars.

"Wouldn't it be nice if my mother's dolls were worth a fortune?" I remarked. "But I could never sell them while she's alive." I gazed in the direction of her house and wondered why she never outgrew her fascination with them. Not wanting to get into that with Mike, I asked him, "How long did you deal with your wife's situation?"

"Years," he said softly. "It was a gradual process."

"She was fairly young for Alzheimer's, wasn't she?"

"It started in her early sixties." He paused and glanced at a photo of her on one of the kitchen walls. She looked to be in her twenties. "We were high school sweethearts."

He put down his fork. "I swore I wasn't going to put her somewhere, Jo, even when she became violent and didn't know who I was. Then one night she pulled a knife on me, and the doctor said, 'You can't handle this anymore. For your own safety and hers, you have to put her somewhere.'"

Again, I said nothing as I let this sink in. It was no wonder he hadn't visited Mama Jo. It probably reminded him of what he'd gone through with his wife.

"I went to see her every day," he said as he looked through his dinner. "I'd bring her a green apple. Her favorite. Every day. Gosh, that was tough. Found myself crying for no reason." He looked up. "I was on an antidepressant for a while. It sure did help."

What a tender man, I thought. I could see what my mother saw in him. At the same time, how do you compete with a high school sweetheart?

"Do you think my mother has Alzheimer's?" I asked.

"That's hard to say. Probably not yet."

"Do you think she's depressed?"

He paused. "She hasn't been very happy the last few years, but she's a tough one, all right. Very independent lady."

Just like me. I wondered if independence was all I'd made it out to be.

A week later, Arthur and I were on the fourth Dumpster, and the place still looked the same. We entered Bitch Mode.

Complicating matters were my two cell phones stuffed like pistols into the side pockets of my jeans. Without fail, one would ring, then the other, and then I'd hear the annoying beep of another call coming in as I spoke to friends and business associates, and fielded questions from the contractor back in North Carolina who was renovating Mama Jo's bathroom ("What shade of grout do I want? There are shades?").

Gone was the urban diva in her pointy-toed boots and tight French pants. Now I looked like I'd been working under a car all day—which wasn't good when I showed up at a local radio station that I'd brokered a deal with to do my announcing work in one of their studios. And I kept thinking that bugs were crawling on me.

When I reached periodic moments of madness, I would find a new ear to bend. One pal listened and calmly said, "And to think this will never happen to us."

Arthur's outbursts were more frequent as well. Picking up a Beanie Baby in the shape of a cat, he yelled, "All I see everywhere is wasted money! She could have at least given some of it to the church!"

Tense moments were offset by warm ones, like finding our grandmother's cookie jar that we always raided when we visited, or more photos from our time in Anchorage.

"Yeah," I sighed dreamily. "Alaska."

Arthur said thoughtfully, "It was the only time we ever felt like a real family."

"Nothing was the same after we came back." I perked up when I said, "I wonder if we'll find her Alaskan yo-yo. No one could work it like her."

I could easily envision Mama Jo holding two strings a few feet long with furry balls on each end. She would start swinging them until they were moving back and forth so fast they were a blur, making a terrific whirring sound as they whipped through the air. As a five-year-old I could watch her forever, especially when she was wearing her fringed leather jacket. The fringe moved in time with the yo-yo.

Arthur worked on putting together another corrugated box with packing tape. "I think Mama Jo was happiest in Alaska because it was the first time she was away from Florence and Granny."

I thought about that as I gulped down some bottled water. "She did claim she married Poddy so she could finally get out of the house. Seems like she just traded two controlling people for one."

Arthur said, "She sure seemed to have been having a good time when she was single, though."

We'd discovered a box filled with photos from the 1940s of our mother on dates with many good-looking men—some in uniform—dining or drinking at various D.C. hot spots, like the Starlight Roof, Casino Royal, and the Tradewinds. On the bottom of one was written: "Say yes." It was signed Billy Somebody. From her rigid body language and the fact that he was the least attractive in the bunch, I assumed my mother said no.

"Oh, my God," I said. "Is this what I think it is?"

Arthur peered at what I had found: two savings bonds in each of our names. We called the bank and were told they were now worth about a thousand dollars each. "Look at the date," I said. "She bought them the summer of 1969. She had no money, and she bought us these?"

"Maybe she got something in the divorce after all."

Or maybe it was her way of showing her love for us, even when we didn't show it for her. Again, I choked up.

We found more Alaska memorabilia. I cautiously asked Arthur, "Do you think the guy with the dogsled team who wore a purple parka was her lover?"

"What?" he said, obviously thrown by my question.

"Don't you remember her leaving us in the car while she went in and visited some of her male friends? Though maybe that was more when we moved back to Virginia."

He stopped what he was doing and stated emphatically. "No."

Apparently, Arthur and I had very different views of our mother.

"Maybe it was some Eastern Star lady's house," I said to placate him, but why would she not bring us inside?

And who was the dashing man in a uniform who kept turning up in photos, some taken at the Washington, D.C., apartment Mama Jo shared with her mother and grandmother? I showed a few pictures of him to Mama Jo when we visited her one night. She said simply, "He was an oral surgeon at Walter Reed Hospital that I worked for when I graduated from secretary school."

"He's very handsome," I said. "Why didn't you marry him?"

"He was already married."

What was he doing coming to their place?

I could feel my brother's discomfort as he jiggled change in his pocket, just like Poddy used to do. "We need to get going, Jo," he said, clearly not the Story Junkie I was.

After we left the nursing home, I said to him, "I didn't even notice the smell in the room this time."

His mind seemed far away when he said, "We get used to all kinds of things."

The thought went through my mind that maybe Mama Jo would be better off staying where she was. Or was it I who'd be better off?

Arthur had to leave for a job interview in North Carolina. It was agreed that he and Janet would come back to do the final sweep and I'd pay Janet's cleaning business a nice sum out of the sale of the house. For the backbreaking work it would require, I wished it could have been more. Later I would give Arthur shares in a stock I found that were worth quite a lot. I was eternally optimistic that my voice-over business would be fine as soon as things settled down and I could focus on it. He still hadn't landed a full-time job, and I wanted us all to be on good terms. It was critical to the success of Operation Mama Jo.

Ginny, my mother's friend, came by after Arthur left. She was close to my age, quite petite, with long hair that framed an attractive face. What struck me most was how normal she seemed. I had put doll lovers in the same category as some of the weirdos I'd seen at comic conventions I'd gone to with my ex-husband. Sometimes I felt a sibling rivalry with Ginny. She was like the daughter I could never be, the one Mama Jo could still play dolls with.

There was one doll in my mother's collection that I adored and would never part with. Ginny and I bonded over our mutual admiration of "Mammy." My great-grandmother Granny had made her to honor the former slave who raised her as a child on an Arkansas farm in the late 1800s. On the one hand, it was a touching honor. On the other, her name was lost to time, like the slave who built the shelf unit I'd found. Mammy's head was made out of a coconut, and in her lap were two little white baby dolls. Though an outdated stereotype, I thought she was an outstanding example of folk art that also connected me on a personal level to another era.

Ginny knew not only a lot about dolls in general but a lot about my mother's collection. She said, "That bedroom that's filled with boxes from floor to ceiling is all dolls." She swept her arms around the house as she said, "All those boxes over there . . . all those over there . . . all those in there. And there. And there. They're all dolls, doll clothes, doll furniture, or dollhouses."

I sank back on the sofa, slack-jawed. I knew my mother had a lot of dolls, but this was mind-boggling. Even more staggering was that after two weeks and several Dumpsters, I was now learning this. That's how much we still had to go through.

Pointing to the dolls crowded into a corner of the living room, Ginny said, "Those aren't that special. She hid the ones she really loved."

That sounded crazy to me. What was the point of having a collection if you didn't enjoy it? I said, "If there are any dolls you really want, please let me know. You've been so good to my mother."

She thought about that. "I'd love the Ginnies. I collected them as a kid since they had my name." I had no idea what she was talking about and would later learn they were highly collectible.

"Don't worry about it now," she said. "Let Mama Jo take pleasure in them while she can. But there's a dollhouse in the attic I'd like."

Oh, my God. The attic. The attic! I'd completely forgotten about the attic! I went up there with a flashlight in hand. It was packed solid, floor to ceiling, with more stuff.

I screamed. Then screamed some more.

The devout Florence, my maternal grandmother, another hat lover

11

"We Don't Really Know Each Other That Well, Do We?"

I had once asked my mother why she didn't call Florence "Mom," and she replied, "I was an only child. I never heard anyone call her anything but Florence."

I was reminded of this comment as I unearthed countless photos of Mama Jo and Florence dressed up in evening attire at various Eastern Star events. It was as though they were a couple, not mother and daughter, even though my mother was considerably younger than everyone else. My mother said her father was a Mason and had tried to get Florence to join the Eastern Star, the female counterpart. For whatever reason, she put it off. When he died, she regretted not having joined but wouldn't do it on her own. She waited until my mother was old enough, eighteen. They had been loyal members ever since.

Mama Jo tried to interest me when I turned that age. She'd said, "You can go anywhere in the world, and if you need help, or just a friend, you'll always be able to turn to a Star member. There are chapters everywhere." It seemed like too much of a commitment to hang out with a bunch of old people for a reason I'd probably never need.

Going through my mother's stuff served as a constant reminder of how different our worlds were and always had been. I was born in a hospital and grew up in one postwar suburban development after another as my father moved around for his job. My mother was brought into this world in a small wooden house built around the turn of the twentieth century. I saw it when I flew out to Kansas City from New York in the late 1980s for the burial of Florence, my grandmother, in the family plot. My mother's former modest house was ramshackle and abandoned. She'd married up quite a few notches. She slid down a few when she divorced my dad, but not as far down as this.

Granny, my matriarchal great-grandmother, whom my father referred to as the Bull of the Woods, was responsible for my mother ending up in the nation's capital. Granny told her daughter Florence, a plain, sullen widow, to get a government job. Between being hard hit by the Great Depression and Florence's inability to even think about another man after losing her husband at twenty-nine, Granny said it was the only way to have financial security. She certainly wasn't going to work outside the home. She expected Florence to be the breadwinner after her own husband had died.

Florence took a test and was offered a job at the U.S. Mint in Washington, D.C. She moved there first. Granny and my mother eventually followed. Uncle Sid stayed at their small ground-floor apartment sometimes, too. He was closer in age to my mother than to his teenage sisters, and they often double-dated. Mama Jo was under strict orders to never call him "Uncle" when they went out.

My mother attended secretary school and eventually landed a job at the Civil Aeronautics Administration (later known as the FAA), working down the hall from the man who would become my father. As they say in the real estate business, there are only three things that matter: location, location, location.

Now in my mother's Richmond home, I examined a small metal tubular object I'd never seen before. It said it was a cream lifter. Etched on its side were the words: "You can whip our cream but you can't beat our milk. Avon Sanitary Dairy. Phone —504."

A three-digit phone number? I had no idea they ever existed. How old was this thing?

I thought of the sweeping technological changes that had occurred in my mother's, grandmother's, and great-grandmother's lives (Granny had grown up with covered wagons, for God's sake)—and how they refused to embrace so many of them. No flying in an airplane. No touch-tone phone service. Florence had driven a stick-shift car her entire life. The last one was a cherry-red VW Beetle that had plastic covers over its white seats.

I also thought of the seismic social shifts, like staying in one place with one person and at one job and making a change only if you were forced to, not by choice. Some psychological studies have shown that happiness rises when choices decline. I balked at this notion at first, but understood it better when faced with the simple decision of what orange juice to buy. There were dozens of choices where there used to be two—quart or half gallon.

The difference between my jacked-up "better" world and Mama Jo's hit me again when I visited her at the assisted-living facility and said "Pick out a color" as I laid out dozens of paint chips of every hue on her bed. "Choose whatever you like for your bedroom, bathroom, and doll room."

She stared at them, then quietly said, "I've never lived in a house with different colored rooms."

Could that be true? I mentally flipped through the houses we'd lived in, and the ones she had lived in since the family split up. She was right. "Do you not want any colors? I can just paint the walls white."

Her thin finger pointed to a color chip. "That one."

I examined the delicate light-pink rectangle closely. "It's called Confection."

"Pink is my favorite color."

"I didn't know that. Which room is this one for?"

"You would look good in pink," she said.

"I'm a New Yorker. Everything I wear is black."

The bed made a scrunching sound when I moved that I hadn't noticed before. I assumed they must put protective plastic on everyone's mattress.

She kept smiling and reached for my hand. Hers was small and soft, like a child's. Damn, she could be so cute! Why hadn't I seen it before? Still, it seemed as if I was visiting someone else's mother.

I asked, "Which room do you want painted in Confection?"

"All of them."

I told her she could think about it some more, but she didn't seem to be nearly as concerned about it as I was.

I either saw Mama Jo or spoke to her every day. We referred to the assisted-living facility as "the Resort." She now seemed so Zen-like in her acceptance of her situation that it was eerie. I asked her if she still wanted to come live with me.

"If you still want me to," she said. "We don't really know each other that well, do we?"

Was she just making an honest, lighthearted comment? Was she issuing a waring?

I stopped in to see the director of the place to pay her more money. There wasn't much left in Mama Jo's bank account. The work on the renovation of her future bathroom was living up to my Law of Pi: however long you think something will take to finish, or however much you think it will cost, multiply it by 3.14. The bathroom was now up to five thousand dollars and two weeks over the completion date.

After settling things financially with the director, she told me that a few years before, she'd been through the same thing with her own mother. "What's the strangest thing you've found so far?" she asked.

"A single Wheat Chex wrapped in a tissue that was inside a jar that was packed in a tin can that was inside a box."

She said, "We found scores of white plastic balls from inside roll-on deodorant containers."

"They come out?"

"That's what we said."

The director then segued into what she really wanted to talk about. "Your mother should be using a walker. We had a physical therapist work with her, and her balance is not good." I knew a fall at her age would be disastrous. Then she took a deep breath, and said, "Also, she's incontinent and needs to wear a protective undergarment at all times."

This sad news was not only disheartening for the hassle it meant for me, but for what it would do to Mama Jo's already low self-esteem.

As I began to leave, the director surprised me when she said, "I really hate to see your mother go." She told me that a woman had arrived the other night in the same agitated state my mother had been in at first. "Your mother went over to her and sweetly said, 'It's good for you to be here so your family doesn't have to worry about you.'"

I stopped in my tracks. "My mother said that?" She seemed even more a stranger.

I lost track of the number of Dumpsters I went through, but it was at least ten at $250 each. Major work still needed to be done on the yard and on the house, and I had an endless punch list back in North Carolina, including having a handicap ramp installed leading to the front door, and they, of course, weren't cheap. I begged Arthur to come back to Richmond and finish the job of clearing out Mama Jo's house before I lost my mind. He and Janet soon switched places with me.

Janet reported by phone that Arthur had the same reaction to the attic as I did—plus he started throwing objects down the stairs, even glass ones, while yelling at the top of his lungs. "I said, 'Chill out, honey! You could have hurt me!'"

I was so glad I wasn't there. But neither was I thrilled to be in my new place when I opened the door to the garage that was now packed to the rafters and spied a snake on one of the boxes. I had the man putting down tile in Mama Jo's bathroom kill it and throw it in the woods out back. Then I realized that I'd better identify it, and contacted the superfriendly neighbor, and minister, Van.

When we found it in the woods, it was being eaten by another snake! "Oh, they're just black snakes," Van said. "You want them. They eat mice. It's the copperhead you have to watch out for. They're poisonous." He peered at the one being devoured. "You know, that just might be a copperhead."

Right near the end of their time in Richmond, Arthur called and announced, "I found the divorce papers."

Excited, I asked, "What did they say?"

In as edgy a state as I was when I left, he tersely replied, "You'll see." Then he said, "I also found some papers that I can't figure out at all. Some DNA tests that you, Mama Jo, and Aunt Julie had done?"

I inhaled sharply. "Uh, what do you think they're about?"

"All I can think is that Mama Jo wanted to see if you were related to Julie because she didn't want you to see her because she was a lesbian?"

Either my brother was even more conservative than I thought, or he could never imagine his mother being unfaithful. I quietly said, "Mama Jo was having an affair with your pediatrician and didn't know who my father was." I filled in his silence with, "The DNA test was to see if I was related to Julie."

"That's enough! Don't tell me any more!"

"I was."

I wondered what else I'd learn about my mother, and my other family members now deceased, during whatever time she had left on this earth. I had a feeling there was a lot more than just tangible objects to rummage through.

12

A Bird Let Out of Her Cage

Mama Jo and her favorite rocking horse,
Constance Rozelle

All told, it took six weeks to clear out Mama Jo's house. It felt like six years. On the first evening in June, Arthur and Janet picked her up at "the Resort" and headed to North Carolina with one last stuffed U-Haul in tow. A professional mover had already brought down the bigger pieces of furniture.

Though my life had already changed dramatically, it was now a matter of hours until the real, irrevocable change would occur. Living with Mama Jo had all been speculation, theory, before. The truth was, I was a nervous wreck.

I examined her new pink living space and the empty white shelves that would soon hold her dolls. I was reminded of a touching story a man once told me. He and his wife were waiting to adopt a child. The call came that she'd be ready for them the next day, way before they had expected her. "I stayed up all night and painted her bedroom," he said. "I wanted it to be perfect when she got there."

That's how I felt now. There was no other way to put it: Mama Jo was such a little girl in so many ways, and I wanted to be a mother so much, it wasn't far from the actual truth. How well this role reversal would work for both of us was another matter.

Mama Jo, Arthur, and Janet finally pulled in around midnight. My mother seemed so frail as we hugged for a long time in the driveway. She slowly, very slowly, made her way into the house, reluctantly using a metallic green walker with a basket in front and a platform in the middle that could be flipped down and used as a seat. Once inside, she politely asked, "Where's my cane?"

I put the fancy black one in her right hand, and her left hand reached for mine. We were now officially joined at the hip.

The ever ebullient Janet said, "Mama Jo didn't say a word when we left Richmond, and after thirty minutes, Arthur said, 'What's wrong? You're so quiet.' And I said, 'I think you're in shock.' And she said, 'I feel like a bird let out of her cage!'"

However, the happy mood began to feel forced as I gave Mama Jo a tour of her new home. I suspected it could have been Buckingham Palace and she wouldn't have been enthusiastic. It simply was not her home with just her things in it. And Mike next door.

The first stop was her bedroom, which was nearly twice the size of her last one, and bright and airy. "Does that quilt look familiar?"

"Granny and Florence made it out of my schoolgirl dresses."

Janet said, "I put up the curtains, and Arthur did the shelves for your dolls."

Mama Jo nodded noncommittally, and the words of the social worker began to haunt me. *Hoarders turn violently angry if put in a new, clean place*.

I said, "I found a nice lady through the local doll club to help get the collection organized."

My mother said nothing. Would she prefer the dolls stashed out of sight so no one could steal them? Was she just tired?

We moved into the biggest room in the house. The locked wooden glass display cases that Mama Jo had had custom-made for dolls (and never used) awaited their occupants. She barely noticed them. She was too busy delighting in the sight of her childhood rocking hobbyhorse.

"Constance Rozelle!" she cried. "She's named after two girls I knew in grade school." She moved closer and rubbed her hand over the wooden horse's smooth head. "What happened to your mane? And your bridle?"

The three of us looked at each other warily. Was she going to have a Mama Jo Meltdown over this? I cautiously said, "That's the way we found her."

Arthur added a little defensively, "We brought everything that was doll related."

What if some of that hair we found at her house belonged to this horse? Too late now. I put a hopeful spin on the situation by saying, "I'm sure they'll turn up," then tried to focus her attention on the empty display cases. "The whole room is for your dolls, Mama Jo. We just have to unpack them."

Janet encouragingly chimed in, "Won't that be great?"

Mama Jo leaned on her cane and seemed to be searching for something kind to say. "It'll be nice to see them."

"It's been a while, hasn't it?" Arthur asked.

We were all talking in that you're-really-in-bad-shape-but-we're-all-pretending-you're-fine voice again.

Mama Jo just nodded. Was she peeved? Or just lost in that big, mostly empty room? Or maybe, I hoped, moved beyond words? I couldn't tell.

We walked into the dining area, and I pointed out the wall that had been extended and the door that was added so she could close it and have total privacy in her "wing."

"Do you like the color of the walls here?" I said, indicating the dining area. "It's called Neighborly Peach. I think it might be a bit much." I'd gravitated toward bright colors, figuring it would be cheerful to someone who was depressed.

"I like it," she said with a hint of a smile. "It's warm."

Her teak dining table was bare for the first time in years. My wicker chairs with leopard print cushions were around it. Some of our furnishings were so different, I'd feared a decorating disaster, but they blended fine. I held my breath, hoping she wouldn't ask where her dining chairs were. They were in such bad shape they had to be tossed.

I turned on a light so she could see the back porch. I said, "Be careful when you walk out because it's a big step down. The backyard is fenced in so Lupe has a safe place to roam. She's declawed—something I stupidly did when I thought I'd never live anywhere but in an apartment in Manhattan for the rest of my life." I glanced at Arthur. "Guess I was crowbarred out after all."

"Guess so," he smiled back.

"Where is Lupe?" Mama Jo asked, finally showing some life.

I called her name, and we heard the tinkle of a bell coming from the open kitchen next to the dining area. I'd discovered the hard way that Lupe was a frighteningly inquisitive cat. At twelve weeks old she'd managed to sneak into the refrigerator and stay there for six hours. She'd worn a bell on her collar ever since. I spied her way on top of one of the kitchen cabinets, one black paw hanging over the edge. We all laughed, but it tickled Mama Jo the most.

"It'll take a while for her to warm up to you," I warned.

"That's okay," Mama Jo said. "I'm the same way."

In the middle of the kitchen was a tiled island with a four-burner cooktop. I hoped my mother wouldn't be upset that it was gas, which scared her. I also hoped that I wouldn't be sorry I hadn't gotten around to childproofing it, as well as the doors leading outside. My biggest fears were that she would sneak out and try to drive the car, or get lost wandering around the neighborhood, or walk onto the porch and fall.

I showed her the large laundry room that was off the kitchen. She stopped in front of the new front-loading washer and dryer. I'd sprung for the extra cost of matching pedestals so they'd be higher and easier for her to access. I had a feeling the only things she might be capable of doing were washing a few dishes and running the washer and dryer. It wasn't just to take a load off me, but to let her feel like she was helping in some way. I'd made sure the appliances were as simple as could be—no computerized settings.

"They're beautiful," she said.

"Here's the best part of all," I announced as I guided her through the laundry room and opened the door to the garage. I turned on the overhead fluorescent light, and she took in the boxes upon boxes, trunks upon trunks. "It's all your things, Mama Jo."

She scanned the large space that was packed to the rafters. In a tone I still couldn't quite read, she said, "That's a lot of stuff."

Arthur and I exchanged a look that silently said, "It ain't nothin' compared to what it was." Was she thinking the same thing?

I said, "I prefer to look at it as an embarrassment of riches."

She said softly, "I like that description."

"We'll get through it," I assured her. "One box at a time."

Arthur and Janet were putting on a good show, but I knew they were ready to collapse. They were soon on their way after another group hug and prayer filled with thanks and good thoughts for the future.

Then it was just the two of us.

It was late, so I helped her get ready for bed. I'd found some never-worn green-and-blue-plaid flannel pajamas at her house in a bag that said "Meals on Wheels" on it. She recognized the PJs and knew they'd been given to her with one of the dinners they had brought her. I clung to the notion that maybe her memory wasn't that bad after all.

Her antique mahogany bed was high off the floor, and she needed a footstool to help her up. It was faded and torn. "I should reupholster that stool, don't you think?" I asked.

"You don't have to. I'm just glad to be out of the mess I was living in."

I crossed my fingers that she'd keep thinking like that.

I took off her favorite light-blue tennis shoes with Velcro tabs that had been run through a washing machine when she refused to let them be thrown out. They had no odor now. As I helped her out of her clothes, she looked at me and said, "Thank you," as though she were talking to a hired aide, not her daughter.

She was wearing adult diapers. I could detect they weren't clean. I also noticed that my mother's legs were somewhat bowed. As I helped her to the bathroom, she seemed to walk more on the outside of the soles of her feet, though she expressed no discomfort.

I tried to see how much she could do on her own. I opened the drawer in the new cabinet next to the toilet and pointed out the Depends and pads. Then I soaped up a warm, wet washcloth and offered it to her. "I don't know when they last gave you a shower in that place." I also showed her the containers of wet-wipes that I'd picked up. I'd made sure they didn't say "baby" or "diaper" on them.

"Would you like me to leave you alone?" I asked.

She nodded and I left, but stayed close by. I knew this could be a long wait. As a child, I dreaded hearing the words "I need to use the ladies' room" when out shopping with her. She would take so long that I'd leave and wander around the store. I could have been abducted!

After a while I heard water running and knocked on the door. "Everything okay?"

"Yes."

"Would you like me to come in?"

"Yes."

She was hunched over the sink, washing her hands. I handed her a towel, as if I were a restroom attendant, and opened the cabinet over the sink. "Here's your Paquins." It was a hand cream she had used forever. I untwisted the top and held out the container so she could take a dab of the silky white cream. As she moisturized her hands, turning one over the other, I put it back in the lower drawer so it would be easier for her to retrieve.

"I can reach it where you had it," she said. I put it back above the sink. She smiled and in the sweetest of voices remarked, "You're such a good daughter. I'm so lucky to have you."

A wonderful feeling flooded me. It came not just from winning her approval. I felt needed and appreciated in a way I never had before. I felt a sense of purpose. I wasn't remotely angry with her anymore.

I helped her back to bed and kissed her goodnight. She hugged me tightly and again said, "Thank you."

"Thank you, Mama Jo. I was tired of living alone."

She broke into her elfish grin that now melted my heart. "Me, too."

I reached the door and put my hand on the light switch. "See you in the morning. Just shout if you need anything. I'm in the room right above you."

"Where's Lupe?"

"Inside the house somewhere." I reminded her again that she didn't have her claws and to make sure she didn't go out the front door. "The back door is fine."

"I understand."

But would she remember? Worrying about my hellion of a cat was another issue I had to grapple with. But some other time. Right now I just wanted to look at my mother's sweet little face poking out from under Granny and Florence's beautiful quilt.

"Good night," she said.

"Good night." I paused. "Do you have enough covers? Too many?"

"I'm fine."

"I need to get a lamp for your nightstand. It's too bright in here with just the overhead light."

"Can you leave the light on in the bathroom?"

How dumb of me. She'd surely trip and fall if she got up during the night. I turned it on, came back, and gave her another hug goodnight.

"Where am I again?"

"You're home, Mama Jo. In North Carolina."

"Oh." She seemed surprised.

I asked tentatively, "Is that okay?"

"Have I ever been here before?"

Suddenly, I was overcome by a disturbing image of my mother being released from her cage, and me stepping into it.

13

Trapper Jo

Roughing it in the Alaskan wilderness and loving it, circa 1960. Note the matching jackets on me and Mama Jo.

The next morning, several hours after I'd been up, Mama Jo was ready to rise. She was still in her bathrobe and PJs. I helped her to the dining room. Before she sat down, I pointed out two paintings that I wanted her to know were still around. They were portraits of an Eskimo man and woman that I liked for purely sentimental reasons. They'd been on display in every house we'd lived in after Alaska. She'd had them since the divorce.

Gazing at them, she told me the story behind them. "There was a big going-away party for us when we were leaving Anchorage. They gave the painting of the man to your father and the one of the woman to me. I stood up and gave a thank-you speech. When I was done, your father looked at me and said, 'I had no idea you could talk like that.' Of course I could. I'd been a Toastmaster and was in the Eastern Star. I did things like that all the time."

I wasn't aware she could do it either.

I served her one of her favorite meals: a toasted English muffin with cream cheese and a light sprinkling of cinnamon. She enjoyed it once I turned off the overhead fan that scared her. She was afraid it might fall from the ceiling and decapitate her.

When I offered her a cup of coffee, she said, "I only drink tea."

"That's right. I forgot." I ticked off the types I had on hand, and she picked Irish Breakfast. "Since I'm Irish," she explained.

There was Scotch-Irish on my mother's maternal side, and she occasionally referred to "getting my Irish up" when she was irritated, but I didn't know she considered herself Irish. I certainly didn't call myself that. I was a Mixed Breed White Girl—Scotch-Irish, French Canadian, and Alsatian.

I made her tea in a cup that had cantaloupes encircling it that she recognized from her home. She said meekly, "Next time could you put less milk in it and not so hot?" Like a waitress aiming for a good tip, I was determined to get it to her liking and made her another cup. And another. Each time it was too hot. Lukewarm suited her fine. In contrast, I liked the temperature of my coffee near tongue scalding.

We ate in silence, and I reflected on how nice it felt to be in my own house, not a rental, how accurate the term "putting down roots" was. I grabbed my calculator that was nearby and did some math.

"Wow." I stared at the final number.

"What is it?" she asked.

I explained that I'd just counted up every house or apartment I'd ever lived in (twenty-eight) and divided it into my age (forty-seven). "I've moved an average of once every 1.68 years!"

We stared at each other, probably thinking the same thing: what completely different lives we'd led.

"What about me?" she asked.

I did the calculations. "You've moved once every 4.37—but most were when you were married to Poddy. If you take those out, it's once every 11.71 years."

I was definitely ready to stay put, but why did I have to end up here? Not being able to get in my car and reach Manhattan in an hour still did not sit well with me.

"Look," she said, her blue eyes lighting up at the sight of something in the backyard. "A squirrel is talking to Lupe."

He was on the porch looking for food as Lupe eyed him intently through the glass door. Her bushy black tail thumped away. I played along. "What's the squirrel saying?"

"Good morning."

"There are lots of them here. And a woodchuck."

"What's that?"

"Like a groundhog. I saw him the other day down by my storage shed that's beyond the fence. He was so cute sitting on his hind legs with his nose in the air." My tone changed when I said, "The neighbor's teenage son who cuts our grass offered to shoot it." Mama Jo stopped chewing and pulled back in horror. "I told him of course not. Who would want to kill such a cute animal?"

My English muffin was, typically, inhaled by now, and I wanted to get the day going. I had endless techie issues to deal with and more boxes to unpack, and I needed to find a doctor for my mother (all the geriatricians I'd called were closed to new patients) and get a handicap sticker for Mama Jo (but I first needed a doctor to sign off on it). I also wanted to give her a shower, and then cruise around the area so she could see where she lived now. At the pace she was eating, we wouldn't get on the road anytime soon.

The squirrel was gone, and Lupe looked at me with her big yellow cat eyes and let out her high-pitched squeak. I knew she wouldn't shut up until I let her out, so I did and reminded my concerned mother that she was okay because the backyard was fenced in. Beyond it were woods that were beautiful to look at but teeming with wildlife like foxes and coyotes that would love a defenseless little declawed pussycat for a meal.

I did the dishes to kill time, but when I finished, Mama Jo was only halfway done with her breakfast. I went upstairs to my office to tackle the day's "tediocity." It was bad enough when it was just my life to deal with. Now I had Mama Jo's, too.

When I returned to the dining room, she was on her last bite of breakfast. Slow eaters drive me nuts, and at the same time, I wish I were more like them. When she finished, I started to help her to the bathroom. She stopped and surveyed the backyard.

"Those two tree trunks look like legs," she said. "Daddy longlegs."

You wanted a child, Jo. You got one.

I would learn that my mother was quite the anthropomorphizer. The flowers talked to each other, the dolls talked to each other, and everything talked to Lupe.

Giving my mother a shower for the first time was not something I looked forward to. I thought she'd find it demoralizing and fight me. But she didn't. Perhaps her stay in the assisted-living facility had gotten her used to accepting help.

In my youth, I'd thought she was beautiful in a pale and voluptuous way but for some vivid blue lines in her legs. When I'd asked her then what they were, she'd said, "Varicose veins. I got them when I was pregnant with you and Arthur." It was my earliest memory of thinking, "There is no way I will ever bear a child." Looking at her body now, those veins were nowhere to be found.

"Your skin is like cream, Mama Jo. Do you use a lot of moisturizer?"

"Only on my hands."

"Not even on your face?"

She took just the right comedic beat. "Nothing could help all these wrinkles."

"Stop it," I chided her mildly as I took off her glasses and guided her to the shower. "You look great."

She gave me another disapproving look and grabbed onto the hand bar outside the sliding door to the walk-in shower. I'd bought a plastic chair for her to sit on and hoped she could reach it okay. I wasn't sure if I should have already been inside the shower to help her in. But then what if she fell stepping in? I needed to be behind her. Once she was safely on the chair, I detached the showerhead and let the water warm up. I wasn't surprised that I could take it a lot hotter than she could.

"It has different settings," I said, as I tried out each one on her. "I bet the pulsating one would feel good on your back." Instead, she jumped in pain from it, and I apologized profusely. We settled on the softest one of all.

I watched the water cascade down her small, round shoulders, and over her breasts that had shrunken with age and her round belly that protruded even more because she was hunched over. I lathered up a washcloth, but it proved too rough for her. I used a bar of soap directly on her smooth skin instead.

"This is Yardley lavender soap that I found at your house," I said. "Wasn't that Florence's favorite? I could instantly smell her bathroom when I held it to my nose."

"I can't find it anymore."

"I'll look on the Internet for it."

"The what?"

"Something you access through a computer that links you to the world and is a great way to waste time."

"I don't need any help with that."

I let the gentle rainlike warm water cover her back for a good minute as she happily moaned, "Aaaaahhhh." I enjoyed watching the pleasure it gave her.

"This is a nice shower," she said. "I feel safe in here."

I hoped she wouldn't ask what the renovation cost. My dream of overhauling the kitchen and master bathroom wasn't going to happen anytime soon. I now knew that when a broker says a house "needs a little updating," what he or she really means is "take out a second mortgage." I also didn't share with Mama Jo that I'd widened the door to thirty-six inches in case she ended up in a wheelchair.

With her eyes closed, I started shampooing and conditioning her short gray hair. In my effort to lighten the uncomfortable situation of a child bathing a parent, I rambled on in the way a nurse does before she sticks you with a needle. "I had no idea tile came in so many different sizes. The contractor sent me to Home Depot to pick out what I wanted, and there were so many choices I couldn't decide. He said that usually people put smaller tiles on the walls and bigger ones on the floor. I've seen plenty of showers. How did I not know that?"

"We just don't see things until we need to," she said.

I was beginning to thoroughly enjoy my mother's succinct responses.

Getting out of the shower was tricky, too. Life with Mama Jo was going to be one trial-and-error event after another.

As I dried her hair with a small towel, I said, "The guy who built your bathroom was cute." That piqued her interest. "Very tall."

"Did he have brown eyes?"

His handsome face came to mind. "I don't remember. Why?"

"I love brown eyes."

My father's eyes were hazel, like mine, a nice way of saying a color that can't make up its mind if it's gray, green, or brown. Apparently, she didn't marry him for his eyes. That got me wondering about the divorce papers that Arthur had found. Have you ever put something valuable in a place so safe that you forgot where you put it? That's what I did with those papers. I was still surrounded by boxes and disorder.

I offered Mama Jo some lavender-scented body lotion, she nodded yes, and I worked it into her skin. She said, "Tell me more about the tall man."

At least she was following the thread of a story. "He's someone Arthur met at church. He knew Arthur and Janet before they even dated. I asked him if ever thought they'd get together. He said, 'Never in a million years!' Guess you never know who you're going to fall in love with."

She said nothing.

It was time to get her into a protective undergarment. I didn't like the ones that broke away at the sides because they were too much like a diaper. Instead, I bought the kind that looked the most like panties and slipped an ultra-absorbent pad inside that could easily be changed. When I reached for her bra, she said, "I need my underwear."

"You already have it on."

"I need my panties." She motioned to her bulky white brief. "To put over this."

I thought that was strange, but found a pair of black ones. You could still see her Depends underneath them. It dawned on me that it gave her a sense of normalcy to have on what she would typically wear.

I held up her black bra. She thrust her arms out as I slipped its straps over them. She turned so I could hook it in the back, and said, "I need this for my big *boo-som*."

When I stopped laughing, she asked, "Am I ever going to meet the tall man?"

Again I was thrilled that she hadn't forgotten what we were talking about. I wasn't, however, thrilled with my response. "He invited me to a church dinner, but he was just interested in saving my soul. Already had a girlfriend." I quickly pointed out, so as not to upset her, "I am religious, Mama Jo. I'm just not, um, hard-core." I had to broach this subject at some point, so I asked, "Do you want to go to Arthur's church on Sunday?"

"Not particularly."

"Is that because it's a Baptist church?"

"Why does he go there?"

"Remember his total-immersion baptism a few years ago?" She stared blankly. "How about a Presbyterian church? Would you like that?"

"We can watch *The Hour of Power* on TV instead."

Me watch a holy-roller show? "Sure, Mama Jo. Just remind me." I crossed my fingers that her unpredictable recall would work in my favor on this one.

I helped her into her pants while she held onto my back for balance. This pair fit, but most of the ones I'd found in her house that were still in good condition were way too big. "I have to buy you new clothes or fatten you up, Mama Jo."

She grabbed her stomach. "You don't call this fat?"

"I call eighty-six pounds not fat."

"Is that what I weigh?"

Once dressed, I asked her if she wanted to use the bathroom before we headed out. She said yes, and after closing the door behind her, I felt a distinct sense of accomplishment from getting her showered and dressed. It wasn't so bad. It was actually tender. Then I looked at the time. Eleven o'clock?! I had a mile-long to-do list awaiting my attention. My shoulders rose, and my jaw clenched as I reprioritized the day.

I opened the door to the backyard and called for Lupe. I had to get her inside before we left. She didn't appear. I walked into the yard to find her. She was nowhere.

I panicked. Where could she have gone? The fence door wasn't open. I scanned the yard again, and then I saw it. A hole dug under the fence.

That woodchuck wasn't so cute anymore.

What was I going to do now, put coils of barbed wire around the bottom of my fence like a high-security prison?

I opened the fence door and called out to the vast woods behind me.

I spit out obscenities.

I felt tears welling up inside at the thought that Lupe might be gone forever.

I dashed around and up the incline to my driveway, and there she was, in all her glorious long-haired blackness, rolling around on the asphalt without a care in the world.

Mama Jo and I never did make it anywhere that day. A man I will henceforth refer to as Wildlife Guy answered my distress call. For $115 he set a trap for the animal I now viewed as a big furry rodent. He called it a gopher. "At least it's not a beaver," he said in an accent that wasn't quite as southern as others I'd heard here. "Those are the most destructive and the only ones we're allowed to kill."

The next day he triumphantly left with his prey, which would be released far away from me. When I relayed its permanent exit to Mama Jo, she responded with concern, "What about its family?"

That hadn't even occurred to me. Alarmed, I called Wildlife Guy. "Could that have been a mother with babies?"

"No, they have babies in April. By now they've grown up and left."

We felt better—until Lupe escaped through a new hole under the fence.

Wildlife Guy trapped two more gophers. He said, "There's really not a lot you can do. They just keep coming back." I gave up. Every time Lupe wanted out, I now had to circumnavigate the backyard to make sure there were no new holes that she could escape through. If there were, I plugged them up with cinder blocks, the only thing I discovered was heavy enough to stop a gopher. It wasn't an attractive solution, but it worked.

As tempting as it was to take my neighbor's son up on his offer to shoot the critters, I didn't. Eventually, however, I tried to trap them myself. How hard could it be? All the guy did was put some pieces of melon inside the metal wire trap and set it near where I said I saw one disappear into a hole in the ground. A trap only cost thirty bucks and could be reused.

On my first try, I bagged a squirrel. Letting him out wasn't nearly as easy as enticing him in. I had to push in and hold up the door attached to a heavy spring while I tilted the trap down. Even with work gloves on, I could easily see a series of rabies shots in my near future. Fortunately, the squirrel dashed out and took off in such a blur of fur that it wasn't a problem.

The possum was another story.

He glared at me from inside the cage and let out a low, scary "Errrrrrr . . . Errrrrrr." He was still doing it as I drove to a wooded area a mile away from me. When I tried to get him out of the trap, he kept clinging to the inside of it. Finally, I shook him halfway out, and the trap door closed down on him. Now I was afraid I was hurting him. I pushed up on the door again and cursed at him. He plopped out, and I grabbed the trap and ran. From twenty feet away I turned around. He just sat there, giving me the evil eye, and uttering his "Errrrrrr . . . Errrrrrr" curse.

As I drove off I decided I wasn't doing this again. With my luck, I'd trap a skunk.

I bought more cinder blocks.

It didn't take long before I had Wildlife Guy's number programmed into my speed dial. Not only did I have snakes and gophers to deal with, I lived in the county with the highest number of rabies cases in the state. News stories of adults and children being viciously attacked by a rabid raccoon or fox that appeared from nowhere were not uncommon. There were plenty of bats around, too.

According to my neighbor Lynette, who had to have the dreaded rabies shots after a bat was found in her house, "You can be bitten by a bat and not even know it because their fangs are so small. And one can spit on you in your sleep and you'd never know it, and that can give you rabies, too." If you don't get the shots immediately after being bitten or spit on by a rabid bat, you'll die. Symptoms may not appear for weeks or months, and then it's too late. She said, "Those shots made me sick as a dog. I had every symptom of rabies except foaming at the mouth."

I asked tentatively, "This bat was in your house here?"

She nodded her head in the affirmative. "And the neighbors two doors down had a whole infestation."

AAIIIEEE!

Wildlife Guy "bat-proofed" my house, and I carried a long metal rod with me when I went on my mind-clearing walks.

My backyard was turning mushy because of moles, Lupe proudly caught a mouse on a regular basis, and local ticks carried not only Lyme disease but the fatal Rocky Mountain spotted fever as well. Then there was the Carolina Jumping Wolf spider that looked like an anorexic tarantula and was impossible to smash because it jumped out of the way and you had no idea where it went. You could only hope it wasn't on you.

Say what you will about the concrete jungle of New York City, at least it didn't force these problems on you. I said to Mama Jo one day after Wildlife Guy had left again, "It's almost like we're back in Alaska."

She said from her chair at the dining table, "The mosquitoes were so big there they called them the Alaskan horse."

"Remember when we stayed in that cabin in the woods?"

"We had to fly in by seaplane," she said. "One day someone knocked on the window in the kitchen. I opened the shutters, and a huge moose was staring at me! I just about died of fright."

"What about when Poddy and I went picking berries? I saw some bear poop and called out to him, 'Look, it's smoking!'" Mama Jo looked confused. "It was so fresh that steam was coming off it! He threw his basket of berries in the air, grabbed me, and ran."

She shook with her inner laugh.

Alaska was a brand-new state then and still rugged and wild. We'd walk out of a movie theater, and a moose would be nonchalantly walking by. Wolverine hides with the heads still attached showing ferocious fangs were casually displayed over the back of someone's sofa like a throw blanket. We watched Eskimos gather around a trampoline made of animal skins and toss people into the air with it. When the earth occasionally trembled, I thought it was wonderful fun.

I said to Mama Jo, "I'll never forget how miserable I was when I started first grade back in Virginia." She had no memory of my distress. I knew my mother's recall was spotty, but how could she forget her child being so severely traumatized?

"You don't remember me crying for two weeks straight and being moved to another teacher?"

"No."

"Or the nightmares I kept having about the Six-Armed Man?"

She gave me a blank stare. "You'd think I'd remember that. No, what I remember is that my ulcers started up again in Alaska. The ground shaking all the time . . ."

Was it the threat of an earthquake or her relationship with my father that had her on edge? Why was she so friendly with Mr. Purple Parka? I recalled her words about my dad on our drive back from Arthur's wedding. *He was like a shell. I could never get inside him.*

"Tell me more about that time," I said. "Why were you so upset?"

After a long pause, she just said, "I can't remember."

How I now wished I could get inside my mother.

14

"Gimme Some Sugar!"

Mama Jo and Arthur in love again

When I wasn't worrying about breaking apart the family units of four-footed fauna, I was worrying about the bringing together of my own two-footed ones. The first occasion came rather quickly—the collision of birthdays of my brother, niece, and sister-in-law's sister in the same week. We were to meet at Arthur's after church on a Sunday at one o'clock. With Mama Jo factored into the equation, I suspected the real start time had been set at two.

"Do you want to come to church with us beforehand?" Janet asked.

"Ummmmm. That's pretty early to get Mama Jo ready. And we have something else to go to later. I think it'll be too much for her in one day."

"Aren't you two a pair! What else are you doing?"

"We've been invited to an ice cream social at a neighbor's house to discuss some issues in the, um, neighborhood." I still couldn't admit that I lived in a development. "What's an ice cream social anyway?"

"Just what it sounds like," she said. "You eat ice cream and socialize."

I set my indispensable Polder electronic timer that hung from a cord around my neck for when I had to start getting Mama Jo ready for our day out. It would be our first test of arriving somewhere on time, or thereabouts. I had bought humorous birthday cards, and as I held each one in front of Mama Jo to read and sign, I tried not to show my shock when I saw how hard it was for her to write. I had to find a felt-tip pen after the ballpoint one required too much effort for her to get it to work. Her signature came out uneven, as though she'd written it while riding in a car going down a bumpy road.

"I don't have a present for them," she said.

"I've taken care of it," I said.

"May I contribute?"

I reached for her hand and said for the tenth time, "Mama Jo, we're a team now. My money is your money and vice versa. I'll pay for my business expenses, and you'll pay for your house expenses until it's sold, but everything else we'll pay for together since we're making about the same amount of money right now."

"That sounds good," she said as she broke into that enormous smile of hers.

I probably shouldn't have reminded her that her house was being sold, but with all that was entailed in doing so, it would be hard to hide it from her. The mention of it didn't seem to affect her.

I was still waiting for the proverbial other shoe to drop.

I was astonished at how easy it was to get her ready. I offered her a few choices of pants and shirts, enjoying my role as valet and image consultant. She picked one, and that was that. I thought of all the times she'd dressed me as a child, and now I was doing it for her. Was she thinking the same?

Before we walked out the door at ten minutes to one, I'd thoroughly learned my mother's pre-outing ritual. She had to: wear pants or shirts with pockets to accommodate folded-up tissues, cock a matching beret on her head just so, carry her purse with the shoulder strap over her head and across the front of her body, moisten her hands with Paquins, and freshly apply her lipstick. When we walked, I had to be on her left, holding her hand only, not her arm or elbow. Her right hand was on her black cane with the fancy gold top.

By the time we made it, very slowly, to my Saab, I understood why she had to have tissues handy. She was so bent over that her nose easily dripped. I'd have to start keeping them in my own pockets so I could whip one out, should she need one.

The car was low and not easy for her to get into. Once in, I clicked her safety belt.

"Would you like the top down?" I asked after starting the engine. "It's a beautiful day." She shook her head. "You never like it down, or you just don't want it down now?"

"I don't like it down."

I looked on the positive side. "No sun exposure that way."

"When can I get my license renewed so I can drive again?"

I pulled out of the driveway, biting my lip. "You have to take a test, you know. I'll give you the book to study." I hoped that would deter her.

"Okay."

Maybe not.

I recalled how annoyed I was when I found out that I had to get a new driver's license and my car inspected within thirty days of my arrival in North Carolina. My new license photo was clear proof of how deranged I was at the time. My hair was sticking out in all directions, and I looked like I was on crystal meth. Even Mama Jo said when she looked at it, "You've had better days." It also disheartened me to not have a New York license anymore. But when I picked up my new license plate, there was one that could be bought for the front of a vehicle that momentarily entertained me.

A WOMAN AND HER TRUCK
IT'S A BEAUTIFUL THING

Then my eyes fell on another:

JESUS INVESTED HIS LIFE IN YOU.
HAVE YOU SHOWN ANY INTEREST?

As I was considering how totally different Greensboro was from New York, one of the clerks announced in her southern drawl to those of us waiting, "Y'all just missed it. Lady was so angry she didn't have her paperwork right, she just leaned right over and mooned us!"

Guess I didn't need to feel ashamed that I was carrying a giant hand flipping the bird in my car that I periodically used on idiot drivers.

Later I threw a hissy fit when my car didn't pass inspection because the windows were tinted too dark for North Carolina standards and I had to pay a few hundred dollars to have it removed. I vented to Arthur, "Why do they even have this rule? So that a cop walking up to a car he's pulled over can see inside? Shouldn't that be more of an issue in New York than here? I like my windows dark!"

He sighed and replied, "Calm down. Every state has different rules. That's all." Then he said, "You're reminding me of a joke, Jo. What's the difference between a Yankee and a damn Yankee?"

"I've already heard it many times since I moved here. A Yankee visits the South, spends his money, and leaves. A damn Yankee stays."

"Don't be surprised if you hear it some more."

My brother lived ten minutes away. To get there, we drove through a part of the county that had an odd mix of brand-new "McMansions" and modest homes from the 1950s, similar to my mom's place in Richmond. We found the horse farms that we passed enchanting, the freshly mown lawns beautiful. I pointed out a small wooden building used for drying tobacco leaves. Winston-Salem, thirty minutes away, was the home of R. J. Reynolds Tobacco Company and where the cigarettes "Winston" and "Salem" came from. I was thankful that public smoking seemed as out of vogue here as it was in New York.

She commented, "Granny liked to ride in a car rather than drive it. Now I understand why. You see more."

I craftily said, "That's right, Mama Jo. Why would you want to drive when you have your very own personal chauffeur? I can take you anywhere you want to go."

She thoughtfully added, "I wouldn't know how to get there, would I?"

"Look!" We delighted at the sight of a strong, lean man pushing a horse-drawn plow through an open field. I easily breezed past our turn. Pulling over and turning around, I said to her, "I like getting lost in a new place. It's part of the thrill of moving. You live somewhere for so long you can practically drive in your sleep. It's boring."

She was smiling. "I agree."

I continued with my pep talk just in case she was still missing Richmond. "You can also wear the same old clothes and tell the same old stories because no one's seen or heard them before."

"You're right."

"Even better is having a romantic tabula rasa."

"What's that?"

"A clean slate. Nobody knows my dating résumé, and I intend to keep it that way." She gave me a skeptical look. "Every move is like a purification process, Mama Jo. The same way I view coming down with the flu."

"I wouldn't go that far."

I looked at her and noticed she had kind of a bug-eyed expression. I did a double take. "Where are your glasses?"

"Guess I forgot to put them on." And I forgot to notice they weren't on. But I'd seen that look before when she was wearing them. Like she was just out of it.

"Can you see?"

"Pretty much. They're mostly for reading."

"Why didn't I get your eyesight?" I said ruefully. I'd been legally blind without glasses since I was in my teens.

"Because God gave you brains and beauty instead."

"Awwwww." I reached for her hand. "That's nice of you to say."

"It's true," she said softly. "I'm so proud of you. You're the best thing that ever happened to me."

I was beginning to think the same thing about her.

When we arrived at Arthur's house, my nephew, James, now eleven, was playing basketball in the street of his cul-de-sac with his friends. It was your usual suburban setting with similar houses clumped together, ideal for raising kids.

I popped out and gave him a wave. He'd visited me in New York on several occasions, and we'd had a fantastic time. Now that I actually lived here, though, he didn't quite know what to make of our relationship. He still gave me a great big smile that an orthodontist would undoubtedly love one day soon, but he didn't go out of his way to strike up a conversation with me. The same was true with my niece. Perhaps they just didn't know how to act around their grandmother, who was probably the first seriously diminished elderly person they'd ever encountered.

Arthur answered the doorbell wearing an apron that said "Grill Master." He registered surprise. "You're the first ones here!"

Janet's greeting was even better. With arms spread wide she sang out, "Gimme some sugar!"

We slowly made it to the living room. Mama Jo was so small, she looked more like a pillow sitting on their big leather sofa than a human. Janet offered us some real sugar in the form of a glass of "sweet tea," a popular southern drink that was basically brewed tea with a lot of sweetener added before it's chilled. Mama Jo had one sip and summed up what she thought of it: "I like my tea hot, thank you."

The moment prompted me to relay when Mama Jo visited me in New York and she ate sushi for the first time. "She took one little taste and said, 'I prefer my tuna out of a can.'" The story wasn't nearly as funny as when I told it in New York.

Janet started telling us about a great place to shop with the word "meals" in its name. I asked, "Is it like a food court at a mall?" She looked as confused as I was. "Didn't you say it was called 'Something Meals'?"

She let out a big laugh. "Meals! M-I-L-L-S! It's a shopping center."

Soon the house was full of people, most of whom we didn't know, chattering in their lovely southern accents. Many casserole dishes covered the kitchen table, including a gelatin one that was bright green and was referred to as "congealed salad." I hadn't seen such a thing since my grandmother used to cook back in the 1970s. After we bowed our heads and Arthur rambled on with a very long grace, I took a small portion to be courteous and ended up going back for more.

Arthur's hamburgers were three times the size of any I'd ever seen. One guest commented, "Boy howdy, this burger's so good it'll tongue-slap yer brains out."

Everyone fussed over Mama Jo as she sat there looking a little bewildered and not saying much. Janet said she'd take her to get her hair permed. Her energetic mother, Wanda Lou, offered to stop by and see her when she could. Noticeably not in attendance was the other guest of honor: my niece, Chris.

She finally ambled in with her baseball cap on backward and gave an obligatory fast hug to those who expected one.

Then came coffee and desserts, plural. Birthday cake and homemade ice cream served up from big, cold metal containers were just the start. Wanda Lou had also baked cookies and made fudge. As the birthday presents were opened, my body shut down from all the starch and fat I'd just put in it, and I dozed off. I popped back awake when I heard someone use the word "Negro." It was an older member of the family. One of the younger folks was chiding him for saying that word, but it still drove home that I wasn't in New York anymore.

I wasn't even sure I was in the twenty-first century.

There was a lot of good-natured ribbing in this group, and I knew my turn was coming. Janet made a reference to my being "high-maintenance." This was the same term my real estate broker had used, amiably, when I explained that I'd never bought a house before and I wanted to make sure I could contact her through e-mail and her cell phone because I'd have a lot of questions. Still, I acted offended to my sister-in-law. "How so?"

"You have to have half-and-half in your coffee. Regular milk isn't good enough."

"That's high-maintenance?" said one family member. "That's just making your coffee taste good. And she's thin enough not to have to worry about it."

Given how much, and what, I was eating, I wondered how much longer I'd be considered that. Mama Jo's comment was a loud, long burp. Everyone burst out laughing.

When Janet said, "You're like a different person, Mama Jo," I added, "Sometimes I think my real mother is back in Richmond and you're an impostor."

"Like a bird let out of her cage!" Janet sang out. "I'll never forget you saying that." Mama Jo grinned from ear to ear. "What do you say I not only take you to get your hair permed, I'll do your makeup too. You'll be Coochie Mama Jo, then!"

When my mother finally stopped bobbing her head while she did her inaudible laugh, she said, "I'm so happy to be here."

Everyone gave us each a long hug, then a group hug, before we left.

After passing that social test, we were on to the next one.

The ice cream social was held on the back porch of my neighbor Lynette's bat-free house across the street from me. There were again three big, cold metal cylinders of freshly made vanilla, chocolate, and strawberry ice cream awaiting us. I'm not a big ice cream lover, but how could I say no to another round of the fresh-made kind?

We'd gathered to talk about the maintenance of the welcoming sign for our development (which I hadn't even noticed—probably another mental block) and to address the issue of construction trucks barreling down our main road on their way to the new development next to us. I had no clue as to what I could contribute to either of these discussions, but I was curious to meet my neighbors.

A sheet was handed out that listed everyone's names. Mine, by itself, jumped out. All of the nearly twenty others were married couples.

Lynette announced, after everyone was served and I'd taken two big bites of delicious ice cream, "Van is going to lead us in prayer."

Prayer? Now? I quickly put my spoon down.

Van was my snake-inspecting next-door minister neighbor. "Dear Lord," he said, as everyone bowed their heads and I tried not to sneak peeks at the others, "thank you for giving us this time to fellowship with our neighbors. We have so few opportunities to do so. And we ask, Lord, that you guide us through the solving of our issues in a kind and thoughtful manner. We pray that you . . ."

I couldn't in a million years imagine anyone in New York leading a neighborhood gathering in prayer. The closest we might come was raising our alcoholic drinks in a toast. As weird as this group prayer was to me, I also liked it. It was the thoughtfulness of it, I guess. And the way that it momentarily connected us.

While everyone was enjoying the ice cream, Van turned to Mama Jo and me. "Seen any more snakes?"

I leaned behind my mother so she couldn't see my face and violently shook my head to signal to him not to talk about it.

"What snakes?" asked Mama Jo with alarm in her voice.

"Oh, just one," I said. "It was killed. No big deal. Haven't seen one since."

That wasn't true. I'd caught Lupe stealthily approaching a gray mound in the back yard, went out to investigate, and found it was a long coiled snake with flies all over it. It appeared dead, but I still grabbed Lupe and dashed inside. I looked back, and it was gone.

Wildlife Guy told me black snakes play dead when they're threatened. They can even smell dead, which explains the flies. "He was just afraid of your cat," he said. "Call me the next time you see one, and I'll get it." For sixty dollars.

I said to Van, "Do you know how to get rid of gophers?"

And there I was, talking about gophers while consuming way too many calories in what seemed like light-years away from my previous life, especially when Van got on his favorite subject.

He said, "People who don't have God in their life are often lonely. I used to be an atheist and read all of the morbid thinkers like Sartre and Camus. Even they said you have to believe in something. We are the only life form that can bring a purpose to our lives. It doesn't make sense to strive and strive and then die without any meaning to it."

A few weeks before, his teenage daughter, Cassie, had come over to help me with a few things. She was gorgeous and wearing a clinging T-shirt that said "My Heart Belongs to Jesus." She had told me that her father had been very successful in the business world but one day locked himself in a closet for thirty days, then emerged saying he was now going to dedicate himself to God, completely freaking out her mother and siblings. "We were ready to leave him," she said, "but the Lord worked on us, and we stayed." She also claimed she was never going to date. "If the Lord wants me to get married, he'll bring me my husband." I enjoyed watching her innocently drive the repairman who was present at the time stark raving mad. (She did indeed marry, still a virgin, to a wonderful guy.)

As Mama Jo slowly and silently worked on her three scoops of ice cream, Van continued to give me lengthy answers to my questions about religion that were just my way of making polite conversation on a subject I really didn't know much about and was his area of expertise—what I would do in any social setting. "So why do we need the New Testament, Van?" I asked. "Wasn't it all laid out in the Old?"

"The Old Testament laid down the rules. Jesus told us how to apply it to life in the New." I don't remember the rest of what he said. It went on for some time.

After we left, I said to Mama Jo, "Well, that was different."

She looked at me and said, "You get into a conversation with a preacher, he's got to preach."

My father and his sister, Julie, ages nine and five

15

On Probation

That stranger-in-a-strange-land feeling hit me every day. Once, as I charged into Staples with my list of things to buy, I heard a man say, "Good morning, ma'am," and I kept charging. "Good morning, ma'am," he repeated.

I turned toward the red-shirted Staples employee and pointed to my chest. "Me?"

"Yes, ma'am."

I looked around. "Did I do something wrong?"

"No, ma'am. I was just going to offer you this shopping cart if you needed one."

Another culture-shock moment came when the cute young man behind the register at my local supermarket nicely said, "Thank you for shopping at Lowe's, ma'am. Did you find everything you were looking for?"

"Pretty much. Well, actually, I didn't see any goat cheese."

He registered surprise. "I've never heard of that kind." He's just young, I thought. "Please write it down on this piece of paper, and we'll be sure to get it for you."

As he scanned a bulky package of Depends, I almost said to this all-American hottie, "Those are for my grandmother." When the transaction was complete, I reached for my full shopping cart to push it along. The equally adorable bag boy asked, "Would you like help out to your car, ma'am?"

"Uh, sure." No one had made me that offer in about twenty years.

I stepped aside as he took over, and pulled a dollar out of my wallet. When I offered it to him, he said, "We can't accept tips, ma'am. Thanks anyway." I loved the manners but could do without the "ma'am."

"You have a blessed day," he said as he pushed the empty cart back to the store.

I had heard that phrase often down here and thought it was charming, but I could never say it with the proper conviction and delivery, any more than I could say "Au revoir" to someone who was French.

I was temporarily doing my voice-over work out of a local radio station that had offered me a weekend on-air position. When the program director told me they paid part-timers a whopping ten dollars an hour with no benefits, I was stunned into silence. Not only was that a fraction of what I'd been paid in New York (and a fraction of a fraction after taxes), if I factored in what it would cost to have someone stay with Mama Jo while I worked, I'd be losing money. "Given your background, we might be able to do fifteen," he said encouragingly.

I declined his offer and concluded that my days as a DJ were, without question, officially over. It was only a slightly emotional moment, along the lines of parting with an outdated outfit you once loved but knew you'd never wear again.

Back home, I had to have something called an ISDN line put in that would allow me to speak into my microphone, send the signal to a recording studio in New York, and sound as though I were there. I didn't lose my mind trying to get this done, but I did lose my cool. After having my yard torn up and ten people in three states ask me the same questions, and they still couldn't get the lines to work properly, I finally shrieked into the phone at one of them, "I CAN'T TAKE THIS ANYMORE!" and hung up.

Mama Jo called out from her bedroom below. "What's wrong?"

I made my way down the stairs with a big smile on my face and floated into her room. "I just had a nervous breakdown, and I feel great!"

My freak-out also worked. Ten minutes later someone very high up at the phone company called and had it all straightened out. I hung up with an ethereal "Thank you." The glowing effects of my primal scream therapy lasted an entire twenty-four hours.

A kindred spirit arrived in the form of Ted, a local radio engineer I hired to help set up my home studio after the ISDN lines were in. In the good old days, every radio station had its own engineer. Now, with consolidation, an engineer may oversee five stations or more. Ted wasn't too keen on helping me until he discovered I lived only two miles from him and there was no man of the house. Ted was single.

There was an instantaneous connection, but no chemistry, as we say in the dating world. Radio guys feel like brothers to me, and dating one would be incestuous. He seemed to feel the same way about me. I would also discover that Ted already had his hands quite full beyond his work.

He was a little older than I was and a transplanted northerner who, after eleven years here, still felt out of place. As we tried out a new software program that was supposed to mimic a very expensive piece of hardware, I said, "I can't believe how big a role religion plays here. It just seems to be everywhere. You know, 'Have a blessed day' and ads in the Yellow Pages that say a business is Christian owned. But I don't feel like anyone's forcing it on me in a big way."

"You're on probation," he said. "Just wait. If you haven't joined a church in six months, it'll be a different story."

He told me that he had lost several girlfriends because he wasn't a true believer. "I dated one woman for three years and had no problem at all with her being involved with the church. But the fact that I didn't feel it on the same level . . . I was history."

Ted had an interesting religious upbringing. He was raised Jewish, but just as he was to be bar mitzvahed, his father converted to Christianity, as did his mother. "They asked me if I wanted a bar mitzvah party or a new stereo," he said. "You can guess which one I picked." For a while, he did embrace Jesus as his personal savior and even taught Bible-study classes. "But it didn't feel right," he said. "Nor did being Jewish."

Ted and I were of the same tribe: Radio Geek. And we both felt like foreigners here. He opened up to me even more. I found out he was seeing a twenty-year-old African American exotic dancer named Champagne. But it wasn't going well. What a surprise.

"Champagne?" I asked, not even trying to hide my amusement. "I have to meet her." Story Junkie needed her fix.

"Uh, can you go talk into your microphone while I adjust the E-Q here?"

"I'm serious. I want to meet her."

"We'll see."

"Ted," I said, as I chattered into my microphone that was situated in my walk-in closet, "maybe your problem is that you were never bar mitzvahed. You never officially became a man. No wonder you're in a relationship that can't go anywhere. Why don't you go to a synagogue and meet a nice, appropriate girl?" Then I added, "Are there any synagogues here?"

"I don't like Jewish women," he called out. "They remind me too much of my mother."

The voice test ended, and while he fiddled with knobs and clicked and unclicked boxes on the computer screen, I opened the Yellow Pages directory. There were two synagogues. How many churches were there in Greensboro? Well over two hundred.

The too-good-to-be-true software confounded Ted. I'd had my new computer built by a local guy to save money.

I griped, "Once again, I tried to save money and it ended up costing me more than if I hadn't tried to save it in the first place."

"A shrink would call that neurotic," he said. "You keep doing the same thing and expect a different result."

"I call it 'God Wants Me to Be Rich but He's Just a Little Backlogged.'"

Four thousand dollars and a week later, everything was working. Best of all, I got to meet Champagne.

She and Ted came over one night for drinks before they went out. The four of us sat around making small talk. Mama Jo hardly said a word but seemed to be fine having new integrated company. Champagne was definitely a looker and quite demure.

After they left, I said to Mama Jo, "Ted thinks Champagne is using him."

She said, "She probably is."

When I explained his religious upbringing to her, she said, "He's spiritually bilingual."

I liked that term. "Yeah, like Poddy. Half Jewish, half Protestant."

She looked over her wire-rimmed glasses. "Jewish?"

"You didn't know that? His mother's father was a Reformed rabbi! But he and Julie were raised Ethical Culture."

"What's that?"

"Spiritually bilingual."

She sat and absorbed what I had told her while I got my head around the fact that she was married to him for two decades and was clueless about this. True, my father, having been a victim of anti-Semitism, had hidden his heritage. It was Julie who told me. But you'd think a wife would know this.

She said, "Now it makes sense. I was listening to a radio broadcast from my church in D.C. when his mother said, 'Turn that off!' I didn't. She walked across the room and turned it off herself."

"Was this when Poddy's parents lived with you?"

"Yes. But not for long."

She had told me once that they hadn't been married long when his parents called, my father spoke to them, and then handed the phone to her. He said, "Talk to my parents. They're coming to live with us." No discussion. It was an order, soldier.

I could just see Mama Jo sitting there with them and not one word being spoken, or her hiding in the bathroom. The care of his parents was soon put completely on Julie and Charlotte. Things were never quite the same between my father and his sister until I entered Julie's life as a teenager.

The spiritually bilingual Ted later told me that Champagne thought I was cute. It was the way he said it that made me ask, "Cute as in sweet, or cute as in hot?"

"Hot." I sensed he was feeling me out for a threesome.

"How nice" was all I said and changed the subject.

And I thought I was moving to Greensboring.

Champagne was also the source of continual drama for Ted, like when her former (she claimed) boyfriend smashed his car window. "Ted," I said, "everyone loves drama. That's why we go to the movies. But after two hours, it's enough."

I would discover over time and many dinners that when Ted talked about his withholding, emotionally distant mother and the women he dated, they sounded like the same person. His annoyed tone was the same; his phrases were the same. "I'm a very generous guy, but I have to have it returned." Or "She's very self-centered."

Shaking my head over margaritas at his favorite southwestern restaurant, I said, "You're repeating your reciprocity issues with your mother. You're choosing women who can't return your affection." I tried to soften my acerbic analysis by saying, "I know all about this. For years I've been choosing men who mirrored my issues with Mama Jo."

He looked confused. "What issues with your mom? You seem to get along great."

For most of my life, no one seeing me interact with Mama Jo would have said that. I crammed another Tostitos chip and guacamole in my mouth to force open my throat. I finally said, "It wasn't always that way."

I told him my saga of falling for men that, like my mother, had lost their fathers when they were young, had no brothers, and the mothers never remarried. The problems we would invariably have were just like those with my mother. I said, "Why not move your mom out of that nursing home in Florida and in with you?"

The shocked expression on his face was priceless.

"On second thought," I said, "just get bar mitzvahed. You can do it at any age, you know. I'll throw you a big party!"

"I think you've had too much to drink." Glancing around the southwestern decor of the restaurant, he said, "I should move back to New Mexico. I had the best time when I lived there. The people are just more open."

Whoever said "Wherever you go, there you are" was right. But I also wondered if Ted was right, too. Sometimes staying in a place where you don't fit in only makes your life more difficult, which was why I would no doubt be moving right back to New York as soon as Mama Jo's time on this earth was over.

Eklutna Lake, Alaska, 1961. Mama Jo won five dollars for this photo in a local contest.

16

Can't See the Trees for the Forrest

"Ya gotta real mess here." Landscaper contestant number 1 had few teeth and was wearing a John Deere baseball cap. He was dressed in jeans and an old work shirt. "Ya got these here trees that was damaged by the ice storms that needs ta come down. And ya gotta lotta mulchin' to do."

"Do you mean composting?"

He pushed his cap back and gave me a surprised look. "Mulch is what you put on the flower beds to keep the weeds out, the moisture in, and make 'em look nice and purdy." His parting words were, "I'll get you an estimate." I never heard from him again.

Landscaper contestant number 2 was a crisply professional African American man in his forties who arrived carrying a clipboard and pen and wearing a shirt with his company's logo on it. He took a while walking around and scribbling things on an official-looking form. His final analysis was, "You have a real mess here."

I'd bought the house in the dead of winter, before I knew how much of God's green earth I'd taken on. He handed me his estimate, and I gasped. "Seven thousand dollars?!"

"Then we can talk about a monthly maintenance fee."

When I told my brother this, he said, "That's ridiculous! I know someone at church who might be interested."

Landscaper contestant number 3 had long, stringy gray hair. I would later learn that he once had a serious substance-abuse problem.

He had clearly been through something. He seemed genuinely humble and reliable now.

His estimate was fifteen hundred dollars. "But you need to hire a tree guy to take down the damaged ones," he said. "You really should do that, or you could have a much bigger problem on your hands if they fall on your house."

"You're hired."

"Thank you, ma'am. Just tell me what kind of mulch you want."

"There are kinds?"

He gave me the same funny look the first guy had. "I suggest you stop at a nursery, take a look, and let me know."

"I don't have time! Just pick out something."

He backed off. "No, no, ma'am." He'd obviously made the mistake before of trying to predict a woman's unpredictable mind.

I went to a nursery and stared at six-foot-high mounds of mulch: black, brown, red, and all sizes of nuggets. This was too hard. I asked the man working there for advice.

He said, "Just depends on what you like, ma'am. There's also pine needles." He pointed to an even bigger mountain of square bundles that I had thought were hay. "Local folk seem to go for the pine needles more than out-of-towners. They're cheaper, but you have to replace them more often." Still proudly clinging to my I'm-not-from-here attitude, I went with the medium-size bark nuggets.

Ted gave me the name of his tree man, Forrest. What Ted didn't tell me was how cute he was. Little did I know that when Forrest ambled up to my front door wearing wraparound sunglasses with yellow reflective lenses, I'd have more problems with trees than I ever thought possible—and I wouldn't mind a bit. A visit from Forrest set my pheromones afire.

Until he quoted me his fee.

I flirted to get his price down. He flirted to get it up.

Story Junkie/Single Woman went to work and found out Forrest had been drawn to this line of work because "I thought climbin' a tree would impress women." He had married two that it had worked its charm on. "Never doin' that again—no way."

"How come?"

"No woman has everything I'm looking for."

"I've often said that about men." Smile, smile, smile. "Now how much could you do for five hundred dollars?"

"Five? I quoted you nine, and that's a deal."

"All I can afford is five."

"You don't have to pay me all at once."

"How about we do a trade? I'll be the voice on your answering machine. It doesn't sound very professional. I'll make you sound like a huge company."

"That's my mama on my machine."

"Oh." I recovered with, "And I'm sure she'd like you to make more money, wouldn't she?"

"That's not gonna happen if I keep gettin' customers like you." Smile, smile.

Forrest was also a huge NASCAR fan and told me that he had turned his basement into a shrine to his favorite sport. The floor was a black-and-white checkerboard design like the flag that's waved at a race. And he had memorabilia in glass display cases on the walls, including uniforms that belonged to Darrell Waltrip (whoever that was). A part of me was dying to see it, but I knew that would be asking for trouble.

He said, "Did ya know Kevin Harvick lives just down the road?"

"Kevin who?"

His jaw dropped. "He took over Dale Earnhardt's team when he died!" That name I knew. Vaguely. "But he's movin' out soon. Bought himself a big piece of land a few miles away and is puttin' up a home over twenty thousand square feet. I'm clearin' the property."

"That's a lot of house."

"Sure is." He took off his sunglasses and looked straight at me. "You could have three wives in a house that size, and they'd never even see each other."

"Then you'd better make a lot of money, Forrest, because that sounds like exactly what you need."

"So you'll go for the nine hundred?"

We finally agreed on a price, but when I told Mama Jo what it was going to cost, she was more upset about the act itself. "Why cut down any of them?" she asked.

"They're damaged, Mama Jo. Four people have said the same thing. If we don't cut them down, they could fall on the house."

"Are they going to cut down the two daddy-longlegs trees?"

Taking down the one that was leaning toward the house had been suggested. "Absolutely not," I said to her. If it fell, it fell.

She kept checking out Forrest's crew with a disapproving look as they buzzed away. She stared at the place where one tree had been. It hit me that she probably saw herself in that tree that was no more. It was damaged and had been eliminated because of the harm it might do. I missed it as well.

When Forrest knocked on the front door to collect his check, he thanked me and said, "When was the last time you had your septic pumped?"

I was somewhat familiar with the underground tanks that store human waste from when I lived in my New York cottage. Once I had engaged a guy in conversation who was pumping mine out, and he told me he'd heard of a guy drowning in one. We couldn't figure out how that happened unless he'd had a heart attack in the middle of doing his job. What I did know was that earned my vote as the worst possible way you could die.

"Pumped? No clue," I answered Forrest. "Why?"

"It's comin' up in your front yard. Don't ya smell it?"

"This is a joke, right?"

He pointed to the newly, expensively, mulched area of my front lawn where the remaining trees were. "See how they're taller than those trees over yonder? All that waste is the best fertilizer there is. But maples are the worst trees you can have near your septic, next to willows. The roots seek water like crazy. How old is this house?"

"About eighteen years."

"Yep, I bet your drain fields are completely clogged by now. You'll have to take out all of those maples, dig up the old drain fields, put in new ones, and relandscape the whole front yard. I can do everything but the drain fields."

I felt faint as I began to calculate the thousands of dollars this would cost. Plus the heartbreak of losing the beauty and added privacy my front-yard trees gave me. If cutting down one was upsetting, how would it feel to lose all ten, and have to look out at my neighbor's house that had trees everywhere?

"But don't worry," he smiled. "I'll give you a good price."

And what was a drain field?

Drain fields, I learned, are big black plastic tubes with holes in them that run from your septic tank into your yard. Solids stay in the tank, but once the bacteria there causes them to decompose into a liquid state, the waste runs into these pipes and splurts out of their holes. I had never given much thought to how any of this worked, but the idea of poop flowing into my property, even if it was underground, was pretty damn crude.

The first specialist I talked to on the phone said, "You have maples near your septic? Why, that's like invitin' the devil into your livin' room. You're gonna have to build an outhouse soon. I wouldn't spend a dime until you get rid of those trees, every one of them. Then get yer tank pumped every two years. I'm just telling you the truth. I'm a Christian man." He added one last caveat. "And don't be callin' the health department. They'll spend your money like it grows on trees. Make you go through all kinds of stuff to get it right."

"Why would I even think of calling them?"

"You have to have a permit if you change anything. So get rid of them maples, and we'll lay new drain fields."

"I'm not getting rid of any trees," I practically yelled at the guy. "Can't these drain things be pumped out?"

He said no. I insisted they could be. Finally, he gave me the name of someone who might be able to do it.

That man considered the job and said, "You'll have to do this every year."

"What would it cost?"

He thought long and hard as I prepared myself for a ridiculous amount. He said, "Well, I think the most I ever charged anyone was two hundred bucks."

"You're hired."

When he was done, the problem was worse. My fresh new mulch was torn up in many places with red clay mixed in with it, and now when the septic effluvia appeared, pools of it formed in my front yard. Before it was just an even ooze everywhere.

I studied the open land to the left of where the trees and mulch were. Why hadn't they put the drain fields there? A neighbor I consulted said it might not have perked right. Of course I had no idea what that meant.

I called the Department of Public Health and said, "I'm thinking of putting a weeping willow tree in my yard and need to know where my drain fields are." This was not a lie. I did want to do this. Someday.

They faxed me a copy of my septic-tank inspection certificate. It had a lot of information that made no sense to me and a hand-drawn sketch of my drain fields. Now I could see why pumping them out would be impossible. The labyrinthine way they were installed made them look like intestines sitting near my house. I didn't see anything on the certificate about why they were put there in the first place instead of in the open area.

I called my real estate broker, the one who had said in her honey-coated voice when we first spoke, "I get it. You're high-maintenance." If she wasn't thrilled to hear my obviously annoyed voice, she surely hid it. I said, "A neighbor told me the previous owners had the same problem a few years ago, and the whole front yard was torn up. Wouldn't this fall under full disclosure?" I was also seeing how neighbors sure do know a lot about everyone who lives near them.

"Uhhhh, well, that depends. I believe if the problem was fixed, they don't have to," she said.

"I paid four hundred dollars for my home inspection. He could see those were maples near the septic. He could have warned me."

"Hmmmm. You have a point. Wait, it was winter. There were no leaves on the trees. He's not a tree expert." Her voice didn't get edgy once. She was as sweet as the first time we spoke, many, many months before. "I am so sorry you're having this problem, but drain fields aren't part of an inspection. They're all underground. Let's just see how it all shakes out." She was probably contemplating changing her phone number at this point.

I entered Mama Jo's bedroom carrying Granny's well-used wooden bed tray with pink and yellow peonies painted on it. It easily slipped over my mother's small frame. On it was a plate with one of her favorite lunches: a grilled cheese sandwich. I said, "I have no idea what to do about this septic problem, Mama Jo. It could be a huge expense."

She pushed herself up in the bed some more. "When I lived in Kansas City we had an outhouse. We used the pages from an old Montgomery Ward catalog for toilet paper."

"Eehhk. That must have hurt."

"Not the pocketbook."

The knowledge that just one generation behind me used an outhouse year-round was startling. She had also told me that they saved every scrap of aluminum foil and pressed them into a ball, and when it was the size of a fist they could redeem it for a dollar. When we were cleaning out Uncle Sid's house after he died, I found a pencil next to his telephone that had been used right down to the eraser.

She said, "Our outhouse was also where the coal was stored. Sometimes you'd be sitting there, and all of a sudden coal would come pouring in from a delivery."

"I thought your father was a plumber," I said. "Didn't you once tell me something about gold faucets?"

"He was a steamfitter, and we didn't have those fancy faucets. They were in some rich folks' homethat he worked on. We had indoor plumbing in our house, but when he died, we moved in with Granny and Sid and Pamp, who didn't."

"Pamp?"

"My grandfather, Sid's father. I couldn't say 'Grandpa' when I was a child, so I called him Pamp." I mentally filed that away, and when I returned later to retrieve the tray, she said, "Did I ever tell you that Florence said I was conceived in this bed?"

With delight, I said, "No, you didn't." How could I ever get rid of it now?

She said, "I remember sleeping at the foot of it, on a little cot, and tickling my father's feet." She added thoughtfully, "After he passed, we moved into Granny's house, and Sid and I ended up sleeping in the hallway with our beds end to end. I tried to tickle his feet, too, but he didn't like it."

I thought of the rejection she must have felt from her uncle right after her father had died, and sleeping under such conditions.

I started to leave the room. She stopped me when she said, "Do you know what Sid used to say when we were out and he had to use the men's room?"

"No," I answered warily.

"I need to let my lily drip."

If the saying is true that laughter is the best medicine, then bathroom humor deserves a Nobel Prize. Once when she was taking forever to finish up, I said, "What are you doing, digging a hole to China?" She said, "Yes, I haven't been there in a while." But my favorite was when I was helping her to the bathroom, and she passed gas and said, "That's my butt whistle." I replied, "Sounded more like a fog horn."

I still had to figure out what to do about this septic situation. I looked in the Yellow Pages and saw an ad for a septic company that offered "Soil/Site Evaluations." I was not happy when they arrived with a copy of my septic-tank inspection certificate.

"You didn't need to get that!" I cried. "I already have one. Now they're going to make me spend my money like it grows on trees!"

A man who had spent a lot of time in the sun without sunscreen said, "Don't worry, ma'am. We deal with the inspectors all the time. They're not that bad."

Was I dealing with the Septic Mafia who were in cahoots with each other?

Another man walked around my yard, poking the ground with a metal rod. He informed me that my drain fields actually went way beyond the house over to the edge of my property a good distance away, where the land was clear of trees.

"The distribution box is in the wrong place, and it's pumping your waste into the maples. If we put a distribution box over there, where it's just grass, the waste'll go thataway."

"Why didn't they do that in the first place?"

"I have no clue, ma'am. I didn't do the job."

I held my breath. "And what will that cost?"

"Lemme think. We gotta pump out the tank, bring in a backhoe . . ." I'm seeing thousands of dollars evaporating into thin air. "Should run you 'bout seven hundred dollars."

I exhaled. Only seven hundred. "That'll be just fine."

When I relayed this to Mama Jo, she said, "Knock on wood, Uncle Remus, Uncle Remus."

"What's that supposed to mean?"

"Just something Granny always said when something good happened. We won't have to cut down the trees now."

When the job was finally done and the man said "Thank-y, ma'am" when I paid him, I surveyed my spared maples with great satisfaction. Wait. Did I see something move?

I reached for my phone to call Wildlife Guy. A long black snake was slithering up one of them.

Mama Jo around the time her father died, 1929

17

Just an Angry Old Irishman

Given how warm my sister-in-law, Janet, was, I was surprised by the curtness of her relative Annie when I spoke to her over the phone about looking after Mama Jo part-time.

"Yeah, I'm a CNA," she said in a raspy voice. That stood for "certified nursing assistant."

"Good," I said, "because in case I'm able to get her insurance policy reinstated, you have to be one. You're up-to-date on your certification?"

She haughtily replied, "I'd have to be to work at the hospital. I do overnights on the weekend in the hospice ward."

Caring for people at death's door had to be a depressing job, and her hours were the least desirable of them all. I'd soon find out it was probably the best shift for Annie because it meant she had the least contact with humanity. Pretty much everyone rubbed her the wrong way. Being a New Yorker, I did not have a problem with that.

Most of the time.

Annie was short, overweight and walked with a side-to-side, movement due to hip problems, yet still managed to move pretty fast. She dressed in the uniform of a medical professional: loose elastic-waistband pants in a color like blue or violet, with a loose-fitting matching top in a colorful design. At first she was so grumpy, I asked, "Are you sure you want to get up this early, given the hours you work?" When I was starting out as a DJ I had to work the graveyard shift. It completely knocked me out of sync with the daytime world.

"I never sleep anyway," she said. "Doesn't matter when I work."

Annie came from a large family, and she quickly lost me as she ran down the names and order of all the siblings. Two of them hadn't spoken to each other in years. Another two were "so close they peed through the same straw."

One morning she came in really ticked off. "Last night this couple come traipsin' in at three in the mornin' with a toddler and a baby in a basket. They was stinkin' drunk. The man passed out on the floor, mouth wide open. I kicked his feet right outta the way."

"Uh, you came here straight from work?"

"I got an hour's sleep. That's enough. Anyway . . ." She went on about how so many kids today are raised by an aunt or grandmother "so that when one of them's in hospice, forty people show up saying the woman is their auntie. Oh, do they love to boss us around. But once auntie dies, they get gone real fast."

I wasn't following this at all. "Why?"

"They don't wanna be stuck with no bill!" she cried as if I were as dumb as dirt.

But the human beings she detested the most were men. We were sitting in Mama Jo's bedroom when I asked her where Mama Jo and I could go to meet some who were single. She crossed her arms tightly across her chest and said, "That is *nau-zee-ay-ting.*"

Trying not to laugh, I asked, "How come?"

"It took me forty-two years to get rid of my husband," she said. "Kept waiting for him to die but he never did, so I divorced him. A man is the last thing on earth I want."

She had an obsession—one I did not share—with the TV show *Fear Factor*, and I often caught her changing the approved programs to that one. We had an ongoing battle about it. Mama Jo would not take sides. I thought she was just being too polite to disagree with Annie. She'd told me she didn't like the show. But when Annie reported that Mama Jo sometimes stuck her tongue out at me after I left the room, I wondered if perhaps I was obsessing over my mother's care just a little too much.

Charlotte, Aunt Julie's partner, was the Queen of Micromanagement. She had warned me from her dealings with Julie's stroke aides that they would often end up doing things their own way, no matter what they were told. "You'll find that each one has her strengths and weaknesses," she airily said. "It's all part of the experience."

I remembered that Mama Jo had loved to watch *The Young and the Restless* when she lived in Richmond and referred to it as "my soap." Annie sat through one episode with her and reported back to me when I was in the kitchen, "She don't know who anyone is. It's like she never seen it before."

"Let her watch it. Maybe it'll come back to her."

After she left for the day, Mama Jo said to me, "I haven't seen my soap in a long time—that's why I didn't know who the people were."

My mother may have lost weight and several inches of her height, but she'd not lost her hearing. Nor was her memory as bad as everyone had thought. She was now on the proper dosage of Synthroid for her hypothyroidism, plus the antidepressant Zoloft, and Aricept, which helped slow down memory loss. Things like the current date and who was the vice president of our country (typical questions given in neurological assessment exams) she couldn't answer, but, then, she didn't need to know these things, did she?

I gave her a shower twice a week, even though she had virtually no body odor. "How come you don't sweat, Mama Jo?" I asked one day as I was getting her undressed.

She took just the right beat before answering, "Because when you're old, everything dries up."

I asked her if it was okay if Annie gave her a shower, and she answered with a firm, "No." I told her I just didn't have time that week to do it. She finally agreed. But according to Annie, "She got dressed when I was in the kitchen doin' dishes and wouldn't get out of her clothes for me to give her a shower."

My mother complained to me in private, "It's like I'm in high school again and everyone's staring at me because I have no boobs."

Having had body-image issues from my eyeballs to my ankles—and especially with my non-Barbie-doll boobs—I could more than relate to what she was saying, but there was so little I could delegate when it came to her care. "Please let her do this. Do you have any idea how much I have to do?" My voice rose as I said, "I have to grocery shop, cook, fix everything around this house, pay our bills, unpack all this stuff, try to get my business going again, work on—"

She snapped, "I'm sorry I'm such a pain in the neck!"

I left the room and beat myself up for talking to her that way. But I was ticked off. My world wasn't anywhere close to being back to normal. Once I calmed down, I returned to her room with a cup of tea and some freshly baked cookies.

In a small voice she said, "I'm sorry."

"No, I'm sorry. I didn't mean to make you feel that way."

"I appreciate everything you do for me."

In a softer tone, I said, "Thank you, but I'd really appreciate it if you could help me out on this one thing." I could tell from her expression that she still didn't want someone else to give her a shower. I decided not to push it because my mother, to my surprise, had become the quiet eye in the center of the storm that was my life.

As she watched television or a DVD of *The Wizard of Oz* or *Gone with the Wind*, I imagined this was what an at-home parent must feel like when a child with a mild illness stays out of school. Caring for my mother wasn't overtly taxing, but I had to be constantly thinking about her. When did she last eat? How much did she eat? Does she need to go to the bathroom? What was that coughing spell about? Is her movie over yet? It was never-ending attention that at the same time had a pleasant grounding effect on me.

She still sometimes grew testy when she knew someone was coming over to be with her while I went out. "I don't need a babysitter," she said. "I can be by myself."

"What if you fall?" I'd say, trying not to get snippy back. "What if there's a fire? Who would you call? Do you know our address? How many times have I left you alone, called to check on you, and then called back and the phone was busy because you didn't hang it up right?" Seeing the look on her face when I said all that made me feel bad, again, but she was my responsibility. I couldn't pretend all was fine when it wasn't.

I added to my shopping list a phone that might be easier to hang up. I also put up a sign next to her bed with emergency information.

She stopped fighting my hiring "babysitters" when she had a dizzy spell in the bathroom and fell. I heard a sickening thud and came running. She had fallen in a way that her forehead landed right on the track the shower door ran on. Fortunately, the only damage was a horrible bruise, but what if no one had been there?

Having full-time care for Mama Jo wasn't in the budget, so I had Response Link installed as a backup. It required Mama Jo to wear a necklace that had a big red button hanging on it. When she touched it, an ear-piercing alarm went off that summoned help through a box next to her bed. I felt somewhat better having this contraption, though every time I put it around her neck, she'd ask, "What's this?"

She did hit it accidentally once when I wasn't there, never answered the Response Link person's query, and the entire local fire and police departments showed up. At least I knew it worked, but I now felt even greater pangs of paranoia when I left her by herself. I felt marginally better when Annie rasped to me one day, "Takin' care of your mama is easy. She's not in bad shape at all compared to what I've seen."

For now, I thought, for now. Whenever I envisioned the future, I felt distinctly uneasy.

I brought a few boxes of dolls in from the garage and asked Annie to help unpack them while I went out to do errands. The doll expert I'd found to work on the massive project of appraising the collection wasn't available for another month. I wanted Mama Jo to see them so she knew they were okay.

When I returned from the outside world, I could tell something was wrong. They were both glaring.

"I didn't do it on purpose!" Annie cried. "And I ain't touchin' those dolls no more."

Now what?

The older dolls had their extremities and heads covered in bubble wrap. Somehow a finger on one of them had come off as Annie was unpacking it. Mama Jo was inconsolable. I knew I should have done it myself.

I put the finger in a special envelope and marked it "DO NOT THROW OUT! FINGER INSIDE!" Then I called her doll friend Ginny in Richmond.

"It already came off once, and I glued it back on," she said.

"Please tell Mama Jo that. She's really upset."

After they talked, Mama Jo contritely said to Annie, "I'm sorry I got mad. I'm just an angry old Irishman."

From that day forward, whenever Annie arrived for duty, she'd greet my mother in her sandpaper voice with, "How's my angry old Irishman today?" and Mama Jo would break into a big smile.

I came to find that Annie had many qualities in the plus column.

1. She was so punctual I could set my watch to her arrivals.
2. She would work on an as-needed basis with little advance notice.
3. She wouldn't let a dirty dish sit in my kitchen sink for more than thirty seconds.
4. She was often outrageously funny.
5. She was the only person I trusted enough to give a house key.
6. She rolled up her sleeves and did whatever had to be done (outside of touching the dolls), from planting pansies to the laundry.
7. She dearly loved my mother. It was me she wasn't all that crazy about.

More than twenty-five years in show business had given me a pretty thick skin, so I didn't give her opinions of me a second thought. And like a mama bear protecting her cub, all I really cared about was how my mother was cared for.

Still, I needed a backup in case Annie wasn't available or she up and quit on me. Janet put me on to a woman named Suzie whom she knew through her church. It was becoming clear to me that church down here was the equivalent of Pilates and yoga classes in New York: network central.

Suzie's ebullient nature was the opposite of Annie's, but she wasn't as flexible with her schedule. "I need at least five hours every time I come out," she said. "What with the price of gas, my husband says it's not worth it to come all the way up there for less."

This statement irked me for two reasons. First, she was using her husband as the "bad cop." Not having one, I resented that. Second, "all the way up there" was a mere thirty-minute drive, tops. Probably more like twenty. I was used to daily commutes in New York that were four times as long.

She added, "And if I don't have set days, that's fine for now, but if another job comes along that does, I'll have to take it."

We agreed to try one evening and see how it went.

Suzie was forty-five minutes late, too late to take Mama Jo around the corner to her new doctor to have some blood drawn to check her thyroid. His office was closed by then. I had also planned on making it to a movie at a certain time, and this screwed up everything.

"I had no idea you lived this far!" she said. With her red lipstick and long dark hair, she did not look in her sixties. And, as they colorfully put it in the South, "She could talk the ears off a mule." I kept inching toward the door, making noises with my keys, adjusting my purse on my shoulder. Finally, she let me go.

Driving to the movie, I said to myself this wasn't going to work. I have no patience for people who are late. But when I got home later and saw Suzie heating up my mother's pajamas in the dryer before getting her into them in the most loving way while repeatedly calling her "Mom," and how much Mama Jo liked her (and her toasty PJs), I softened my stance.

In time, Suzie also clued me in to the magical effect of the cable channel Animal Planet. Mama Jo could watch it all day and all night, though she liked it more during the day when the shows tended to be warm and fuzzy. At night they turned more menacing, as they revolved around reptiles, sharks, and shocking pet abuse.

Suzie, however, continued to have "time-management issues." There was always an excuse as to why she was delayed, from one grandchild projectile vomiting at school to being stuck behind "two cee-ment trucks." Another time a flock of geese crossing the road held her up twenty minutes. I would get so furious waiting for her, especially if I had to be somewhere, like my own doctor's appointment, I'd think about popping an Ativan (which I hadn't touched since my mother moved in with me).

Whenever Suzie, finally, walked through the door to my mother's bedroom after she arrived, she'd sing out, "Hello, sunshine!" and start singing her a song appropriate for a five-year-old. Though Mama Jo claimed she didn't want a babysitter, she loved this woman who treated every visit like a playdate.

And she was a liberal. "I bet I'm the only one in the entire congregation," Suzie said proudly. Her trump card was that she was the only other person Mama Jo would let give her a shower. She stayed, and I came to really like her—except when she was late.

Tania was the other aide I hired for weekend shifts and fill-ins. I found her through a local senior-resource organization. She was the only one who called me back in a timely manner and was polite and well spoken. I checked her references and had her stop by for a trial outing with Mama Jo. "All I'd like you to do is take her to a play," I said. "I bought tickets, but now I can't make it." I just needed a night off to chill out at home by myself.

Tania was a large African American woman with beautifully plaited hair and wild acrylic fingernails. After my mother's racist comment on the way to her Richmond lawyer, I was afraid Tania might not be well received by Mama Jo. If she had a problem with her, she didn't show it. I chuckled as I watched them slowly make their way to the car, my mother's left hand in Tania's right one as she towered over her.

While they were out, the house felt eerily empty. I yakked on the phone to friends up north, and before I knew it Mama Jo and Tania were back home. After Tania had gone, I turned to Mama Jo for her reaction. She broke into a wide smile. "You should have seen how people got out of our way when they saw us coming."

Shortly after that, Mama Jo ordered a black Madame Alexander doll out of a doll magazine. She was named Paris, but my mother changed her name to Tania, which really tickled her namesake.

On another occasion, while Mama Jo was in the bathroom making her final pit stop before going out with her, I asked Tania how long she'd been doing this kind of work.

"Too long," she answered with a sigh. "I feel like I'm going nowhere fast in a hurry. I need a real job with benefits. The ones with elderly people don't last. It's not just bad for paying bills, but I get so attached to them and then they die." She said "die" with such sadness. "I'm too old for this kind of unpredictable life."

"Old? You don't look old."

"Honey, I'm old as crib dust."

"I bet we're about the same age, Tania, so I'm not going to agree with that statement."

With her brown eyes widening, she said, "Your mother is so sweet. And she's in good shape. She's going to be around a while." Now that's what I wanted to hear. "She's funny, too," Tania said. "The other night I was giving her an Aricept. She asked what it was for. I said, 'To improve your memory.' She said, 'In that case, give me four.'"

I added, "When I was filling out the medical forms at the doctor's office the other day, she said, 'I'm glad you know what I'm doing.'"

"She is better. Before she seemed like she didn't know where she was."

I said, "I think the Zoloft has made a huge difference. I always suspected she needed an antidepressant."

"Don't we all," she said wearily. "Don't we all."

I wondered what Tania's life was like when she went back to the apartment she shared with the teenage son she'd raised alone. What did she and the other aides think when they pulled up to my nice house? I had to walk a difficult line with those who came into my home to care for my mother. Our relationship was so intimate, yet it was a job. I had to keep Story Junkie at bay. I feared if I got to know them too well, I wouldn't be able to see them as employees.

18

The Return of the Little People

My mother's "living doll," circa 1962

Pat, the local doll expert, at last arrived to tackle the five hundred–pound gorilla that was my mother's doll collection. I had no desire to help her. For one, the local TV weatherman had predicted a scorcher of a day after a nice temperate spell and commented, "Isn't that a fine how d'ya do?" I also wanted to stay far, far away from those creepy dolls.

Pat had gray hair cut in a short bob, an easygoing temperament, and a warm smile to go with it. Her light voice evoked my aunt Gladys, the one who made wax dolls and used the freshly cut hair my mother had saved to construct doll wigs. I had told Pat the collection was big, but when I led her to the two-car garage, she cried, "This is all dolls?!"

"Pretty much." I hoped her next sentence wouldn't be "We need to renegotiate."

I pushed a button and raised the garage doors to let in air and light. After the loud grinding of the door opener stopped, she said, "Let's see how far we get today."

We?

I tried getting on Pat's good side by offering her some cookies that I'd just baked and that Mama Jo called "my favorite fruit."

"No, thank you," she said. "I'm diabetic."

So much for that plan. "Sooooo, do you want me to . . . help a little?" I crossed my fingers that her answer would again be, "No, thank you."

"Of course!"

"Uh, let me finish up this voice-over job that just came in, and I'll be right back."

It was like trying to get a teenage boy to clean up his filthy room. I simply didn't want to do this. I was paying her an hourly rate. Even knowing it would save money if I assisted had no impact.

Pat soon hired a doll-loving, upbeat-friend named Dorie to help. With their sunny personalities and me now off the "assistant" hook, the atmosphere livened up considerably. I was given the job of making sachets with coffee grounds to help reduce the overpowering musty odor that I was afraid was going to forever permeate our home. I took a square of a paper towel, poured a scoop of coffee into the middle of it, joined the corners, and twisted a tie underneath them. I made at least two hundred of these and dropped them into trunks in boxes that once held dolls, and hid them around the doll room like Easter eggs. To my surprise, they worked.

Mama Jo periodically left her room, cane in one hand, and checked on us. I thought of her scrutinizing Ronnie as he cut her shrubs back in Richmond. It was that kind of look. As we tried to engage her in conversation about the dolls, she didn't have too much to say. She seemed kind of dazed, as though she didn't quite get that these were her dolls. I often wondered if I should even be bothering.

Her face finally lit up. "Patsy! There you are!" She lovingly touched the doll's face and clothes like she'd probably done a thousand times before. Patsy was about a foot tall and made from a hard material referred to as composition, or "compo" for short. Patsy was wearing a short pink dress with intricate blue embroidery and a soft beige overcoat and matching hat. Her shoes, socks, and shoelaces matched the coat as well. Her hair was short and strawberry blonde, her painted dark eyes looked to the right, and her tiny rose-pink mouth was barely visible when surrounded by her chipmunk cheeks.

"She was my first doll," Mama Jo said. "Florence made us matching outfits."

I thought that was really weird and began to back away.

She said to her company, "My mother, grandmother, and aunt made lots of clothes for the dolls." She went around the room and pointed out their astonishing craftsmanship. The lacework on the baby christening gowns was so perfectly detailed, I couldn't begin to imagine how long it took them to do it.

Finding my great-aunt Gladys's handmade wax dolls was a real treat. There were even adorable small cherubs to hang on a Christmas tree. There was also a dark-skinned girl that Mama Jo said Gladys made when she lived briefly in Panama. I was surprised the wax hadn't melted by now. We found a book that had a chapter on Gladys in it. "She has a UFDC doll club named after her," Mama Jo said proudly. Pat and Dorie were impressed. I had to admit, so was I.

The United Federation of Doll Clubs was the most respected of doll organizations, with officially sanctioned clubs all over the world. To join one in your area wasn't easy. You didn't just show up and say, "I love dolls. Let me in." You had to be sponsored by an existing member and approved by the club.

For years my mother paid my dues for whichever club she belonged to. The UFDC glossy magazine, *Doll News*, would arrive at my house wrapped in plastic. It would go straight into the garbage. Now I was finding out that people collected them.

A group of cloth dolls that didn't look like anything special turned out to be dolls that Florence, Granny, and Gladys made during World War II when the commercial production of dolls had been interrupted. Mama Jo said, "They sold them for a few dollars." When I took a closer look, I saw that some of them had light-red patches on their knees to look like they had skinned them. Someone exclaimed, "How cute!" It was me.

"Teddy!" Mama Jo said as Dorie admired an old teddy bear. "I've had him since I was born." She pointed out that his four paws were roughly stitched up with red thread. "His stuffing started coming out, and I kept bothering Florence to fix him. Finally, she grabbed him and sewed him up with whatever thread she was using."

"There's a card with him," Dorie said.

Written in my mother's adult handwriting were the words: *A too-loved Teddy Bear, early 1920s. I held his hands and he danced too much.*

I was still absorbing the poetic way my mother put that when a large Shirley Temple compo was unearthed, causing her to cry out, "Shirley! Where are your sisters?"

I was instantly transported to grade school when my mother sometimes woke me up in the middle of the night to curl my hair into ringlets so that I'd look like Ms. Temple. Was I ever cranky when she did that. Why didn't she do it when I was awake? Because she never got around to it until then.

I went back to the dining room to make more coffee sachets and get away from the bizarre vibes those dolls were giving me. I could hear my mother's soft, often cracking voice calling out her dolls' names. "Otis! Shirley! Matilda! Shirley! Billy! Shirley!" How many Shirley Temples did she have? I came running back in when I heard "Patty Playpal! Penny Playpal! Peter Playpal!"

"I used to play with them," I said as I stared at, but didn't touch, the life-size dolls that Pat was arranging around a small table for a tea party. Even Lupe was drawn to the doll room. She curled up in a purple Victorian baby carriage and went to sleep.

"A Greiner papier-mâché!" Pat said with awe. "He was the first to patent doll heads in America." She inspected the doll's back. "The label says March 30, 1858."

"Was she one of Granny's dolls?" I asked Mama Jo.

Sitting in a chair in the middle of the room, she stretched out her arms for Pat to bring it to her as if it were a baby. "I got her when I lived in D.C."

"When was that?"

She gave it considerable thought. "From 1938 until I married your father. I forget what year that was."

She couldn't remember the year she got married, but she could recall seeing a newspaper ad that a woman was looking for new homes for her dolls. "Florence and I took the bus to see her. It was a long ride. She was old and getting ready to move into a nursing home." Mama Jo nodded at the old doll. "She gave her to us when she saw how much we loved her."

The parallel between this woman's situation and Mama Jo's hung in the air, and she sunk back into her chair, noticeably deflated.

"Have you found Mammy yet?" I said in my happy DJ voice, as though everything was fine. I described the coconut-head doll my great-grandmother had made to honor the slave who raised her.

Dorie said, "I think I saw her and the rest of them in the garage."

"Rest?"

"There was a whole family."

I shrieked with delight over the discovery of a grandmother, father, mother, daughter, and tiny baby. Studying the last one, I wondered how Granny ever found a coconut about the size of a billiard ball.

We put them out with Mammy, who was seated in her rocking chair with her two little white babies tied to her with a string. All agreed her bandanna had seen better days and she needed a new one. I'd never taken a close look at Mammy before and was soon admiring her dangling red earrings, matching bracelet, and fake diamond ring. There were two perfect holes drilled in her head that held glass eyes. They even had eyelashes on their eyelids that opened and closed. Her hands were made from smooth brown leather. Her feet were covered with black leather button-top high boots made for a small child.

Mama Jo gently touched the babies in Mammy's lap. "Their names are Homer and Hildegard. They represent Sam and Sarah, the twins Granny lost."

We listened intently as she slowly told us about Granny's first pregnancy. There was a snowstorm, and the doctor couldn't get to her house in time. Her twins died soon after childbirth. "She had another little boy after Florence and Gladys. His name was Iver. He died when he was about three or four. I can't remember from what. I wasn't born yet. When Sid came along years later, she was so happy to finally have a little boy. I think the reason Sid never married was because he was so spoiled by his mother and sisters. No woman could ever live up to that treatment."

I pulled out an old sepia photo I had found that had two young girls and a little boy in it. "Is this Iver with Florence and Gladys?"

Her mouth dropped. "It's the only photo of him I've ever seen." It made me smile until she said, "It was probably hidden all these years because it was just too painful for them to look at it." She studied it a while and then said weakly, "I'm going to lie down."

The rest of us went back to hunting through Mama Jo's treasure trove. In addition to dolls, there were toy pianos, miniature tea sets, a mini four-poster bed (and linens and quilts made for it), and boxes of doll books. But all of it blurred in my mind as I thought about Granny losing three children, Florence and Gladys losing their little brother, Sid being smothered with too much affection and never marrying. It also struck me that there's no male equivalent to the term "spinster." "Confirmed bachelor"? Somehow that didn't have the same negative connotation.

The collection spread beyond the designated doll room into several closets, two bureaus, and a large playroom off the guest bedroom. It was all strangely fascinating to me: a mix of history, family folklore, fantasy, and fetishism. I put a few 1960s and '70s pop-star dolls in the guest room I called the "retro room" because its furnishings were from those decades. But no dolls were allowed in the rest of the house! I made one exception: I thought it just the right whimsical touch to display the Arnold Schwarzenegger action figure near the front door with one arm raised, as though he were the official greeter and protector of the premises.

I would learn that the color of a doll's eyes, outfit, and hair all play a role in its value. Whether the mouth is open or closed affects it, too. Often dolls that looked outright ugly or cheap to me were noteworthy and interesting to a doll lover.

It took a month for Pat to get the doll collection completely sorted through. At one point my mother said, "Collectors have a lot of money and no sense." Another time she was lying in bed looking at the dolls on the shelves in her room and said, "It's odd having these little people looking at me."

"Do you want me to take them down?" I asked.

"No," she said casually. "I'm never alone."

Ultimately, the collection numbered several hundred dolls, but not too many were considered highly valuable. My mother didn't look at dolls as an investment. Her reasons for purchasing a particular one were often emotionally based, like it looked like Arthur when he was a boy, or it was wearing a pink dress (her favorite color), or it cried when you squeezed it. She had several teddy bears dressed as postal carriers because Uncle Sid had worked as one long ago.

Alas, it was not the six-hundred-thousand-dollar clock collection I had hoped for. And as eBay trading assistants and stores made it easy for anyone to clear out their attic and sell on the site, prices plummeted unless you had something very rare in mint condition and happened to be selling it right at the moment when at least two people with bucks to burn just had to have it. The Diana Ross doll that was going for four hundred dollars when Pat started appraising the collection was going for less than forty bucks two years later. Not that I could ever give up ownership of a Diana Ross doll, nor the likenesses of Michael Jackson, Frank Sinatra, and Elvis.

There was nothing I could do with the collection anyway with Mama Jo still around, especially when she said one day after gazing at them lovingly, "I hope they stay together."

"Of course," I said, without adding, "for now." But the doll clothes and furniture I parted with easily—secretly, that is. They weren't staring at me with big, imploring eyes.

I also sold most of the Barbies. I still despised her.

In High Point, a town nearby, was the Angela Peterson doll museum (now the Doll and Miniature Museum), which had been started with the huge collection of its founder. I thought it interesting that she died estranged from her children. Did they feel she loved her dolls more?

In time, to my amazement, I began to love the doll room in our North Carolina home. It was irresistibly kooky. And the expression on a visitor's face when he or she walked into the room and was rendered speechless by the sheer number of dolls gave me a huge kick. I actually found myself wondering how I would ever part with these "little people."

Mama Jo and I joined the local UFDC doll club, and everyone seemed perfectly normal and nice. I learned a great deal and longed to share some of Mama Jo's dolls with the club. But due to rules of the management where the meetings were held, the doors to the building had to be locked shortly after the meeting started. Getting Mama Jo anywhere at a certain time still wasn't easy, especially in the evening, when her energy was flagging (and mine).

She also said, "I don't know anyone." It was the same reason she made it to one Eastern Star meeting in each local town and never returned. I pushed her to make new friends, but she didn't seem interested, so I waited for a cue she had changed her mind before bringing it up again.

It never came.

Me, the nascent Story Junkie, getting my fix, third grade

19

A Quiet Happiness

My ally at the Bureau of Insurance in Richmond called, and I held my breath, fearing what was sure to be more bad news. When she said, "I don't believe it. They've reinstated your mother's policy," a glorious feeling of triumph surged through me.

"Wow!" I shouted to Mama Jo. "This must be how lawyers feel when they win a case!" She gave me her big toothy smile in return.

First, though, I had to cough up several thousand dollars to cover the premiums she had missed. It was a modest policy, as these go, with a whopper of a deductible (forty-two hundred dollars) that had to be met first, and with limited benefits thereafter for care in her home, not in a facility. But anything was better than nothing.

I spent hours gathering up 135 pages of paperwork on what I'd spent on Mama Jo's aides so far and what each aide had done when they took care of her. The claim was denied. They said that the aides needed to come through a certified health care company that they had preapproved. In all of my previous phone calls to them, why did no one tell me this?

The insurance company had a branch in Greensboro. I set up a time to come in. I arrived with my dossier only to find the office empty. No furniture, no telephones, nothing. Fury set in. I entered an office down the hall and was told they had moved to the building next door. I felt relief and more anger. I had just spoken to them. Surely they had known they were relocating.

I was quite on edge by the time a man with a southern oh-so-polite voice sat me down in his office. "I'm sorry, ma'am, but you simply didn't follow the rules for this kind of claim."

I burst into tears. I not only felt like I'd failed a test that I'd studied so hard for; but eventually I might have to put my mother on Medicaid and in a nursing home because we didn't have the money to care for her at home. No doubt the fact that I was going through "the change" added to my wild mood swings.

I related my tale to my friend at the Bureau of Insurance. She told me, "Stay calm and write down everything that transpired. Include names and dates, if you can, and send it all to me."

The insurance company finally agreed Mama Jo had met the deductible and that they would reimburse us for what we had spent so far beyond that amount. From now on, the aides had to go through a nursing care company that had been preapproved. The downside was that the nursing company charged twice what I had been paying, which translated to half the hours of care I had been getting. At least it was coming out of someone else's pocket and I didn't have to do any paperwork. Also, they would use the aides I had already hired, so I wouldn't have to retrain anyone. I made sure my aides' earnings did not decrease.

Annie, however, refused to go along with this arrangement. "Those places treat people like me like dirt. Believe me, I know."

I explained that this agency had a great reputation and they were being superflexible. She still wouldn't do it. Suzie agreed, as did Tania after saying, "That insurance company sure took you around the cow's tail and back." However, I had to find a way to stretch out the life of the policy. The way my mother was improving, she could live for years. I still used Annie, but not as often.

Every day at five thirty I'd quit working. "Work" consisted of a few voice-over auditions and maybe some actual work, and the tediocity/emergencies of my life. I'd also eat up time on the Internet with e-mail and researching things like becoming a doll appraiser. Maybe that would be my next career? Or a home inspector.

The issues with my house were endless, and I was getting quite an education on what to look for the next time I bought a house—if I ever did.

I certainly couldn't rely on the voice-over business. The technology that had allowed me to leave New York and still be able to work had also made it easier for a lot of other people to do it. Supply was greater than demand.

When my day was over, Mama Jo and I would watch *The Andy Griffith Show*, which aired, incredulously to a New Yorker, between two local newscasts. We'd laugh our heads off over this quaint comedy. In one episode, bachelor Barney Fife comments that men who put off getting married tend to get irritable. I said to my mother, "Maybe that's true for men, but marriage made me more irritable."

Her answer was a long rocking of her tiny frame as she silently laughed.

I told her about a narration I once read for a documentary on how various animals procreate. "Male and female elephants live separately," I said. "They come together over the watering hole to mate and then go back to their own camps. The offspring stays with its mother forever if it's a female. If a male, he leaves when he goes into 'must.' I think that's short for must have sex. Then he lives with the other males from then on."

She raised her eyebrows and looked at me over her glasses. "Fascinating."

"Do you think men and women should live separately? I do sometimes."

She sat back. "I have to think about that." Her eyes moved around while her mental gears churned. Finally, she said, "No. We're not elephants."

After *Andy Griffith*, we'd watch the local news and the national news, and then she'd enjoy *Wheel of Fortune* while I made dinner. We ate during *Jeopardy*. At first I loved showing off by calling out the answers. Then Mama Jo's silence caused me to start biting my tongue. The game went too fast for her. But she didn't want me to change the channel. "This show makes me feel smart," she said, "and dumb at the same time."

It was a far cry from *Sex and the City* nights with my New York gal pals. If only they knew that their flirty "Samantha" was turning into the goody-goody "Charlotte."

Often while Mama Jo was watching the Animal Planet channel, or a movie, I'd tackle unpacking another box. When I found her birth certificate and the receipt from the doctor who delivered her, I ran downstairs to show them to her.

"Look, Mama Jo," I said. "You were delivered at home for just thirty-five dollars!"

"That was a lot of money back then." She paused and looked at me quizzically. "What year was that?"

"1921."

"What year is it now?"

"2004."

"Am I that old?"

"Hey, I'm going to be fifty next year."

"That's impossible."

"That's what I say."

I read another document to her, the certificate of birth registration. "What's an attending accoucheur?"

"Someone who delivers a baby."

It was another generational marker that I duly noted. Mama Jo probably had no idea what a Lamaze class was.

One evening I found the 1937 diary she kept when she was fifteen and started reading it to her. On January 13 she wrote, *Florence left home about 9:30 for the train to Washington, D.C. She took with her a cold and her suitcase strapped with Sid's belt. I slept by myself. My back was rather cool, as were my feet (as usual).*

The part about Florence moving to D.C. for her government job was sad. She was leaving the city she'd lived in for most of her life and would be alone for a long time until her daughter and mother joined her. My mother had written her entry in such an understated, visual way that I again encouraged her to try writing some more. I also smiled at the mention of my mother's typically cold feet. I seemed to have inherited more than her love of a good turn of phrase and cookies. But something else struck me. I asked her, "Did you and Florence sleep in the same bed?"

She thought about my question. "My choices were either there or in the hallway. I preferred a bedroom. Wouldn't you?"

I found this piece of information as interesting as when Aunt Julie had told me that she slept with her mother until she left home after high school. I had wondered in the past if Julie slept with her because she preferred to sleep with a woman, or did she prefer to sleep with a woman because she had slept with her mother? Now I considered that it was probably just because they had limited space in their small Brooklyn apartment.

I, on the other hand, never had to share a room, much less a bed, with anyone until I lived with my first love. I was assigned two roommates in college, but moved out in a hurry to my own place. I had to wonder if having my own bedroom as a kid was a privilege that disconnected me from others, or did it help me grow up faster? It certainly made me love plenty of personal space and alone time.

Over the course of that week I read my mother the entire contents of her diary. She often had an expression of not knowing who the people were that she had written about. It could have been anyone's diary. Occasionally, she'd recognize a name. Often, she fell asleep. Overall, it was pretty boring, but that was exactly what charmed me. The sauciest entry was: *Who should I see in the library but that short little wavy haired guy. When he saw me he smiled and blushed "red as a beet."*

When I read that she had been a reporter for her school newspaper, I contacted the alumni association and tried to hunt down stories with her byline. I was unsuccessful in my quest. She may not have given herself credit. That would have been like her.

At the other extreme of my mother's diary was my teenage journal that I unearthed among my things. I wrote, *I don't know what i'm looking for, or am in need of, or want; but i sure know that i don't have it.*

I remembered why I didn't capitalize "I." It was about taming my ego. If I didn't capitalize "he," except when referring to God, or "she," why should references to myself be that way? Reflecting on how monstrous my ego would grow as a DJ, it was hilarious to see that I once thought that way.

A real sign of the liberated times: *Comment overheard: "Man, these girls around here just don't put out." If a woman has sex she's considered to be "putting out," but what is it called if a guy has sex? Natural. In other words, women are not supposed to have the same sexual urges and freedom of expression as men. how incredibly sexist!!*

I chuckled when I read: *I have the tendency to do the following: If someone is partially screwed-up, i see them as totally screwed-up . . . Why am i so impatient? It's like i plant a seed and the next day i come yelling at it "Why aren't you a flower?"*

Other times I cringed at what I wrote. *Why is it that i don't want to live with other people, but i can't live with myself? . . . Hurry 9:00. The rates go down.* That was a reference to wanting to call Aunt Julie in New York to pull me out of my despondency.

There was something familiar about: *I'd much rather read a book and feed my mind than smile at a stranger and exchange some light, meaningless conversation.* It reminded me of Mama Jo's summation of nursing homes: "I'll smile at you if you'll smile at me."

One entry was about a dream I had where I was sitting in my mother's car and a cigarette was burning in it somewhere. The car was going to explode, and everyone was running away from it but me. *Suddenly, the whole front blew up and at first i panicked but i knew i had to keep myself together or i wouldn't get out. Then i woke up and i knew exactly what the dream meant. The cigarette burning symbolizes the tension i feel with my mom that is slowly penetrating deeper and deeper until finally it's just going to explode. And when that happens i'm going to have to be very calm and everything will be cool.*

And then I started capitalizing the I:

How I view myself—

I don't want to be dependent on others. I don't want others to be dependent on me.

I love my mother but I love myself more.

I feel my needs are more important to me than her needs.

Is this right? Wrong? What?

I could have written that not so long ago. But not now. My mother's health and happiness were all that mattered to me.

I didn't share my diary with Mama Jo. It was embarrassing, and I didn't want to stir up that depressing time in my life. I'd rather read about hers, which seemed so sweet and innocent.

At night, after I'd tucked in my mother, I'd often go to my bedroom and journal if I had the energy. Sometimes my entries were written in the middle of the night.

3:30 a.m. I woke up and heard her walking around downstairs with her cane tapping the wooden floor and the bottom of her sneakers squeaking.

"Mama Jo?" I called out.

"Did you call out 'Mama'?" she answered.

I got up. Led her back to her bed. "You just had a bad dream."

"I heard someone say 'Mama, help me. Mama, help me.'"

Maybe I had said it in my sleep.

Six nights later: *2:40 a.m. She's up. "I heard someone knocking on the door."*

Three nights later: *1:40 a.m. "Someone's knocking on the door!"*

All was quiet for a few weeks. Then:

2:45 a.m. She stood at the foot of the stairs and yelled "hey!" then opened the front door. "There are kids down here sizzling something!" There was no one there. She kept insisting she heard a "sshhhhhh" sound, like a heater. All I heard was the refrigerator humming. "I can still hear it," she said. "Shhhhhh." Finally figured out it was her emergency monitoring system. They ran a test and confirmed something wasn't right. I wonder if they eavesdrop on customers.

One entry in particular had me reaching for a Kleenex.

Tonight, after I gave her a shower, shampoo, changed the probes on her heart event box (we're trying to pinpoint the cause of her increasing dizzy spells), and got her into bed, she said, "I'm such a nuisance."

"No, you're not. Think of how lonely I'd be if you weren't here. Think of how purposeless my life would be. I'll look back on this time as some of the best years of my life."

She said, "You're right. It's a quiet happiness. I've never felt more completely relaxed than since I came here."

I thought again about those studies that say the fewer choices we have, the happier we are. I also wondered why it is that our parents, whom we should know the best and care for the most, are often the most inscrutable and hardest to love. Maybe it's Mother Nature's way of helping us to make our own lives and, later, to cope with their loss.

Then I found the divorce papers. I did not share them with my mother.

They were typed on onionskin paper and stapled to a stiff paper that was a pretty sky blue. What a lovely presentation, I thought. My father was the Plaintiff, my mother the Defendant. Some of it caused me to clutch my chest.

Wife hereby waives any and all rights to alimony . . . It is in the best interest of the minor children that Plaintiff retain custody, control and management . . . Defendant has been guilty of extreme cruelty to the Plaintiff.

All I could think was that we were the ones guilty of extreme cruelty: my father, brother, and myself. We chose to move away. We never reached out to her or even expressed our frustrations. We should have been in family therapy, but people didn't do that back then like they do today. Only "crazy" people went to "shrinks."

Was my mother's having an affair deserving of this punishment, especially if my father "was a shell" and unaffectionate? Was he faithful throughout the marriage? My mother didn't think so. Was it simply because she chose not to follow "orders" and come to Miami?

A long-forgotten memory came rushing back to me. She was pulling into the driveway of the second-to-last house we lived in. It was late. She was returning from another of her long absences doing "errands." She had no merchandise with her. I must have been eleven or twelve. I confronted her. "You were with a man, weren't you?" She was speechless at first, then denied it. But I knew. And I condemned her for it.

A few years later, during our first Christmas in Miami, she and Florence visited us. My best girlfriend back in Virginia also came down. Of course I wanted to hang out with her, not them, and the high point (or rather low) was us getting caught shoplifting at the mall. Luckily, the store owner didn't call my home, and I was so frightened by the experience I never stole again.

Years later my mother said to me, "I waited for you to say you missed me when I was down there. That's all I needed to hear, and I would have stayed."

It never occurred to me to say such a thing then, and that awareness now had me doubled over sobbing. Then I found the marriage certificate for her second union. It was dated two weeks after the divorce from my father. She was starting a new life with a man who was smitten with her. Maybe she felt reborn at the time but sorry later when his drinking and smoking wore the bloom of romance away like acid on a fresh coat of paint.

I was fascinated by my mother's love life, from the Catholic boy she told me she loved in Kansas City whom Granny and Florence forbade her to see, to the young swains in D.C. taking her to the Starlight Roof in the 1940s, to my father, her extramarital affairs, her second husband, and her former neighbor Mike.

It was clear whom she loved at the end of her life.

Mike still wrote sweet e-mails, always carefully crafted to both of us. I read them to her, and they always made her smile. All she usually said afterward was, "He was the best neighbor I ever had." It tore me up every time. No matter how much our bodies may age, the heart never grows old.

One night after we watched an episode of *The Bachelor*, where the three final ladies were given the opportunity to spend the night with that season's stud in the Fantasy Suite, I asked my mother, "Do you still think about sex?"

She peered over her wire-rimmed glasses. "Depends on who it's with."

I confessed, "I just think about penises. They're not attached to anyone."

Just as the silence that followed my comment was becoming awkward, she wryly said, "I think you need to get out more."

With the chaos of the last year calming down, it was time for both of us to start having some fun. There'd be plenty of time for lovemaking later in my life—I hoped.

One Friday, after *Jeopardy*, I said, "Let's have an adventure, Mama Jo. Want to see some male strippers?"

"Hot dog, yes!"

Babyitis

Mama Jo's first dip in a hot tub, Hot Springs, North Carolina

He was wearing only two things: a lime-green thong bikini bottom with a string of blinking lights on the front of it—and a smile. He was heading straight for Mama Jo.

He removed her eyeglasses, danced his flawless, sculpted body before us while wearing her specs, then folded them up and dropped them down his pants so that she had to reach in to get them.

We gave him a very nice tip.

Mama Jo and I had discovered Male Fantasy Night at the Inzone in Kernersville, the next town over, affectionately known as K-Vegas to its inhabitants. The behavior of the women-only crowd that night was so raunchy, I yelled over the ear-shattering music to my mother, "DO YOU WANT TO GO?" and she yelled back, "NO!" and kept grinning.

I didn't want to leave either. The men were not only gorgeous, but their routines were expertly choreographed and rehearsed. Every visual and audio cue was nailed perfectly. The most original dancer was the guy who came out straddling an inflatable tractor and proceeded to strip to Kenny Chesney's "She Thinks My Tractor's Sexy."

I asked a pretty young blonde next to me, "COME HERE OFTEN?"

"FIRST TIME. MY BOYFRIEND'S THE COP CALLED ECSTASY. I'VE NEVER SEEN HIS ACT BEFORE!"

"DOES ECSTASY HAVE A DAY JOB?"

"HE SELLS INSURANCE."

I had the impression she was more intrigued by the idea of her boyfriend being an exotic dancer than the reality of it as I watched her amused countenance turn to a glower when he simulated various sexual acts with members of the audience.

We finally left, and as I buckled Mama Jo's seatbelt, I asked her what she thought of the dancers. "I had corns on my eyes from staring so much."

On the way home, I couldn't help but notice how many churches we passed. I loved to read the sayings they had posted in front. My favorite, so far, was: "It's time to turn before you burn." I'll be sure to do that—after I take in a few more Male Fantasy Nights.

Other adventures we had included plenty of wine tastings at local wineries, and a trip to Hot Springs, near the Tennessee border, to celebrate my birthday. We had a wonderfully sybaritic time parboiling in one of the town's famous hot tubs (she'd never been in one before) until it was time to get out.

She couldn't.

Bare naked, I struggled and groaned and grunted and tried every kind of leverage trick, but nothing worked. I was afraid I'd have to call for help but managed at the last moment to move her butt to the side and roll her over and in the clear. We couldn't stop giggling after our panic subsided.

We saw tenor saxophone great Dewey Redman play with the University of North Carolina–Greensboro Jazz Ensemble for a mere five bucks. We joyfully stumbled upon the jazz vocalist René Marie. A riveting one-man show by an ex-con who mastered the art of embroidery while in the joint and authored *Sins and Needles* forever changed my view of felons, jail, and that craft. We saw local plays that were as good as anything on Broadway. The only difference was the actors weren't famous. One theater gave away tickets to *A Streetcar Named Desire* to the male and female patron who did the best "Stellaaaaaa" and "Stanleeeeey" screams.

Mama Jo and I checked out the down-home, all-you-can-eat Hillbilly Hideaway and stuffed ourselves on fried chicken and banana pudding. We dined on fancier fare at the O. Henry Hotel restaurant, named after Greensboro's native son.

With all the episodes of *The Andy Griffith Show* we were consuming, a visit to Mount Airy, Andy's nearby birthplace, was in order. The line was too long at the actual Snappy Lunch eatery, but we stopped in the town museum which had a room dedicated to him, and another to the Siamese twins Chang and Eng, who had fathered twenty-two children when they lived in the area. I was so captivated by their story that *I* suggested we buy a doll of them. Mama Jo agreed since we had nothing like that in the collection. I asked the lady in the gift shop if they sold such an item. She looked at me like I was nuts.

Perhaps I was.

Mama Jo and I started each of our ventures into the outer world by popping a peppermint into our mouths before pulling out of our driveway. Mine would be gone within a minute. She somehow made hers last thirty.

We frequently became lost exploring our new home state because I became so caught up in our conversations, often while I held her small soft hand (which had never been manicured until she lived with me).

"Mama Jo," I said as we headed off to a place called Bridal Veil Falls, "according to a Cherokee legend, any maiden who walks behind this waterfall will be married by the following spring. Do you still want to do it?"

She smiled. "Yes!"

When we finished singing along to "Chattanooga Choo Choo" on the satellite-radio '40s big-band channel, I said, "Tell me about meeting Poddy. Why were you attracted to him?" I was still hoping for some evidence that they were once in love.

She told me, again, how handsome he was in a uniform. She said, "I knew he'd be a good father, and he was." She didn't add any of the melancholic comments that she had shared with me in the past. I still didn't hear her say she loved him.

We stopped in a Cracker Barrel restaurant for a bite and resumed our conversation over frosty mugs of root beer and a big plate of chicken 'n' dumplins and turnip greens. "I bet Granny loved Arthur when he came along," I said, thinking of the two boys she'd lost.

She brightened at the memory. "Oh, yes. She called him Precious. I'd leave her to watch him, come back, and they'd still be playing."

"I thought she couldn't walk by then. How did she babysit?"

"She stayed in bed and bunched up her blanket into different shapes so Arthur could pretend it was a mountain with roads on it. He'd race his cars all over and make up people and houses in his head." Again she relayed a tender, simple pleasure that filled me with a nostalgic lightheadedness. After consuming another dainty bite of her buttered biscuit, she said, "I didn't know what to do with a little boy. And your father didn't know what to do with a little girl."

I thought about how picking up on that might have affected my brother, and me. I'd found a photo of me at age three with shaving cream all over my face, trying to be like Poppa. Janet had told me that Arthur once became visibly upset talking about how Mama Jo would dress him up as a kid whenever she went out with him. "He felt like her accessory."

I motioned to Mama Jo that she had some crumbs on her mouth. She wiped them away and said what she'd been saying to me every single night when I put her to bed: "You were the answer to my prayers. I wanted a little girl so much."

It was wonderful to hear her say that, but it also hurt. Not only would the day come when I would no longer hear it, but I would never have a child I could say it to.

I went from never wanting to have children when I was younger to what I would describe as raging ambivalence. I remember the exact moment my uterus turned into a gaping maw chanting, "Feed me sperm!" and my ovaries two little fists angrily shaking along in time. I was reading an article on egg donor programs that said women over thirty-five weren't accepted because eggs start to deteriorate at that point. I was thirty-six. The biological clock I thought I'd been born without went off like Big Ben.

I went through various tests to make sure all was working right, hormonally and anatomically, should I meet Mr. Right in the next two seconds.

"You're a DES daughter," the fertility expert told me.

"A what?"

"Your uterus is in the shape of a T," he said. "It's a sure sign your mother took the drug DES when she was pregnant with you."

I had heard of the banned drug DES and its ugly side effects but had never paid close attention to it. While my consequences were not as severe as some, the odds that I would conceive and bear a child were now considerably longer. My odds of developing cervical or breast cancer, however, were better than average.

I called Mama Jo, who was living in Richmond then, and asked her if she knew anything about this. She said, "They told me that the combination of my blood type and your father's could cause a miscarriage in a second pregnancy. It was a little red pill. I didn't want to take it, but I did. I didn't want to lose you."

As an adult, I was incredibly touched to hear that. But I was bothered she hadn't tuned in to the extensive press about it. She could have warned me.

And then I fell in love. Of course, he fit my usual pattern: father died when he was young, no brothers, mom never remarried while he was still living at home. He had so much baggage, I felt like I was trying to get a seat on a plane that could never take off. But I still loved him.

The biggest problem, to me, was that this man, in his fifties, had already been down the rosy path of parenthood several times and didn't want to go down it again. I wasn't going to get pregnant "accidentally on purpose" even if I could. I had so much uncertainty about my mothering skills, and adoption is not an easy process, that I needed him to want this child, too. I needed him to convince me all would be fine. After several years we were still in the same place. I could imagine our child in a little dinghy, slowly drifting away until he or she (the gender would change) disappeared over the horizon. We painfully drifted apart as well.

I started talking to friends about adopting a baby girl from China. At the time, their adoption laws for older single women were more relaxed than in other countries, and girls were put up for adoption far more often than boys. I was floored when friends wrote in recommendation letters what a good mother I would be. Was that true?

Mama Jo's reaction was, "Chinese babies are so cute."

"And expensive," I replied. "Try twenty-five thousand dollars before I buy the first diaper."

"I'm sorry I can't help you."

I fumed inwardly, *You could if you sold some of those damn dolls*.

My oldest friend, Michele, had some advice, "You never had physical affection in your family. Chidren need that."

Aunt Julie and Charlotte were the sole dissenters to my life-changing plan. Julie said, "You'll have a hard time doing this. You work too much and make too little. A child is a huge responsibility."

I freely admitted it wasn't a logical decision. It was pure raw-gut emotion. One moment, I was sure I could handle it. Where there's a will, there's a way, and all that rah-rah American can-do pluck. But I also knew myself well enough to know that I had a lot of my mother in me. If too much was added to the mix, I splattered. I would will my Babyitis to go away. It would always return.

Why couldn't I meet a guy who would be a great father and husband, who I wanted to marry, who also wanted to marry me, and who wanted to be a father again or for the first time? Why should this basic biological setup that billions of people have managed to pull off elude me? The number-one fear of human beings is public speaking and I had not one drop of it. But be a mother? Even with a mate, it terrified me.

I said to Mama Jo now as we plowed through our Cracker Barrel feast, "I don't remember you ever saying things to me like 'When you grow up and get married and have children,' or giving me advice about how to treat a man. Did you not want those things for me, or did you sense I just wasn't cut out for it? Or did you say them and I just tuned them out?"

It was a pretty deep question to ask, and she gave it considerable thought before answering, "I always thought you were very smart." That was all she said.

Did she mean I was smart enough to make my own decisions? I was a thinker and not a mother? At times I wished she had pressured me to give her grandchildren. But I suppose if I'd wanted a child that badly, I would have had one. I couldn't put the blame on her. I needed it to just happen, without thinking, like someone leaving a baby on my front step.

Watching my little hunched-over Mama Jo, who was practically swallowed up in the booth seat before me, lapping up her mashed potatoes and gravy in this unpretentious restaurant in the Bible Belt, I realized that's about what had happened.

I leaned forward so she could hear me loud and clear in the busy restaurant, "You were the answer to my prayers, too, Mama Jo."

She worked on another small bite, then said, "I think I love you more every day."

Then it hit me why I was so traumatized when I went off to the first grade. It was separation anxiety. I didn't want to be away from my mother. No wonder I was so happy with her now. I had returned to that preschool time of just the two of us.

After our meal, as we slowly made our way to the car, I found myself wanting to be more like her: sweet, composed, and gracious. It wasn't just the Zoloft that made her that way. In the photos I had turned up in the move, I'd seen the same quiet inner beauty in her as a child and young woman. I had to have it somewhere inside me, too.

21

A Long Line of Skillets

Granny, a.k.a. the Bull of the Woods, surveying her modest Kansas City kingdom

It wasn't easy finding someone to fix a typewriter, but I finally did and set it up on the table in the doll room with a ream of clean white paper and a large-print dictionary next to it. I turned it on, and it started humming, awaiting her command.

She sat down. "First I have to think about what to say."

"Don't think too much," I said, "or you'll never write anything. Just get down whatever pops into your head and put it into shape later."

I left and went upstairs to my office to do some journaling of my own. I froze when I heard: Click . . . click . . . click, click . . . click.

I saw the two of us whiling away the hours with our writing. How much more perfect could it be?

She stopped. I cocked my head, waited.

Click . . . click, click, click . . . click.

This was thrilling.

She stopped again, but this time for good.

I dashed downstairs to see if she needed something or was stuck and I could somehow help her. She had gone into the bathroom. I read what she had typed.

The Beginning:

Many things happen in our lives and sometimes we wonder why. After having my immediate family move away to lead lives of their own, I looked around at all my accumulated junk and thought "I can never get anywhere with all this junk but what do I do with it?"

The answer came from out of the blue, a most unexpected surprise.

"Mama Jo," I called to her through the bathroom door, "that's a fantastic start! Keep writing!"

She wrote no more.

Over the next week, I cajoled her in every way I could. "Write it for your grandchildren. Write it for the kids they'll have one day. Write it for me."

"Not today," she said softly. "Not today."

I crossed my arms and pouted. Then with a mischievous grin, I said, "All right, then, let's have an adventure instead."

She peered over her eyeglasses and gave me her skeptical look as she waited to hear what I wanted to do this time.

"It's a beautiful day. Let's find a winery we haven't been to yet."

She broke into a big smile. "How soon can we get there?"

Mama Jo wasn't much of a drinker, which had significantly curtailed my own consumption. We'd do a wine tasting for one when we visited wineries which ranged from funky to right out of an upscale magazine. She tended to like the sweeter wines; I liked the dry ones. At the end we'd be given our glass with the winery's name on it as a souvenir. Our collection was rapidly expanding.

As I was drinking less, Mama Jo was losing her fixation on accumulating more stuff or dolls. It was an occasional occurrence now. Once when we were antiquing, she spied a statue of an Indian about two feet tall that she had to have. As he headed back to his new home with us, I asked her why she liked him so much. "Because one of my father's sisters married an Indian named Jim Crow."

"Jim Crow? Like the segregation laws in the South?"

"That was his name. Jim Crow. One hundred percent American Indian."

"Do you remember anything about him?"

"Nope. Just that he was tall and had jet-black hair." She was searching for something on the floor now.

"What are you looking for?"

"My cane! It's gone!"

My head went back and forth between her and the road ahead. She was frantic. "Are you sure?" How did I not notice?

"I must have left it in the last place we were in."

We went back and couldn't find it. She would not calm down. I mentally retraced our steps and when I last saw her with it. We had a lot of backtracking to do.

She said, "An insurance salesman gave that cane to Granny when we lived in D.C. He watched how she made her way across the room by grabbing onto the furniture and brought her that so she wouldn't have to get around that way. I have to find it!"

I made one more look in our last stop and found it in the ladies' room stall that she had used.

Back on the road, I thought some more about Granny. She died when I was four, and my only memory of her was that of a big white bedridden blob ringing a bell when she needed something. She scared me. I had a new image of her now. She once walked.

Mama Jo touched my soul again when she said, "Granny could tell how old the child was that lived in the apartment above us by the sounds that he made. Like, 'Oh, he must be two now. He's walking a little faster.' She was a nurse. She knew about children."

I'd heard a lot about my corncob-smoking, whiskey-drinking (Four Roses was her favorite brand) great-grandmother, but nothing suggested she was very sensitive, other than doting on my brother, "Precious."

"How come she had problems walking?" I asked.

"She was five feet tall and about four feet wide. Got that way after she had Sid at age forty-one." I knew what was coming next and never grew tired of hearing it. "Granny went into the delivery room, and another woman who was there in labor looked at her gray hair and asked, 'What are doing here?' She said, 'The same thing you are.'"

My great-grandmother may have been old, for then, to have a baby, but she was young when she took part in the Cherokee Strip Land Run of 1893. Just seventeen, she staked out her own plot of land while commandeering a covered wagon. Mama Jo told me how beautiful Granny was then with her long red hair, white skin, and piercing blue eyes.

"I bet she had a lot of suitors," I said. "Why did she choose Pamp?"

"When she found out he had no siblings and that his parents were dead, she said, 'That's the man for me. No in-laws.'"

I had a good laugh over that one, but something occurred to me. "How come Pamp isn't buried in the family plot in Kansas City if he had no other family?"

She stayed quiet as we kept on I-40 and I tried to keep our little wagon away from the big eighteen-wheelers that could easily crush us. Finally, she said, "Granny said he had 'itchy feet.' He'd hop a train somewhere, or go check on one of his properties. He died on one of those jaunts, in Nebraska. Granny said, 'He can be buried right where he dropped.'"

Story Junkie went on red alert. I knew someone whose father had another family no one was supposed to know about. He was always disappearing to check on his properties, too. Granny's reaction to Pamp's death sounded like that of a woman glad to be rid of her husband. Then again, she'd lost three children. That would harden anyone. "I hope we find a photo of him," I said. "I don't have a mental image, like I do of your father now."

I'd opened a cedar chest and found it full of items relating to Mama Jo's dad, including his 1929 obituary. He'd received a special recognition from the White House for his work with carrier pigeons during World War I. At his funeral, his pigeon-fancier friends released thirty-six of them (the age he was when he died) into the autumn air—just as the stock market was beginning to plummet. When I showed these things to Mama Jo, she said, "Granny said it was a blessing my father died before the crash. He wouldn't have been able to take it."

My mother claimed that before he passed, he would give Florence a hundred-dollar bill to shop with. That was the equivalent of more than a thousand dollars today. When I had asked why each white linen napkin that I'd unpacked had a dot of red thread sown into one corner, she'd told me it was so the cleaners wouldn't mix them up with someone else's. They'd once sent their napkins out to be washed and ironed? I was gaining a much clearer understanding of how drastically my mother's life changed after she lost her father.

"What do you remember about him?" I asked her as we kept driving.

"The last time I saw him was in the hospital." He had been admitted for pneumonia. "I sat in his lap. He looked very tired. He told me how much he loved me. When he died, Florence and Granny couldn't stop crying. I never did, though. I said to them, 'Why are you crying? He's just gone to be with God in heaven.'"

I hoped I'd be able to think that way, too, when I lost her.

I'd also found her father's paperwork for various patents that he held with his father, who lived in Canada. One was for a draft regulator Mama Jo said he invented so Florence wouldn't have to go downstairs to turn on the furnace when it was cold. It was like the precursor to the thermostat, and was inspired by what I considered to be a gallant motivation.

Mama Jo had once told me, "When he died, his relatives from Canada swarmed down on us and convened at a lawyer's office. Florence couldn't make it for some reason. She either had to work or just couldn't take the pressure. We saw nothing from those patents, and she was so disgusted that she threw out the papers."

But I had found them. Had a fortune slipped through their fingers? I had tried to research what happened to my grandfather's patents but turned up nothing other than the fact that they did exist and I could go on the patent office Web site anytime and look at the schematics.

Another document I found was from a New York company offering a considerable sum of money for the rights to one of my grandfather's devices, but it wasn't signed. Maybe he had signed it, there was a windfall, and hope of more to come. Had Mama Jo's father died without a will, leaving a legal nightmare, especially with dual citizenship and dual ownership of his patents with his Canadian father, which Florence in her grief, anger, and lack of sophistication couldn't face? Black Tuesday struck just days after he died. Everyone must have been in a state of shock and terror. Florence's was quadrupled.

My mother said Florence never looked at another man once she became a widow. "No one could compare to my father." Now I wondered if it was just a matter of her never trusting a man again.

There was a pattern here. My mother's father, her maternal grandfather, and her own two husbands had left their wives in one way or another to fend for themselves. Aunt Julie on my paternal side had married a man when she was young, but divorced him and "married" a woman. All were women who were ultimately disappointed by men and who learned to live without them back when women didn't do such a thing. And there was Uncle Sid, who never married. He undoubtedly had his share of disappointments, too.

The evidence was growing that perhaps I wasn't wired to live a so-called conventional life. Maybe the matchmaking adage "every pot has a lid" doesn't apply to someone who comes from a long line of skillets. Arthur was an aberration, a Darwinian glitch to ensure our oddball strain continued.

Who wants to be a pot with a lid anyway? They boil over.

I now looked at Mama Jo in the seat next to me. She seemed lost in a pleasant reverie. I asked her what she was thinking about.

"Meat."

"Meat?"

"Granny used to send me back to the butcher when the meat I picked up for her wasn't fresh enough. She said she grew up on a farm and knew what fresh meat should look like. One day the butcher said to me, 'You are the most particularest people I know.'"

So that's why I'm so picky. Being a perfectionist Virgo and a demanding New Yorker only made it worse.

I noticed that Mama Jo was studying something in the sky. "What is it?" I asked.

"Just cloud gazing." She explained it was an activity that she and Granny indulged in on their porch in Kansas City. "We'd sit there and describe what we saw in the clouds."

"What do you see now?"

"A reindeer resting on the ground with its front knees tucked under and looking over at a cat with a big face, a large mouth, and wearing sunglasses."

"Gee, is that all?"

"Florence used to say to us when we were doing this, 'It's a good thing I know you two are sane.'"

I was about to suggest we play our car-ride game of thinking up five objects and spotting them as we drove. It was to kill time, but also to keep her memory sharp. I'd suggest things like a purple car, an American flag, or a motorcycle. She'd add to the list impossible items like "a horse by a lake." Before I opened my mouth to speak she said quietly, "Where do clouds go?"

That was much more interesting to dwell on as we tootled along in her Escort. I'd finally broken down and sold my Saab. It couldn't hold a wheelchair, didn't make financial sense anymore, and was another thing I had to maintain and worry about. Who cared what I drove here anyway? It was another Yuppie Liberation moment.

My cell with the New York phone number became history when its contract expired, saving me money but also severing one more tie with what I still called home. Ditto when I canceled delivery of the Sunday *New York Times*. I lived in the boonies in their estimation and had to receive it by mail. It just wasn't the same reading it on another day.

My dedicated fax line went bye-bye, too, and I raised deductibles to lower insurance premiums as I looked for more ways to economize and preserve our savings. All it would take was one bad fall, a stroke, or a steep mental decline, and I'd have to send Mama Jo somewhere costly for who knows how long. Medicaid's five-year "look-back" period still hung over me like the sword of Damocles. Theoretically, I'd have to hand over the proceeds from the sale of her Richmond house before Medicaid would step in to cover the expenses.

I was even shopping at Wal-Mart. I was astounded by the low prices and array of merchandise, from power saws to, yes, goat cheese. On one visit I brought my Chanel Vitalumière foundation and held it up to each brand Wal-Mart carried, trying to match it. (FYI: Revlon ColorStay is acceptable if applied with a forty-dollar Chanel foundation brush.)

What shocked me even more than my shopping at Wally World was how much I'd spent in the past on things I didn't need, or could buy for less elsewhere. I shared this with Arthur and Janet. She said, "You mean you're getting just like your brother. He can squeeze a quarter out of his behind."

He sweetly replied, "I'd better, honey, because for every one you spend, I have to squeeze out two."

Luckily, Arthur was gainfully employed again. My financial outlook, however, continued to be bleak. I told him in confidence, "I might have to sell Mama Jo's dolls. Is there anything you want, like the G.I. Joes you played with, before I do that?"

He seemed revolted at the thought. "No! I have all the family stuff I want. Just do what you have to do. And remember, no one ever added anything to their life by worrying." It was one of the most comforting things he'd ever said to me.

"Ted Weems," Mama Jo said as she pointed to the satellite radio that I'd had installed in the Escort.

I returned my thoughts to her and where I was driving. "Excuse me?"

"I bet that's Ted Weems on the radio. He always had a whistler on his records."

She still didn't understand that you could look at the screen of the satellite radio, and it would tell you the artist and song title. I pointed that out to her, again. She was right about the artist.

We finally pulled into our driveway singing along to "Sentimental Journey." That is, when the words weren't caught in my throat.

Mama Jo in her 1960s Sunday best

22

What Stays. What Goes.

"Oops. Sorry," I said meekly.

Mama Jo and I were "double-dating" with my brother and his wife at a nice Italian restaurant. Once again I'd started eating before our meal was blessed. I was sincerely trying to adopt this custom because I liked momentarily channeling a higher power before mindlessly diving into my food, but it was far from second nature for me.

"Dear heavenly Father," he said, "thank you for the food we're about to eat for the nourishment of our bodies so that we may do Your work. And thank you, Lord, for bringing Mama Jo and Jo here, and the good health and loving family and friends we've been blessed with and . . ." On one hand, this was quite touching. On the other, my food was getting cold. " . . . we pray all these things in Your son's name. Amen."

My brother gave his wife an endearing look that made me muse, again, on how sweet he was as a man in love, and how much I'd grown to love him, too. I said with a big grin, "You're like two teenagers."

He said, "I thank the Lord every day for bringing us together."

"I don't know about every day," Janet laughed heartily.

Mama Jo was too deep in concentration trying to cut her chicken to be amused. I took over the cutting, and she said in a put-on kiddie voice, "Thank you, Mama."

Janet said, "I knew Arthur wasn't ready for a real relationship when I met him because it was right after his divorce. I just let him date all the other single women at our church first."

Arthur added in his defense, "They were perfect on paper."

"He means they had a good job and plenty of money," Janet teased.

"But they just didn't feel right," he said. "Then I heard Janet pray, and I saw right into her heart. I knew she was the one."

Who was this sensitive person sitting across from me? "I can't believe how happy you are," I said. "How different. In a good way."

"Again, I have the good Lord to thank for that."

Janet said in a "gitchy-goo" kind of voice that you'd use when handling a baby, "And He's kissed you on the head so much that He's rubbed your hair right off!"

He came back with, "I had a lot more of it before I married you, sweetheart."

"And a lot less of a double chin, too." She reached over and playfully patted his as her eyes sparkled, and the rest of us laughed along. You never knew what was going to come out of Janet's mouth, and obviously my good-natured brother loved that about her, even if he was usually the butt of her digs. I was also seeing that even the nastiest remark was softened when spoken with a sweet southern accent.

If someone had said to me, "Create a woman who is the exact opposite of Arthur's first wife," it would be Janet. The mother of Arthur's children was introverted and unadorned. Janet sported fuchsia fingernails that matched her lipstick, and was fond of jewelry, bright colors, and high heels. She could also be down-to-earth. She'd once saved my brother's life with the Heimlich maneuver when he was choking on a chicken bone. And she did many home improvements by herself. Of course, she had to. My brother wouldn't spend the money to hire someone.

She said, "I have a question for Mama Jo and Baby Jo. I mean, Jo Junior. Does a high sex drive run in the family?"

"Janet!" my brother scolded her.

"Honey, I just want to know if your *prow-ess* is genetic. You are always ready for love."

Mama Jo was smiling as if she knew where all the bodies were buried and wasn't telling anyone. I pondered Janet's question. Did I have an abnormally high sex drive? "I'm afraid I can't give you an objective response," I said in a coquettish tone. Changing the subject before she could begin interrogating Mama Jo, I leaned in and asked, "How did my brother propose?"

Janet was smiling away. "He took me to this really nice restaurant, the Chop House, and told me he thought we should get married. Well, I just about fell on the floor! I thought we were just friends! So I said unless there's a ring, it's not a proposal."

"So I got her a ring and asked her again, and she said—"

"It's not a proposal unless you get down on your knee."

"So I got on my knee. I had to ask her to marry me three times before she said yes!"

I asked Janet why she hadn't married before. "I'm sure you had the opportunity."

"I was a commitment-phobe," she said breezily.

"She dated half of Greensboro," Arthur said with mild annoyance. "Every time we go out, she runs into an ex-boyfriend."

I offered brightly, "You must feel very special."

"Yes, I do." He was gazing at Janet with his love-struck look again.

The waitress cleared our dishes and asked if we wanted coffee or dessert. "I'd like an espresso," I said.

"A what?" wondered the waitress.

This was an Italian restaurant. How could she not know? "How about a cappuccino?"

"No, ma'am, we don't have that."

"How about some biscotti then?"

The waitress furrowed her young brow. "Is that a wine?"

"Yer not in New York City, girl!" said Janet.

Every day I was reminded of that fact, from being stuck behind huge tractors puttering down a main road to dining in places that had "No Swearing Allowed" signs posted. In another quest for espresso, I had asked a shop owner where I might find one. The seemingly civilized man said, "I think the restaurant next door will make anything you want to go."

The following Sunday, I brought Mama Jo breakfast in bed: buckwheat pancakes made with freshly ground flour from the Old Mill of Guilford, not far from our home, that was built in 1767. The clerk wrote your purchases down in a spiral notebook and gave you change out of an old cash register. No credit cards accepted. No machine-generated receipt.

"*The Hour of Power* comes on soon," I said. "You still want to watch it?" I was kind of hoping she'd say no, but these days my desire to make her happy was stronger than my snobbishness.

"Yes, that would be nice."

As I cut her pancakes for her, I asked, "Remember the apple pancakes Poddy used to make on the weekends?"

"Yes."

"And the baked beans he'd let slow cook all day?"

"He liked working in the kitchen. I didn't."

There was no argument there. The only meal she ever made was boiling a bag of premade creamed chipped beef, emptying it on top of white toast, and adding some Jolly Green Giant peas. "I'm surprised," I said, "given what a great cook Florence was."

"All the talent in the family ran out with me," she said wistfully.

"Mama Jo," I reprimanded her, "you have talent. It's just more intangible. You know how to see life in a unique and refreshing way." And it took my living with her as an adult to finally know that.

She stopped in midsip of her tea for a silent laugh. Then she turned a little down again. "I was too slow. They'd give me something to chop and then grab the knife from my hand because I was taking too long." I winced because I'd done the same thing on one of her visits to me in New York. She said, "I also gave up trying to sew when I made a buttonhole and Granny said it looked like a festering pig's eye."

I gasped. "What a horrible thing to say!"

She gave me a "no kidding" look and said, "Sid took one violin class, and the teacher said he was so awful he never tried to play again. He made violins instead. At least he could make something. All I could make was a mess."

I tried to move to another subject. "I wonder whatever happened to that baked-bean pot Poddy used? I haven't seen it in ages. I was hoping to find it in your things."

"His widow probably has it," she said without any bitterness. "Mmmmm. These pancakes are good."

My father's widow did have one special family heirloom that she had given to me on my last visit to her. "Remember that bone from a whale's penis Poddy got in Alaska?"

"How could I forget?"

I teased, "How about I put it next to Arnold Schwarzenegger near the front door? It could double as a very effective weapon, don't you think?"

She nodded while continuing to rock in silence. I told her there was a museum in Iceland dedicated to the penis bones of various animals.

"How do you know that?"

"Someone told me about it," I said, "and I looked it up on the Internet."

"I have to see this Internet everyone is talking about."

"You'll have to come upstairs where my computer is."

Before popping another bite of syrupy pancake in her mouth, she said, "Some other time."

I thought about my father's last wife as I went back in the kitchen to make my own breakfast. She still lived in Miami and had never remarried. Just as Janet bore no resemblance to my brother's first wife, the same could be said about my father's widow and Mama Jo. She was a lean, energetic, warm woman from England who peppered her conversations with the word "love" and spelled it "luv" in her correspondence. I instantly liked her and was glad my father had her in his life. At the time of their marriage, I had just gone off to college, never to return to live at home again.

After my father died (eleven years into their marriage), his widow developed an addiction to ballroom dancing. She turned my father's former office into a dressing room and filled it with outrageous costumes. She enclosed the carport and, voilà, it was a dance studio with mirrors on every wall and a shimmering, rotating mirrored ball hanging from the ceiling. She traveled to competitions with her gay dance partner. I thought it wonderful and zany that she was doing this at her age. More power to her! Also, a little sad. She had probably wanted to kick up her heels when my father was alive, but he was almost twenty years older and not up to it.

One day, when I was still in New York, I'd called to see how she was doing and couldn't reach her. She finally rang me back and said, "I have some news, luv." In her usual chipper Brit tone she told me the following story:

"I was competing in a tango in downtown Miami and so happy that I felt no pain in my leg the whole night." She had had surgery for a circulation problem. "I came in first! Then I drove home, took me glamour off" (her makeup), "got undressed, and just happened to look down. My left foot was all blue! I called the doctor, and he said to go to the emergency room immediately. I drove to the hospital and—oh, luv, it was too late. They had to take my leg off right below the knee."

I couldn't stop blinking as I searched for a response. No wonder the British were famous for keeping "a stiff upper lip."

I was in awe of her indefatigable spirit as she was fitted with a prosthesis she called "me peg leg" and kept dancing and winning ribbons and trophies.

I still found it incomprehensible, yet totally understandable, how my father married two women so completely different. I thought about the photos I'd found of my mother in her twenties. I could see what men saw in her: someone they could protect, someone who looked up to them and depended on them, a woman who had a certain distant quality men find irresistible. I wondered, again, about my parents' courtship—and about their breakup.

I returned to my mother's room and reached for the TV remote. "Ready for *The Hour of Power*, Mama Jo?"

"Yes. I haven't seen it in a long time."

I figured I'd watch a bit of it out of curiosity and then leave the room. To my surprise, I was riveted. The Crystal Cathedral, where it was held, was gorgeous. The thundering church organ was humongous. What seemed like hundreds of singers were incredible. The words to live by proffered by Rev. Robert H. Schuller were unforgettable.

Turn your scars into stars!

Turn your hurts into halos!

Tough times never last, but tough people do!

Schuller's assessment of anxiety was that "40 percent will never happen; 30 percent are things from the past you can't change; 12 percent are criticism or gossip, mostly untrue; 10 percent are about your health; and 8 percent are real problems. Therefore, 92 percent of all anxiety can be cured!"

I turned to Mama Jo. "I guess he never heard the saying that only 86.7 percent of all statistics are true." She didn't seem to find my comment very funny.

We watched the show every Sunday after that. On patriotic holidays they unfurled an American flag the size of a football field while the choir sang the most stirring rendition of "The Battle Hymn of the Republic" I'd ever heard. The weekly guests were spellbinding.

Resentment is like drinking poison and wishing someone else would die!

You can't saw sawdust! Move on!

A young woman recalled how she almost died when a mountain lion attacked her while she was hiking and how God answered her prayers to save her. A handsome young man with no arms or legs gushed about how lucky he felt since accepting Christ and learning the purpose of his life. Shimon Peres said, "You're as great as your faith, and as small as your ego." And what was the president of Israel doing on this program?

Mama Jo told me, "Schuller's mentor was Norman Vincent Peale. His teachings are based on the power of positive thinking."

That's why I liked this show. They didn't preach the usual hellfire and brimstone. Their message felt inclusive, loving, and forgiving.

A hymn would begin, and my mother would say, "Granny and Pamp used to sing that one on the front porch." She'd know the words and sing along in her thin, light voice.

Once I asked, "Is that the same front porch where she'd sit and smoke a pipe?"

"That's the one," she said. "A corncob pipe. I'd fill it with tobacco for her."

"She didn't smoke while she was singing hymns, did she?"

She tilted her head and thought about it. "I wouldn't be surprised."

Of all the hymns, the one I loved the most was "His Eye Is on the Sparrow." When I was in New York, Mama Jo sent me a music box that played it. Two little birds were perched on top. I'd wind it up and find its music cheerful at first, then sorrowful as it slowed down. It made me think of my mother far away in her house of junk, all alone.

During every broadcast of *The Hour of Power* there was a pitch for donations. They always offered you something like the music box in return. For a small amount you could join the Sparrow's Club. When they started talking about the more expensive Eagle's Club, the hair on the back of my neck stood up. In my mother's attic I had found at least a dozen eagles, if not more. Each one was in a different pose and mounted on a heavy marble base that weighed several pounds. I think I kept one. I had "liberated" them during Operation Mama Jo.

How much money had she sent in over the years?

In my mind's eye I saw my mother sitting on the one little cleared spot on her sofa, saying her prayers, and writing out her checks to the Crystal Cathedral. Her appeals to God to be lifted from her squalid house and not be put in a nursing home had been answered, hadn't they? And what about the prayers I'd been saying at the same time when I was in New York? They had been answered too, though not in the ways I had imagined.

New Yorkers think they've seen it all, heard it all, and know it all. But I learned from watching *The Hour of Power*—a Sunday-morning religious TV show!—that being hard to shock was not the same thing as being tolerant. Something was shifting in me, and I liked it. The next time I visited my brother's church, I didn't feel uncomfortable, as I had before. I didn't feel superior. I felt like I was finally learning how to get along with anyone simply by respecting their opinions and realizing that we're more alike than different. I also felt a distinct comfort in honoring the faith in which I was raised.

I sent the Crystal Cathedral a small check, and received a brightly colored teacup that said on it: Don't Throw Away Tomorrow! After having spent six solid weeks downsizing Mama Jo's house, I was a big fan of throwing away as much as possible. But when I recalled all of the precious and illuminating mementos that had been saved, I thought, Don't throw away the past, either.

A photo I took of Aunt Julie when I was sixteen

23

No Greater Gift

"Jo, it's Charlotte." I could tell from the strain in her voice why she was calling. "I'm afraid this is it."

"I'll be right there." The day I had been dreading since I was fourteen had finally arrived. Aunt Julie was dying.

Putting my mother into assisted living for a brief stay wasn't like checking her into a hotel. A stack of forms needed to be filled out by both her doctor and me, and she had to get a shot for tuberculosis. There was no time to do it. I couldn't take her with me. I needed to be able to turn all of my attention to Charlotte, the aftermath of Aunt Julie's passing, and my own grief. Though Arthur's house had no downstairs guest room or shower, Mama Jo stayed with him and Janet, and I hoped for the best. After hastily piling luggage into the car, and Lupe into her cat carrier, we took off for New York.

On the way there, I recalled when Julie visited our broken family in Miami, not long after our move in 1969. She loved the ocean and wanted to go to the beach. I did not. She loved art and wanted to go to a museum. I did not. She wanted to take long walks and talk. I did not.

Finally, she knocked on my bedroom door while I was blasting Led Zeppelin and hating life. My bedroom windows were covered with aluminum foil so that no light would enter my cave. I reluctantly answered her knock. She stood there in a long, white caftan, holding something out to me as if it were a peace offering. It was a joint.

We soon became extremely close, constantly writing to each other, talking on the phone, and making cassette tapes of our thoughts. If my father ever knew she'd offered me pot he'd have flipped—as would my brother if I did that with one of his kids today. Not that I would, since I lost interest in it decades ago. It was bad for my voice, turned me into a blithering idiot, and I needed more energy, not less, to function in the real world.

Julie and I would go on to devour Ram Dass's classic metaphysical tome *Be Here Now*. We chanted. We meditated. We went to packed gatherings in New York City of blissed-out, freaky-looking people singing in Sanskrit while sitting in a lotus position.

Charlotte did not take part in what she called Julie's "hippie phase." The time Julie invited a swami to stay in their home for a week just about drove chef Charlotte nuts due to his dietary restrictions. I often wondered how Julie and Charlotte managed to work out their differences without allowing any tension to show.

In true Julie style, she became friends with Ram Dass and the inner circle of the Highly Evolved and was soon teaching yoga with very little training. That was Julie. She had no formal education beyond high school, yet she taught painting, acting, and "creative arts therapy" to emotionally disturbed kids in institutions. She went on in the 1950s to build a home in the country with Charlotte. They easily got along with their totally different neighbors who referred to them as "the girls."

Julie and Charlotte expanded their little slice of heaven in five-hundred-dollar increments over many years. When they founded an art and cultural center for the community, their neighbors tapped into talents and interests they never knew they had. A badly needed preschool followed that was eventually renamed in their honor. Julie and Charlotte were two of the most remarkable women I'd ever known.

Now Julie was leaving me forever.

By the time I reached her in New York she had lost consciousness and was breathing heavily. I couldn't believe how stoic Charlotte was as I bawled my eyes out. My grief was as much about losing Julie as picturing my mother going through this and having to live without her as well.

The guest room was already taken by someone they'd known since the 1940s. I stayed at the home of a longtime neighbor and friend of the family. She was well aware of my difficult history with my mother and asked how it was going. "It's as though a miracle has occurred," I said. "She's one of the sweetest, funniest human beings I've ever known."

After recovering from her shock, she said, "I'll never forget how she was with you when you visited here as a little girl."

I looked at her curiously. "That was a long time ago. You still remember?"

"She was so concerned about how you played with your dolls. You had to handle them very carefully. She hovered over you, watching your every move."

That was a very different Mama Jo from the one who didn't fight for her children in her divorce. It also sounded a lot like the way I behaved now with her.

At six the next morning the phone rang. Julie was no longer with us.

We rushed over. She lay in bed, lifeless and ashen. She looked more like a stone statue than a human. I lost it again.

Their houseguest, in his eighties, had seen countless friends in the past few years die and kept sobbing, "Enough! Enough!"

Charlotte remained remarkably composed, her voice slightly wavering. She repeated to Julie's still body as we waited for the undertaker to show up, "I have to let you go. I have to let you go." Then she added, "I've lost my job."

Balancing the paralyzing sadness of losing Aunt Julie was the happiness of reuniting with my New York posse. Three of my girlfriends, who had dutifully made quick support visits to North Carolina, took me out to dinner to cheer me up. They knew how much I loved Julie and had been dreading her passing almost as much as I.

After we raised an expensive glass of wine in her honor, I said, "I know I've put on some pounds, but I don't care." I could see their eyes darting among each other. I was notorious for being obsessive about my weight. "I had to fatten up Mama Jo—she was skin and bones. She put on fifteen pounds, and so did I. At first I freaked out and even went to a hypnotist who told me not to think about *losing* weight because when we lose something, we want to find it. Instead, I should be trying to *release* the weight."

They approved of that thinking.

"Obviously, it didn't work. Seeing as I'm still considered thin by North Carolina standards, why bother?" A smile spread across my face. "I think I'm really starting to like living there!"

Tara, the speechwriter who mistakenly thought my minister neighbor might be a swinger, was the first to respond. "Did you say you *like* it there? We've been placing bets as to when the get-me-out-of-here distress call would come."

"Well, I'm not saying I fit in there, yet. For one thing, I don't know how people with jobs, spouses, and kids have time to do anything because they also go to church *twice* a week and on mission trips as well."

"No time for the gym, I'd say," added Meg, a stock market–obsessed TV producer.

"And I'm seeing that it's all about taking sides. Maybe it goes back to the Civil War, but you're immediately sized up as to whether you're from the South or the North, then whether you're Christian or not, Republican or Democrat, if you like eastern- or Lexington-style barbecue, and finally if you're for Duke or Carolina."

"Just don't start rooting for the Panthers," said the feisty Rachel, a media executive.

"If they make it to the Super Bowl, I will."

"That's okay," she said, "because it'll never happen."

I leaned in, and they did as well, waiting for something juicy. I whispered, "You're not going to believe this, but I *love* hearing a southern accent now. It's the New York one that grates on me. And the swearing! Good grief, do people have foul mouths here. You should save a curse word for when you're really upset."

I pulled back, and they did, too, looking rather uncomfortable.

"She's lost her f#&king mind," said Rachel. "May I remind you what happened when I visited you?" She turned to the others. "I go into this barbecue joint to place an order for dinner, and the woman says, 'Ma'am, would you like something to read while you wait?' And she offered me a Bible!"

"Hey!" I cut in. "Don't be dissin' my Prissy Polly's Q, sugar."

Tara quipped, "If you tell me you like the dolls, I'm calling your shrink."

"Uh . . . actually, I am kind of attached to them now."

"The *damn* dolls?" she asked in amazement.

Rachel gasped. "Where have we gone wrong?!"

Meg jumped in with, "I don't think they're that bad. They're kitschy. But what about religion, Jo? Don't tell us you're born-again."

I thought about that as I ate my arugula salad with delicate slivers of first-rate imported Parmesan cheese. I certainly wasn't going to tell them about *The Hour of Power* and that I'd even sent money to the show. "I've become a Christian Buddhist Jew."

"Oh," Meg sighed with relief. "You're a Unitarian. That's fine."

I regaled them with some of my fish-out-of-water stories, and it was as though I was talking about a trip I'd taken to the far reaches of outer space. "And I love it when someone calls me darlin' or swee-pea."

"Sweet pea?" Tara sputtered. "Someone actually called you *sweet pea?*"

"No *t* in there, just 'swee-pea.' But the phrase I hear the most is, 'Why, bless your heaaart.' It really means 'I wouldn't want to be in your shoes for anything.' I hear it a *lot*."

"And how is your mother?" Rachel asked.

I started talking miracles again, and about how she now thought Arthur was the best son a mother could ever have and had no memory of ever being mad at him. "It's astonishing how she charms every person she meets. I wish she could live forever."

They froze with their mouths open and eyes momentarily glistening. I launched into the role of a mom telling cute stories about her child. "A repairman said to her, 'Ma'am, that's the biggest smile I've ever seen.' She quipped, "Yep. I look just like a jackass.'"

Then I told them how much I'd grown to love my brother as well, and recalled the story of us going to Sears to buy Mama Jo a new TV. "When we couldn't decide which one to buy, he suggested we pray for an answer right there in Sears! And we did. I'm a firm believer in prayer now. Not necessarily over TVs, but the big stuff."

They were now looking at each other with deep concern. Rachel took a gulp of wine before asking, "Don't they still have the *KKK* there?"

"I think so, but come on, there's racism everywhere. Even here."

Rachel nearly shrieked, "You're turning into someone I no longer recognize!"

Meg said, "Look, it's wonderful what you're doing for your mother. I'm a mother, too, and I'm very touched. But when that responsibility isn't there anymore, please tell us you're moving back here."

Tara added, "Before it's too late."

I said, "When the cost of living here comes down, I will."

They exchanged that uncomfortable look again.

Rachel turned perky and said, "Okay, enough of that. Tell us what we really want to know. Who are you dating? There's always at least three guys on your radar screen."

I sheepishly confessed, "The closest thing I have to a man in my life is spam that says 'Jo Maeder! Grow your penis quickly and naturally!' Seriously, Mama Jo's my date for everything."

Rachel's exasperated response was, "You have *got* to get out more."

"That's what she said."

Meg's two cents was, "You're turning into Norman Bates in *Psycho*."

"Just go on Match.com," Tara offered.

"Sure," snickered Rachel, "and date psychos instead."

Fun as it was to be with my friends, I had to get back to Charlotte. When asked about her future plans, she would only say, "I'm not going anywhere." Of course, I was concerned about her living alone at age eighty-five. If need be, would I take care of her? Absolutely. I had discovered that there is no greater gift than to be with someone at the end of their life. True, you might get a concrete reward out of it—like an enormous doll collection, or more—but all that I had accomplished professionally had never given me the satisfaction, and appreciation for life, that caring for my mother had. Though a lot of unresolved guilt and suffering in our particular relationship added to the mix, I often heard the "gift" term echoed by others who had been in my place.

Charlotte, who had taken a dim view of my moving to North Carolina, now thought differently. "I think it's great what you're doing," she said. "I sometimes wish I'd done more for my mother."

As I drove away from her home, I wasn't as upset as I thought I'd be. It was her passing I was dreading now, possibly even more than Julie's. For the moment, their house and everything in it were still intact—except for the lack of Julie's glowing presence. A monumental loss, but as long as her "things" were still around, it was manageable. I now understood why my mother found it so hard to part with sentimental objects.

In my car was a wicker tea cozy that Charlotte had given me. A ceramic blue-and-white Chinese teapot fitted snugly into an indentation in its padded interior. Julie had poured me many a cup from it. I would make Mama Jo's tea in it now.

Life goes on.

Upon my return to North Carolina, still no man appeared in my life—other than a guy from Animal Control who removed a raccoon that was wobbling around in my front yard. He guessed, "Might could be rabies, but I think it's distemper."

As he carried the poor thing away in a net attached to a long pole, I admit I glanced at his left hand to see if he was wearing a wedding ring. He was.

I soon began "browsing" Match.com and telling myself I was merely window-shopping.

24

'Til Death Do Us Part

My mother and father at my 1985 wedding.
It would be our last time together.

An older man I knew socially asked me to a Christmas party that his son's company was throwing. I said yes, secretly hoping to meet someone younger there. I didn't. Instead, what I had to show for the one hundred dollars spent on an aide for my mother that night was one of my garage doors rammed and bent courtesy of my date.

"Sorry," he said. "I have poor depth perception. My insurance will pay for it." But I still had to deal with it.

Had it been an isolated event, it wouldn't have been so bad. By now I'd had so many things go wrong with my house and technology, so many administrative hassles, so many Lupe antics (like finding a place in the attic which she couldn't get out of and no human could get into), and so many of Mother Nature's various unpleasant creatures encroaching on my property that I decided I wanted engraved on my headstone: "Now what?"

Here's another example: the IRS sent me a love note saying Mama Jo hadn't submitted a North Carolina return for *three years she didn't even live in the state,* and I had to immediately prove that she had lived elsewhere or *very bad things would happen*.

My radio engineer friend Ted commented, "I can't believe how much stuff goes wrong in your life. It's like one of those *Amityville Horror* movies."

Positive Jo looked at it this way: For any technical malfunction, I said, "I am privileged to have this problem." (As in, I would have no cell phone problems if I didn't have a cell phone, but then I wouldn't have a cell phone.) Other stuff, like bureaucratic red tape that instantly made steam come out of my ears, I told myself, "God is throwing time-wasting tediocity at me until I learn how to take it in stride." It all kept my mind off the fact that I wasn't making much money, had no boyfriend, and my mother wasn't getting younger—nor was I.

Negative Jo said, "No good deed goes unpunished."

The first guy I called about the garage door took several days to come out. He finally arrived in a beat-up pickup truck, took a quick look, and said, "I'll get back to you." He never did. I called the manufacturer, who told me, "We only have one other company in your area authorized to fix it." Within the hour, a shiny truck with ladders and all kinds of tools of the trade came roaring down my driveway.

Out jumped two lean, handsome men in cowboy boots and official-looking shirts covered with patches touting various products and associations they belonged to, similar to what a NASCAR driver wears but not as busy. The one who wasn't driving wore dark CIA-type sunglasses. The one who had been behind the wheel had a thin microphone growing out of a nearly invisible headset earpiece. He had dark hair and wore wire-rimmed glasses that added an aura of intelligence to him. I adore a man in glasses. And he can fix things, too? Oh, baby. He introduced himself as Kyle.

I said, "Are you the *Men in Black* of garage doors?"

He loved that comment and broke into the cutest dimpled smile. "Why, thank you, ma'am. I own this company, and I'll take that as a compliment, though we prefer the term 'overhead doors.' Garage doors are just a small part of our business." I ignored the "ma'am" part as his voice cut through my heart like a warm knife through soft butter.

I repeated "overhead doors" like a foreigner trying to expand her vocabulary in another country.

"Ever see those metal doors that cover a storefront?" he asked. "That's an overhead door. Or the doors that warehouses have?"

"Right."

"Now, let's take a look at the patient."

He and his fellow worker carefully examined my garage door and within five minutes handed me an estimate that they had worked up on a computer that was located in the truck, and printed it out on the spot. They had a printer in there, too? I was very impressed.

When it somehow just innocently slipped out that I was divorced and so was Kyle, I kicked myself for not having on any makeup and wearing sweatpants and a baggy tee.

When they returned a few days later to install the new door, I was looking a lot better, and it somehow just innocently slipped out that Kyle hadn't dated in four years.

"I can't believe it," I said. "Just go on Match.com."

"I *am* on Match.com."

How had I missed him?

"I haven't checked in there in a while," he said. "I gave up. I almost met one woman. I didn't even see her photo, and she stood me up!"

Everyone I knew who had Internet dated refused to meet someone unless they saw what the other person looked like. Kyle was evidently a man who looked beyond the outside package. Then again, he could also be extremely naive. I said, "That's usually not a good sign if someone doesn't want to share a photo."

"I'm through with it all. Taking care of my kids and this business is enough."

"I know what you mean. I'm taking care of my mother full-time. She lives with me, and I don't date either." Another electric gaze was exchanged, this one more intense. "What's your screen name on Match?"

He told me, "Why? Are you on it?"

"Uh, no. I was just, um, thinking about it."

When the garage door repair was finished all too soon, Kyle handed me my receipt with a business card stapled to it. "Let me know if anything's not riiight," he said. "We'll be back in a hurry to fix it."

Kyle roared off in his pickup truck, and my mind jumped immediately to what my female massage therapist had told me recently: "Once you have a southern man, you'll never want another kind. They make sure the lady comes first in *every* way, if you know what I mean."

I had to see Kyle again, and ramming my car into the garage door didn't seem like such a great idea. I signed up for another month on Match.

In his profile, Kyle said he was forty-one and looking for a woman between twenty-seven and forty-five. I was only three years out of his upper range. I conveniently blocked out that I was twenty-one years over his lower number. He said he liked to cycle, golf, and do volunteer work all over the world. And there was that ability to fix things I already knew he possessed. My final analysis was that Kyle intrigued me. Not many men strike me that way.

There was no e-mail address on his business card and I was too nervous to call him, so I had to write him through Match. I've found that men are an odd combination of being highly insecure about pursuing a woman for fear of rejection and needing to pursue her to feel like a man. The solution, ladies, is to create opportunities for him to chase you.

In my e-mail, I complimented him on the job he did and wrote: *Since neither one of us is dating right now, if you ever want to show me the real South just for fun, let me know.*

Soon the e-mails were flowing, and I was utterly charmed. He was more than ready to go "hillbillian" with me and confessed he never gave out his business card unless asked for it. "I said to myself, if she gets back to me in any way, I'll ask her out. That's why I gave you my card." I rest my case on how insecure men are.

In one e-mail, he responded to my offer to come over for dinner with: *How about if I help? Or if you're really pushed I can pick up something.* Oh, the seductive power of those words. Occasionally, he referred to me as Elly Mae, after the blonde bombshell with a thick redneck drawl on the TV show *The Beverly Hillbillies*, and himself as "a goober," which I found hilarious.

Our first date was to the Barn Dinner Theater, where we ate a meal loaded with fat and sodium and then watched a Christian musical comedy called *Peace in the Valley*. By now the highly caloric cuisine and ubiquitous biblical slant here were no longer unusual to me. It's just the way it is. I insisted to Kyle that it was the heavy food, not the show, that put me to sleep for most of the first act. Nevertheless, he still asked me out for a second date.

We went to Indie Night at the Green Bean coffeehouse and watched films by local auteurs, and we cruised around afterward in his awesome truck. I'd practically needed mountain climbing gear to get inside the cab. As we eased up the ramp to merge onto the interstate highway, he said while holding my hand, "When I was a kid and the family went out for a ride, I'd say to my dad right about now, 'Kick it, Diddy!'" And that's just what he did while blasting Led Zeppelin's "Whole Lotta Love."

Da-duh-duh-duh-DUH-DUH-DUH-DUH-DUH-DUH-DUH.

Da-duh-duh-duh-DUH-DUH-DUH-DUH-DUH-DUH-DUH.

It was like a tribal mating call to a woman who was so into Zeppelin as a teenager (and still was) that when the eight-track tape of their first album died, I opened the case, took out the tape, cut it into six-foot sections, and hung them from my bedroom closet doorway like a beaded curtain. Every time I touched the long brown strips I could feel the awesome vibrations of Mssrs. Page, Plant, Jones, and Bonham.

Kyle scored more bonus points when I saw how eclectic his musical tastes were and that he had no problem cranking it up nice and loud if I asked. When he told me how lucrative the overhead-door business was (a lot more than my voice-over business), I was convinced this guy was heaven sent.

He once worked on a NASCAR pit crew and educated me about the sport. I used to think it was boring to watch cars go around and around in a circle, and sick in the head because you're really hoping an accident will happen, but Kyle showed me there was much more to it. "Banking into the turn increases the friction," he explained. "Without it the tires lose traction." He then explained the difference between centripetal and centrifugal forces, but I wasn't listening because I was too busy wondering when we were going to "Kick it, Diddy" ourselves.

A week later, we were curled up on my living room sofa watching the Carolina Panthers in their first Super Bowl appearance. I hadn't dated in so long that I didn't know what to say or do or where to put my hands. Once a world-class flirt, I had somehow completely lost my mojo with men.

"Dadgummit!" Kyle cried again as the Panthers fumbled an easy pass. For the past twenty years I'd been a Giants or Jets fan, but I wanted the Panthers to win this one. I have a soft spot for underdogs. I was also determined that today we were going to have our first kiss. If the Panthers could make it to the Super Bowl, I could have a love life while living with my mother.

"I can't wait to watch the Daytona 500 with you," I said playfully, as he motioned for me to nestle up against him.

"Yer not sayin' it riiight," he chided in his soft southern accent. "It's Daytone-*er*."

I repeated it and then asked, "What else is this Yankee mispronouncing?"

Kyle looked me in the eye. "Everythang."

During the halftime show, I snuggled in closer and purred in my sexiest voice, "I love it when you say 'dadgummit.' Maybe there's a southern belle inside me after all."

Finally, our lips met, and several years of solitude for both of us vanished.

We completely missed Janet Jackson's "wardrobe malfunction."

When our kissing finally ended, he looked dazed. I thought that was a good sign until he said, "You're the first woman I've kissed in fourteen years . . . other than my wife." Seeing my expression he said, "Really, you're the first."

My sultry tone was gone. "Your *wife?*"

He lightly knocked his head with his fist. "I meant ex-wife."

But he'd said "wife." Was I putting too fine a point on it, or was it a turn-back-now red flag? I'd found it hard to believe that another woman hadn't snapped him up. And he saw his ex at least twice a week because of the joint custody arrangement they had. I'd learned all too well that you can't make a man love you when another woman already has his heart.

I pulled away and put my sneakers on.

"I swear I didn't mean to say that," he said. "I'm just not used to being in a situation like this."

"It's okay," I said lightly and softened it with a smile. We weren't going further anyway because, twenty feet away, my mother was in her bedroom watching *The Sound of Music* for the twentieth time. "I need to see how Mama Jo is doing."

I quietly eased into her room and saw her tiny body on top of the bed. She was wearing sky-blue elastic-waistband pants that matched her eyes and a flannel shirt in pastel hues. Her ankle socks, of her choosing, bore Mickey Mouse's face.

I arrived just in time. The credits were rolling on the movie, and she still didn't know how to work the remote. I offered to put on another DVD. "There's *My Dog Skip*, *Paulie* about the parrot,

Racing Stripes about the zebra that wants to be a racehorse, or *The Adventures of Milo and Otis* about the little dog and cat that become pals."

"The last one sounds good."

There were advantages to senile dementia. My mother might not remember her address, phone number, or a lot of other things, but she could happily watch the same film over and over—and that made my job easier.

"Can I get you a cup of tea, Mama Jo?"

She shook her head and then looked at me quizzically. "Is it yesterday or tomorrow?"

I tried to figure out what she was asking. "It's Sunday. Super Bowl Sunday. Why don't you come into the living room and watch the game with us?"

"No, I don't want to intrude."

"You're not intruding," I lightly scolded her as I ran my fingers through a few permed gray curls that were sticking up funny. "Kyle really likes you."

"He really likes *you.*" Her expression said: *I wish I had someone, too.*

I felt guilty and confused by the realization that my happiness was making her unhappy. Hey, I'm sorry, but I have my needs! Or should I have been more discreet to protect her feelings?

She suddenly reached for my hand. "Please don't leave me."

I was thrown by her simple plea. "Why would you say that?"

"I don't want to be alone."

"But you're not alone. You're with me." I bent down and gave her a hug. "Nothing's going to change. It's you and me, Mama Jo. We're a team."

She held me as though her life depended on it—which it did—and I wondered why I even bothered to date. I was, in a sense, already married. So my mother and I didn't have sex and she did nothing around the house. A lot of women are in marriages like that! And unlike my last one that busted up a long time ago, this one really was "until death do us part." Sadly, that day was probably closer than I wanted to admit. As wonderful as Kyle was, he would have to come in a distant second. For now.

Before I helped her to the bathroom, I told Kyle I'd return shortly. With that sly grin that follows kissing someone for the first time, he said, "Take your tiiiime."

The Panthers lost, and Kyle was not happy. With doubts about our future creeping in my heart from every direction like a kudzu vine around a tree it would eventually kill, neither was I. When he bent over to give Mama Jo a long goodnight hug before leaving, as he always did, I could now sense how bittersweet his attention must feel to her.

After he straightened up, he said, "Why don't I take you and your daughter to lunch? Or how about dinner?"

I knew exactly what she was feeling. *What fun. I'll be the third wheel.*

"That'd be great," she said graciously, and patted his hand. He took her cue and held hers a little longer. She said, "You have brown eyes. I love brown eyes."

"Your mother is so sweet," Kyle said at the front door as he was leaving.

"So are you," I replied, and gave our parting kiss my all since it might be some time before I had another one. Kyle again looked bewildered after our kiss.

"What's wrong?" I asked.

Almost breathless, he said, "You have no idea how great you make me feel."

Okay, maybe this would work out.

Once he was gone, I tidied up and couldn't stop smiling. Never did I think this hardened New Yorker would be living in the Bible Belt with the mother she purposely had barely known, rooting for the *Panthers*, and dating a man who sang in the church choir and whose favorite dish was something called Frogmore Stew.

Valentine's Day started off with Lupe jumping on Mama Jo's bed and curling up between her legs. "She's finally accepted me!" She happily observed. I wondered if Lupe knew she felt left out.

She just grinned and said, "We can watch the animal shows together."

When evening rolled around, Kyle proved he was definitely the roses-and-chocolate type when he brought us a dozen long-stemmed red roses, a box of Godiva chocolates for me, a smaller one for Mama Jo as well, and sweet cards for each of us.

His mama done raised that boy right.

He was richly rewarded when Tania took Mama Jo out for the evening. So was I.

I'd blocked out his ex-wife, as well as the warning light that went on when I'd learned that Kyle's father had died when he was in his early twenties, he was the only son, and his mother never remarried. I told myself he wasn't *young* young when he lost his father and that he seemed extremely responsible and mature now. He hadn't made any mention of me meeting his children or family, but that was okay. We hadn't even dated a month. I was feeling so good about things that I was even cheerful with customer service representatives when handling the latest snafu in my life.

Then one night, as he was doing the dishes from a meal we'd cooked together, he said, "I'm afraid to introduce you to my mother or sisters."

"Why? They won't like my cooking? I'll put more salt in it just for them," I joked. He loved to tease me about how I never added enough to anything I made.

He hesitated before saying, "I think they'll have two issues. Religion, and if you'll treat me like a king."

I found the first one more of a surprise than the second. Kyle and I always said grace before meals. When he told me he believed every word in the Bible because, "knowing what I know about mankind, we couldn't have written it if we tried," I agreed that that was one of the best arguments in its favor I'd ever heard.

I said to him now, "I really don't think they have anything to worry about."

He didn't respond. But what bothered me even more was that, occasionally, he still called me "ma'am." It felt like someone using the formal "you" in Spanish or French, a clear way of saying "we're not equals" or "we're not that close yet." Was it because we had met through my being his customer?

His calls and e-mails soon stopped.

Whenever a man I'm seeing goes MIA, I usually don't bother to find out why. The reason is one I rarely care to hear. With Mama Jo feeling lonely, and her being my first priority, I felt more relieved than rejected. Nevertheless, after two weeks I found an excuse to call Kyle. I did want to stay friends. I was very niiiice, as though nothing were wrong.

The topic of seeing each other came up, and he said sweetly that he was going to a Bible-study retreat that weekend. The following weekend, well, that was out, too, because he had his kids, and then he had them again the weekend after that because he was going to *another* Bible retreat the weekend after *that*. He went on about having trouble with a rental property and his computer crashing and his top employee getting sick and then *he* had to have a root canal *and* a crown replaced. I was dutifully sympathetic, and we hung up on a pleasant note. Then I laughed out loud.

I thought of many an episode of *Andy Griffith* where characters went out of their way to not hurt someone's feelings, even if it meant bending the truth. Sometimes they did more than bend, like the one about Aunt Bee's terrible pickles that were called "kerosene cucumbers" behind her back. Since no one could tell her how inedible they were, Andy and Barney removed them from their jars and replaced them with store-bought pickles. When Aunt Bee saw how much they just *loved* them, she decided to enter them in a local contest and, oh, no, she couldn't do that because they weren't her pickles and it would be dishonest, but, naturally, they couldn't tell her. So Andy and Barney ate about a hundred of the commercial pickles so that Aunt Bee would have to make more of her horrible ones.

My mind raced with what Kyle could really be thinking. Did I intimidate him? Was I not to his liking in our more intimate moments? Was he just not falling in love and wanted to get out while he still could? Was his I-haven't-been-with-anyone-in-the-four-years-since-my-divorce a lie and he seduced customers all the time? Or did he simply not see himself with a "Christian Lite" Yankee?

Ted confirmed that passive-aggressive behavior was rampant in the South. "They think they're being polite by not being honest. I think it's just plain rude."

The New Yorker in me agreed with him, but the part of me that watched almost every episode of *Andy Griffith* with a smile on my face didn't. Kyle was so sweet about not seeing me that it was hard to be upset with him. I guess I was learning to be that way, too.

25

"Run. Shoot. Run Some More."

Identical dresses, totally different generations

Through the friend of an acquaintance of a New York friend, I became involved with the RiverRun International Film Festival in Winston-Salem, the second-largest city in the area. I was asked to be a volunteer screener and help weed out the trash from the treasures in the more than one thousand entries that they had received. In no time flat, Story Junkie was mainlining.

I gladly schlepped bags filled with some of the quirkiest films ever made, along with the forms that had my comments and scores on them, back and forth to their office thirty minutes away. As soon as *Jeopardy* ended each night, Mama Jo and I would unleash our savage inner critic. A few of our more caustic comments were: "There's good weird and bad weird. This is the latter . . . Not even the director's mother could watch this . . . Somewhere between Amateur Hour and Better Luck Next Time . . . There was no need to put 'For Screening Purposes Only' throughout the entire film. No one will be pirating this one . . . Vanity production for out-of-work actors . . . Glorified home movie . . . Don't think there's much of an audience for a ventriloquist version of *Spinal Tap*, but what do I know?"

One film I described as *Reefer Madness* meets *The Exorcist* at a Bible college with shades of David Lynch. Mama Jo summed it up with "What was all that crap?" My favorite succinct response of hers came after one interminable feature-length action film: "Run. Shoot. Run some more."

That could also describe my life before I moved to North Carolina.

We saw movies about the personal lives of dwarves (very personal), women who made a living as mermaids at a tourist attraction, the story behind the song "The Orange Blossom Special," a frog-jumping contest, Jews in Baghdad, bass fishermen, cab drivers in Havana, the hideous results of a bite from the brown recluse spider (another local menace for me to worry about), the rapper Coolio playing a sailor in a Croatian drama, a well-known local surgeon changing his gender to female, and one based on the true story of a young Asian boy who was going to die if his eyes were not removed.

When the film about Nat King Cole's piano-playing lesser-known brother ended, I said, "Mama Jo, tell me again about when you saw Nat King Cole perform in D.C."

"I did?"

I vacillated between trying to squeeze every memory out of a mind that was definitely growing less sharp and just backing off and enjoying her company, sensing the time for all that had passed.

My RiverRun work not only gave me quality time with my mother without us having to leave the house, I also learned a lot about the world through these films, most of which would never be widely seen or make one dime for the filmmakers or investors. I don't think Mama Jo retained much of what she saw. She seemed to enjoy just sitting with me and having something to focus on for a few hours.

By now, every morning she'd say, "What do I have to do today?"

Usually my answer was, "Nothing, Mama Jo. You're on permanent vacation."

"Good!" she'd answer. When someone called and asked how she was, she'd say lightly, "Oh, I'm just being lazy."

One night we watched a documentary called *Other People's Pictures,* about collectors of amateur photos that were taken by strangers. They rummaged through yard sales, junk stores, and antique shows to find what they were seeking. There were collectors who only sought photos with shadows of the photo taker in them. Others only wanted ones where the eyes were red dots. Some liked when the heads were cut off. Collectors, or collectomaniacs, as I called them, were still bonkers in my eyes. Would some of them be picking through our photos one day? That thought inspired me to dive into more of Mama Jo's jumble of boxes.

They weren't always such a mess. She'd patiently made three identical photo albums of our life in Alaska, carefully typing captions on many of the photos and putting a great deal of thought into the sequencing. One album was given to Julie and Charlotte, one to Florence and Granny, and one was for our family. I treasured this photo album and wondered why she made no more. Perhaps they were just too much work, or she didn't feel they were appreciated enough.

There's something about an old photo that affects me differently than a digital one. It's the factual information that dates it—the clothes, cars, hairstyles—and something else. One photographer friend of mine says it's because the former are actual physical emanations from the subject versus digitized megapixels. Another put it more poetically: "Film is warmer and more honest. You trust it. You can't trust a digital image."

I found more photos of the married oral surgeon my mother had worked for. Also an eerie mask of her face from the same time period. "A lot of men's faces were destroyed in the war," she explained. "He did those as part of the plastic surgery process."

"Why did he do yours?"

She shrugged. "Guess he thought it would be fun for me to have."

I thought about the horrors my twenty-year-old mother must have seen working for him. I also wondered some more about her and this man. Was he a mentor, or was there more to their friendship?

I visited my own horrors when I came across a photo of my third grade teacher, Mrs. Tarr. I adored her and could still hear her animated voice as she sat in front of the class and read us stories. We'd had a substitute teacher one day, which was unusual. When Mrs. Tarr returned the next, I asked her why she'd been out. She said her husband had been sick. The next week, she was out again. A schoolmate's mother stopped by our house that afternoon. She and my mother spoke quietly. Something was up. In the evening, Mama Jo made me watch the local newscast. The lead story was that Mrs. Tarr's husband had been arrested for stabbing her to death.

Today, every kid in the school would have been offered counseling after such a ghastly event. Not then. Just watch it on the news, buck up, and move on. Maybe my mother didn't believe what she had heard and wanted to see it for herself, but more likely she just didn't know what to say to me. My father had said she was furtive. I think she was just nonconfrontational and ill at ease with strong, unpleasant emotions. She couldn't fight for herself, so she married a fighter, a great match as long as she didn't have to fight him.

Chasing away those grim thoughts were happy family snapshots. Arthur was always smiling and laughing. The dolls added a goofy omnipresence, sitting in chairs at tables or off to the side, silent witnesses to everything.

I found a series of shots of me asleep in a highchair. Mama Jo had not only taken them from different angles but rearranged the objects on the tray in front of me as she played with the composition. It struck me that maybe all that was "wrong" with my mother was that she was a frustrated artist.

I tapped into my own creativity by making photo albums (sans captions) with various themes. One consisted solely of dolls and was placed in the doll room. I made albums for all of my family members with photos of their younger selves.

There were great photos of my father, who was quite handsome when he was younger but looked so old next to me when I was a child. No wonder people thought he was my grandfather. Even more startling was the realization that I was now the age he was in many of these photos.

There weren't many photos of my mother because she was the one who was usually taking the picture. One of her holding Arthur as a baby exuded complete exhaustion on her part. In the few I found of the two of us, she had her hand or hands resting on my shoulders in a way that made it seem like she was protecting me while I was simultaneously propping her up.

Arthur's daughter, Chris, would stop by when she could fit it into her busy life that she never shared with us. She wasn't much of a talker, like her mother, whom she lived with. She loved to watch the RiverRun screeners and then rummage through the old photos, though. I gave her the job of going through albums with Mama Jo and writing down anything she remembered. I whispered to Chris, "When she goes, no one will know who these people are." We both became quiet. How quickly we fade into obscurity.

I'd get angry when Chris would haul in another box of photos from the garage and start going through it after I'd decided I was done with this project. Then she'd start laughing over something she'd found, and I'd easily get sucked into sorting through another box.

We didn't see much of James. He'd crossed over into the monosyllabic world of adolescence and only cared about his friends, basketball, and girls. That little boy I'd had so much fun with in New York when he visited me had vanished. Maybe he'd come back later in life, the way I recognized the adult Arthur in the photographic-boy version.

There were countless boxes left to go through, but some other time. My screening duties were over, and I'd rather watch a Tyler Perry DVD with Mama Jo. After Tyler, we had a Vince Vaughn–a-Thon. Then it was Jim Carrey's work between episodes of *Queer Eye for the Straight Guy* and *Dancing with the Stars*.

I'd cringe when the *F* word was used too much in a movie and ask her if she'd like to watch something else.

"No," she said, "but when did that word become so popular?" She surprised me when she added, "Granny liked to use it, too. Florence was partial to 'shit.'"

I looked at a framed photo of them that was sitting on one of Mama Jo's bedroom shelves, started laughing, and she joined in. Yes, it was just the two of us having a nonstop slumber party. That is, the two of us plus the Grim Reaper standing in the shadows.

When the RiverRun Festival came around, we sat in the front row, she in her wheelchair, for a documentary called *Facing the Audience*. It was about the artist Marshall Arisman, who grew up in Lily Dale, New York, a community of psychics and spiritualists. He could see auras and often painted them around his subjects. When the film was over, Mr. Arisman appeared for a Q&A session. I could have sworn he was flirting with me as he kept glancing in my direction and smiling. I was flattered. When the questions were over, he walked straight over to Mama Jo. It turned out he was admiring her aura, not me at all. "It's the biggest one here," he said. "It fills up the entire room!"

Then I got it. I was living with my very own little Buddha.

She would claim her only resemblance to him was her belly. What I saw was a joyful person who greeted everyone with an all-knowing grin, made pithy remarks, and was happily served by others. Occasionally, someone would make a comment to me about how I was earning a halo or angel wings by taking care of my mother, as though it were an unpleasant obligation. It felt strange to hear that. I didn't deserve any special recognition. I *enjoyed* doing this. It was an honor.

They weren't stuffed animals to Mama Jo.
They were real. And each one needed a buddy.

26

Old Friends, Old Issues

"What do you mean, I cain't throw out this old panty-liner wrapper?" I heard Annie rasp to Mama Jo. "What are you gonna do with it?"

She growled back, "I don't want you throwing it out! It's not yours. It's *mine*."

I sprinted out of my home office and headed downstairs to my mother's bedroom. How was I going to negotiate this flare-up? My mother was about to go on a trip with her friend Ginny to the UFDC summer convention. This annual gathering of doll fanatics was not only a favorite of theirs, but it was going to be held in her hometown of Kansas City, Missouri. Since my mother refused to fly, Ginny gladly offered to drive down from Richmond, pick her up, and drive out and back. All I had to do was get Mama Jo packed. I dreaded doing it so much that I'd brought in Annie to help.

"What's the problem?" I asked.

"I'm just tryin' to clean out the junk in her suitcase, and she won't let me!"

"I can do it myself!" my mother said.

Annie went on as she looked in the suitcase. "Gum wrappers with no gum in them! Old toothpicks with lint on them! Napkins! Packets of sugar!"

"I have a solution," I said and left the room for a moment. I returned with a plastic garbage bag. "Put everything in here and *don't* throw it out. We'll put it in your closet, Mama Jo, where you can look through it anytime you want. Annie's just trying to get you packed so you can go on your trip with Ginny."

"I don't need any help."

I exchanged a look with Annie. Turning back to Mama Jo, I said, "Okay, we'll let you do it then." I nodded for Annie to follow me out of the room and closed the door behind me.

"Thanks for trying," I said. "I'll just tell Ginny to factor in time to get her packed the night before they leave. She has a special touch with my mother."

"Well, of all the dern things," Annie said. "Now I see what you've been talking about. You know, how she was before she got here."

I thought about joining Mama Jo and Ginny on their road trip, or flying out for part of the convention, but I decided to stay home, enjoy my ten days of freedom, and let them have some one-on-one time. It could well be their last excursion.

When I watched them pull out of the driveway in Ginny's car stuffed with Mama Jo's wheelchair and their suitcases, I felt as melancholy as if my last child had flown the coop.

I thought about inviting Kyle over, or a hot young film student I met through RiverRun, or going to see my New York friends. I looked at my trees to see if any of them needed Forrest's attention. Maybe I could convince him to take me to a NASCAR race? No, no, no.

I scanned the boxes of personal stuff that remained for me to go through and couldn't face it. It was too mentally and physically draining. In the end I just chilled out, watched RiverRun screeners that were coming in for the following year's festival, and tried not to see myself one day filling out the comment forms without Mama Jo's input.

There was a moment of alarm when Ginny called from the road and reported that Mama Jo had left her purse in a restaurant where they'd dined and didn't realize it until they were a hundred miles away. "I called them and they had it," she said. "Your mother said it was an old purse and they could keep it and just send back the wallet."

"That purse is brand-new," I said. It had taken us quite some time to find one in a color she liked that was a size she liked and had a strap the right length. "I'll call them and handle it. She'll need it in Kansas City."

I barely heard a word from them while they were away. The few times we did speak, they sounded like they were having a grand old time. But when they returned to North Carolina, I could tell something wasn't right. Did they have a fight?

"It was all gone," Mama Jo wearily stated.

Equally distressed, Ginny explained, "We went to see the house she grew up in, and there was nothing there."

"Nothing," Mama Jo said. "Not even the fire department or grocery store. It was all leveled. Just . . . nothing."

I hesitated to say it, but had to. "Are you sure you were in the right place?"

Mama Jo glared at me. "I know where I grew up."

Ginny said, "I triple-checked it."

I imagined how I would feel in her place. It's one thing to return to a former home and see how built up everything is around it, but finding it and your old neighborhood not there at all?

It haunted us for months. Especially her.

Mike was still sending sweet, breezy e-mails about the weather, family news, and home repairs. From the number of times he said, *It isn't the same without your mom next door* or described her as *special*, I knew there was more going on beneath the surface.

I would read his e-mails to Mama Jo while she listened closely. "Would you like to dictate a response back?" I'd ask. Almost every time she replied, "Just tell him he's the best neighbor I ever had."

In one e-mail he mentioned he'd lost more than twenty pounds, and I was envious. He said he put on his tuxedo for a special dinner at the Elks Lodge, and it didn't fit. He wrote, *I had to buy another pair of pants and tack them up at the last minute.*

Mama Jo grinned. "I bet I wouldn't recognize him now."

One morning, I came into Mama Jo's room smiling and waving a piece of paper while she enjoyed yet another breakfast off Granny's bed tray. "Mike sent an e-mail saying he'd like to come down to visit!"

"He probably just wants to tell me he's getting married."

I had no idea what Mike did in his personal life, but from what I saw when I was cleaning out Mama Jo's house, it didn't appear to be much outside of his family. "I seriously doubt that's the reason, Mama Jo."

"I always assume the worst."

A month later, my heart nearly stopped when he wrote: *How do you think your mother would feel if I came down, picked her up, and brought her back here for a week?*

I read it to her with unabashed glee. "He misses you!"

She was stunned. "Are you sure that invitation isn't to you?"

I held her hand and tried not to get choked up. "Mama Jo, I love living here with you, but if you want to be with Mike, that's fine with me. I want you to be happy."

She gave me a skeptical look. "I don't think I'm going anywhere."

Mike did come through with his offer, and when they finally drove off in his old Caddy, I think I was more nervous than Mama Jo was. Again I fell into a state of loving my freedom but not feeling right without her.

I called a couple of times, and Mike reported where they'd had dinner or what they'd watched on TV. When Mama Jo got on the phone, she was appropriately vague as well. One of his sons was living with him, so I didn't think too much was going to happen. I wondered what she was feeling, what Mike was feeling, and what the son was thinking.

They returned a week later. All was nice and polite as he peppered his speech with "Gosh" and "Oh, boy" as usual. He was staying the night in my guest room, and after he retired I gave Mama Jo a shower that I knew she needed. Sound can travel in strange ways in a house, so I didn't press her about the visit.

The next day, as they hugged good-bye, the full force of their complicated relationship hit me. I was sure we were all wondering if they'd ever embrace again.

"Let's have a cup of tea," I said to Mama Jo after he left.

We sat at the dining table with my cup steaming and hers lukewarm. I waited for her to speak. She gazed into the backyard, lost in thought.

Eventually, I said, "Mike looks good after losing some weight, doesn't he?"

"He's getting younger, and I'm getting older," she said. "I'll never see him again."

As I fought back tears I managed to say, "Do you really think that?"

"Unless he's coming to see you." She focused on a bright-red cardinal pecking at bread crumbs that I'd put out on the back porch. "I wouldn't mind calling him 'son.'"

I practically ran to the sink so she wouldn't see me cry. As I washed some dishes I was numb from the ultimate sacrifice she had offered me, and the sickening truth about age and attractiveness. Why couldn't she have gotten help for her depression sooner? She had a chance at making a life with a man she dearly cherished.

When I returned to the table, I said, "I have no interest in Mike beyond being a friend, Mama Jo. But that's sweet of you to say."

She barely heard me. "His daughter-in-laws made sure I stayed away from him." There was a hint of anger in her voice.

"What do you mean?"

"When I lived next door, they'd give me dirty looks. You can feel when someone doesn't like you."

I'd never heard this before and wasn't sure what to think. Did they see what I was now dealing with coming their way and resented it? Were they projecting their own fears of dying, or divorcing, and their husbands taking up with another woman? Then it dawned on me that Mike had worked for a publicly traded corporation for most of his life. Maybe he was one of those inconspicuous "millionaires next door" and it was all about money?

I searched for comforting words. Before I could find them, she said, "Whoever said it's better to have loved and lost than to never have loved at all . . ."

"Was wrong?"

"No," she said emphatically and looked me straight in the eye. "They were right."

27

Deviant Behavior

Mama Jo on her eighty-third birthday,
dancing with the drag queen Akasha Diamonds

Mama Jo stared at the plunging blue sequined neckline that belonged to a drag queen named Crystal Frost. "I want your boobs."

Crystal quipped, "EBay, honey, eBay!"

For my mother's eighty-third birthday, we were checking out a monthly fund-raising event called Green Queen Bingo, where glorious drag queens put on a show between rounds of bingo to raise money for the Guilford Green Foundation, a nonprofit organization that gave support to the area's gay and transgender community. It was held in a large space called the Empire Room in downtown Greensboro. All of the dolled-up men in women's clothes were fawning over my mother, who was seated near the stage. At one point they stopped everything, and the entire crowd of four hundred people sang her "Happy Birthday."

Then a gorgeous mocha-skinned diva named Akasha Diamonds somersaulted and flipped through Tony Basil's "Mickey," pulled Mama Jo up out of her seat, and got her dancing, to everyone's delight—especially Mama Jo's.

A reporter for the *Greensboro News-Record* interviewed my mother. "What do you think of all this?" Jeri Rowe asked.

She nodded toward Jessica O'Brien, who was onstage in a hot-pink feathery coat, lip-syncing to Helen Reddy's "I Am Woman," and said, "She's my role model."

Mama Jo and I were still in good spirits from our night out when my brother stopped by the next day. I started up a slide show on my TV of the photos I'd taken. After the fourth shot of a drag queen, he grabbed the remote and turned it off. "I don't want to see this. It's deviant behavior!"

I attacked right back. "Arthur, men have been dressing as women for comic effect for thousands of years! Did you stop your kids from watching *Mrs. Doubtfire*? Or *White Chicks*? And this event was for a good cause!" At least *I* thought it was a good cause. I turned to Mama Jo. "What do you think?"

She diplomatically answered, "I never know what's going to happen when I go out with you."

Arthur left in a huff.

We later made up when he gave it some thought and said, "Tom Hanks got his break dressing as a woman in the sitcom *Bosom Buddies*, didn't he?"

I was greatly relieved, but the presidential election was just weeks away, and homophobia was raging all around me. One of the hot-button topics of the campaign was gay marriage. I found myself reflecting on my own domestic partnership.

I was doing everything for my mother that a spouse would do (outside the bedroom, that is), or, more accurately, a parent, yet I wasn't entitled to any benefits someone in those positions would be given. It would be nice to be able to add her to my medical insurance policy for extra coverage, or receive her Social Security or pension checks for a while after she died to help get my life back on track when this was over. I did have a doll collection I could liquidate, but what about the millions of other people in this situation who aren't left a thing? Even my savvy, cost-cutting brother, an asset to any company, had had a hard time finding another position after he was laid off. Imagine being older and looking for work when you've been out of a "real" job for a few years.

As we sat in Mama Jo's bed watching one political ad after another, I asked her, "Are you a Republican or Democrat?"

She finally said, "I don't remember."

I couldn't believe I didn't know this about my mother. I had made sure she was registered to vote in North Carolina, but her party affiliation wasn't divulged.

We watched the final Kerry-Bush debate on a large screen that had been set up at the Green Bean coffeehouse down the street from where we'd played bingo with the drag queens. They also served wine and beer, and I periodically gave Mama Jo a sip from my glass of Cabernet; just another low-key date with my darling mother.

I was wearing a leopard-print coat and my tight black pants and pointy-toed boots, feeling all "back in the New York groove," as KISS guitarist Ace Frehley once sang. I'd brought Mama Jo's metallic-green walker that doubled as a chair since I wasn't sure how crowded it would be, but there were seats for us and I folded it up.

When the debate was over, there were a few young men hanging out in front of the coffeehouse sporting funny-looking hair and tattoos. I didn't have a problem with them, but thought my mother might. So instead of leaving her there while I brought the car around, I pushed her to it while she sat in her walker facing me and holding her little feet up off the sidewalk. We were in one of the older sections of Greensboro, and some parts of the sidewalks were made of brick. I was chattering on when all of a sudden we hit a bump.

Mama Jo and her walker went reeling over backward.

My screams brought the young men running.

She lay there with her eyes bulging, clasping her chest, trying to catch her breath. "Are you all right?!" I screamed idiotically. Of course she wasn't.

Finally, she got out, "I'm fine."

"Should I call an ambulance?"

A part of me was afraid to move her, but she shook her head. "No, I'll be okay."

I wasn't so sure about that, but my need to believe her won out.

The young men carefully helped her into the car. Nothing *seemed* to be broken. I asked them where the closest hospital was, and they gave me directions.

Once in the car she gasped, "I think I'm going to throw up."

She didn't, but I almost did.

In the emergency room I was either crying or barking at the people who worked there to help my mother. She was slumped over to the left side. They wouldn't even give her a Tylenol until a doctor saw her.

Finally, she was asked to rate her pain on a scale of 1 to 10. I knew when she said 7 we'd be there all night. I berated myself for not calling an ambulance when she tumbled. She'd be getting faster attention if I had.

I never should have pushed her on that walker.

I never should have had that wine.

It was all my fault. All my fault.

Dammit.

Finally, X-rays were taken. Looking at the side view of my mother's spine was like viewing the cross section of a nautilus shell, it was that curved over. A front view of her entire body showed her head so bowed down, it looked like she was hanging from an invisible noose. This had not been caused by her spill. She'd been living like this for some time. Had it been so gradual that she had adapted without much pain?

We were informed that she had several hairline fractures and a compression fracture. "It'll just take time to heal," said the doctor.

It was six in the morning when we finally made it out of there with prescriptions for Vicodin and physical therapy. As I finished up the paperwork at the front desk, I turned and saw a stack of the latest *Go Triad,* an insert in Thursday's *News-Record* that covered the local arts and entertainment scene and that was also left as a freebie all over the city. On the cover was the drag queen Jessica O'Brien looking fabulous in her feathery pink outfit.

"Look, Mama Jo!" I grabbed one and quickly leafed through it to see the other photos. And there it was, taking up half a page: my mother dancing hand in hand with Akasha Diamonds, her mouth open in childish wonder as wide as was humanly possible.

I showed it off to everyone like a proud mother, and it boosted our morale, but mine was still severely dampened by the fact that she might never dance again, thanks to me.

Mama Jo's recovery was nothing short of astounding. I was sure her physical therapist being a handsome brown-eyed man that she'd do anything for had everything to do with it. He politely let her have her fantasies.

But she was using her walker all the time now, rather than her cane, even around the house.

Holiday greetings, circa 1940

28

Watching a Photograph Slowly Fade

One evening, long after our night out with the drag queens, I found my mother in her bed under one of the family quilts, gazing through her flowered curtains and toward the front yard. She looked like she was about to break into a smile.

"What are you thinking about, Mama Jo?"

"Dancing with a He-bee She-bee."

Not only did I find her term funny, I was pleased that she hadn't forgotten that outrageous event after so much time had passed. Her mind would, however, become scrambled if I left her in assisted living briefly so I could take a break. New surroundings disoriented her. It was another reason not to leave her there. "You have to take care of yourself, too," friends would say. But I worried about my mother even more when I was away from her. Where was the break in that?

Curiously, her night walking, which I'd thought would surely increase, had subsided, but in the time since her fall, her visits to doctors had stepped up. Each trip took at least four hours to deal with, including getting her ready and travel time, but I didn't care. I would pitch a tent in a doctor's office if it meant she would live longer and be healthier. Her bouts of dizziness and nausea had me worried. She'd been through every possible noninvasive diagnostic procedure and medication. Nothing helped.

Her eyesight suddenly worsened. By the time I got her to the right doctor, her dry macular degeneration had turned to the dreaded wet variety. I was shocked at how quickly it happened. There was a way, maybe, to keep it from progressing that involved injecting her with a dye that turned her skin orange for that day, then zapping her eyes with a laser. It would take several visits and many hours each time to go through this process.

I often wondered if I should do nothing and just let nature take its course, similar to the "she's old, let her die" attitude I had sensed from some members of the medical community. I had been outraged when I encountered it. I understood their position better when I overheard a woman at my gym who was a nurse say, "I can't believe what children put their elderly parents through to keep them alive. Surgery after surgery. It turns my stomach." It didn't make it easier to accept. I saw the children's view, too.

I hadn't subjected Mama Jo to anything that required anesthesia or hospitalization yet, but I was obsessing over her health, taking her to specialists when anything seemed wrong, urging her aides to lead her through a few physical therapy exercises. I was using them more since the day I came home from doing errands and found Mama Jo on the floor, unable to get up. She had tried to go to the bathroom on her own and had fallen. She was wearing the Response Link, but never used it.

Her lack of injury encouraged me to continue to believe she was going to be around for years until the day I took her to our local Great Clips for a perm and haircut. We ran into someone who hadn't seen her in a long time, and in a lowered voice he said, "I can't believe how much your mother has declined."

It ripped a hole clear through my heart. He was right. It was like watching a photograph slowly fade. She was paler, more hunched over, more easily winded when she walked, eating less, sleeping more. She could no longer stand on her toes and watch the bluebirds feeding their young in the birdhouse outside the kitchen window. Our outings had decreased. I said to myself they were too taxing on her, but I was slowing down, too.

"Are we putting up a Christmas tree this year?" Mama Jo asked when Thanksgiving rolled around.

I groaned and was sorry I did.

The first year we lived together, after uncovering the ornaments of my childhood, I had effortlessly lassoed people to help me move furniture, get the tree in the house, string the lights, and do it all in reverse a month later. Now I was weary of cajoling or hiring people to help me out. Arthur and Janet had bronchitis, and the idea of directing my inexperienced niece and nephew as to what to do made me more exhausted. I'd stopped wrapping presents for Mama Jo because it was too hard for her to unwrap them. Instead, I just put them in a decorative bag with colorful tissue paper. Now I was doing that for everyone's presents because it made life easier on me.

The next time she asked me about a tree, I said, "Let me just finish with the Christmas shopping and cards." I had a long list of my friends, her friends, business associates, family, and extended family to honor in one form or another.

The third time she asked, I said, "I'm too tired, Mama Jo. We'll do it next year. I promise." I told myself, *She'll be here then. She will.* I placed a small artificial tree on a table that had white lights and Aunt Gladys's wax cherubs on it. "How's that?"

"That's fine," she said with a weak smile.

I never stopped to think how it made her feel to know there was nothing she could do to make that tree happen. Or how watching me do everything was probably tiring her out as much as it was me, maybe even more so.

Three times she asked.

"Hey," I said cheerily one day, "let's go to the Festival of Lights, Mama Jo! Let's have an adventure!"

She smiled. "Okay!"

This was an annual event Arthur had suggested as an enticement for me to come down for the holidays many years before, and I'd had no interest. Now I'd be happy to do it with my mother. I invited her granddaughter to join us.

On our way there, we turned on the radio station playing continuous holiday music and sang along, easily falling into the Christmas spirit. When we saw the entrance to Tanglewood Park lit up like the Vegas Strip with a grand archway inviting us to drive under it, we all let out a "Wow!" I hoped it made up for the lack of Christmas cheer at home.

We slowly drove through the park in Mama Jo's red wagon, oohing and aahing at more than a hundred displays and nearly a million lights. Even with my mother's failing eyesight she was able to make out most of the mammoth animals, stars, and Santas that blinked and moved. Sometimes she was mistaken. "Is that a cat?" she asked.

Chris, thinking it was funny, said, "No, Mama Jo! That's a snowman!" I turned around to give her a nasty look and then did the same thing myself a few minutes later when she thought Santa and his reindeer was a train. She stopped making comments, and I felt bad. What was wrong with letting her think it was a train? I described the things we saw and tried not to choke up over her loss of vision.

I also found myself imagining the army of people it took to put up these lights and how they would feel when it was time to tear them down. I could at least put up one tree.

We stopped at the Gift Village, and I waited in the car with Mama Jo while Chris went in to investigate. As the Christmas music continued, I held my mother's hand, which was in a pink glove that matched her beret. We sang along to "Walkin' in a Winter Wonderland" and other holiday favorites, her soft voice giving out at the end of most lines.

When it was my turn to gift shop, I zipped through and returned with a few things, including something I'd been on the lookout for for months: a slim wooden table that was the perfect size and color for my brother's guest bathroom. At last, when Mama Jo visited there she'd have something to grab onto. Even though someone was always at her side, the instability of the situation unnerved her.

I wedged the gifts into the back of the car around Mama Jo's wheelchair, and excitedly told her about the table as we pulled out of the space. I reached for her hand and gave her a reassuring squeeze before we went off to cruise through the rest of the park and ooh and aah some more.

The table would never make it to Arthur's house.

The last additions to the collection: the Mama Jo Alaska "Barbie" and the DJ Jo "Barbie"

29

A Tough Little Cuss

The next day, I brought her a container of banana yogurt and a small antique spoon that belonged to her mother, and left her to watch the Animal Planet channel. When I checked on her later she was slumped over to her left. The yogurt had spilled onto the front of her pink pajamas. At first I thought she'd had a stroke and rushed to her, alarmed.

She popped up with a startled "Huh?"

"Do you feel all right?" I asked as I lifted the container off her and looked for a tissue to wipe away the yogurt.

"I guess I dozed off," she said. Noticing what I was doing, she added, "I'm sorry."

"Don't be. You just fell asleep." I dabbed at the stain on her top, concluded she seemed fine, and didn't think much of it.

The following day I brought her yogurt on Granny's tray so she could set it down between spoonfuls. When I returned, she was slumped over again, the yogurt down her front.

Now I was concerned. Not only was something not right, but I couldn't leave her to feed herself anymore. This would be a huge change for both of us. I hoped it wasn't permanent.

When I helped her to the bathroom that night, before tucking her in with her childhood teddy bear, she seemed wobblier and more out of breath than usual and barely made it there and back. The next morning when I came in to help her, she carefully slid off her bed, but when her feet touched the floor she began shaking so violently, I thought she was going to collapse.

"What's wrong, Mama Jo?"

She looked terrified. "I can't walk!"

"Of course you can," I said as if she were speaking nonsense. I reached for the walker that was close by while holding on to her for dear life.

She really couldn't walk.

She was shaking, panting, grasping my arm. She only weighed a hundred pounds but I struggled to get her back up on the bed. Why did this beloved bed have to be so high? It wasn't that long ago that she could step on the footstool and push herself up on the mattress easily and scoot back.

I begged her doctor to make a house call. He showed up that evening. After taking her vitals and trying to get her to walk, he said in his friendly way, "I'll put you on oxygen for a few days. Your levels drop when you exert yourself." As he left, he said to me with a reassuring smile, "I think you'll see a big difference."

The oxygen didn't help.

She was tested her for a urinary tract infection. She didn't have one.

The dosage of her Zoloft was increased. That didn't help either.

Suzie showed up to care for her and when her shift was over said to me confidentially with tears in her eyes, "I know I shouldn't be saying this, but I don't think she's going to make it to the New Year."

I think my heart momentarily stopped. That was only two weeks away.

Annie—who was now fifty pounds lighter, retired from the hospital, recovered from a hip replacement, and feeling infinitely better and not quite as cranky—agreed to go through the nursing agency so I could hire her. Her opinion on Mama Jo was, "She has me stumped. If she had cancer or a specific illness, I could tell you how long she got, but she's just *in decline*. I had a woman like that once who lived a few years on three Ensure shakes a day. So could

Mama Jo. She's a tough little cuss. Those are the ones that hang on the longest."

I was thrilled to hear this and bought a few cases of Ensure fortified liquid meals and turned them into milkshakes by adding ice cream and flavored syrup. Mama Jo loved them.

But she didn't get better. Two days before Christmas, she was officially in home hospice care.

The gruesome reality of what was happening would hit me every day. There was Annie telling me, "You better get that DNR sign posted for your mother!" That was the Do Not Resuscitate order. "They'll intubate her and be pushin' on her chest until she's all red! You'll be furious."

One of the hospice nurses calmly relayed to me the statistical evidence as to why performing an operation on my mother so she could get nourishment through a feeding tube should she stop eating was not a good idea. She stated the odds that she would die from the procedure, and the short time it might prolong her life if she did live through it. She also told me, "Starvation is one of the most peaceful and painless ways to go. The body creates its own morphine."

The hospice people in general were so warm and calm, it was almost chilling. I wondered how they could be so detached. When one became choked up talking about the loss of a favorite uncle, I felt better. She was the one that was part therapist, part docent of death, and focused more on me than my mother. She surprised me when she said, "I feel such a peace when I come here. It's very unusual."

I asked her, "What does it usually feel like?"

"A lot of tension. Family members tend to be more focused on the, um, practical matters." In other words, who's getting what. Thankfully, that had already been worked out. And all that was really left were the dolls.

I often teared up when talking to this woman, even when she said, "You're giving your mother some of the best care I've ever seen." Despite all I did for her at the end of her life, I still wished I'd done more. I should have given her her showers. I should have put up a Christmas tree. Most of all, I should have made this move down here a lot sooner.

I could hear Aunt Julie saying, "Don't shoulda on yourself."

Mama Jo's friend Ginny wisely gently said, "She wouldn't have let you help her before. You both had to be ready, not just you."

We both had to surrender.

My New York pal Meg said, "I've been through this with two aunts. Trust me, by the time it's over you'll be so happy she's out of her pain." Thinking about my mother in any pain at all made me feel worse.

In a soothing southern voice, the woman from hospice told me I was experiencing "anticipatory grief" and that it came from not knowing what was going to happen, how it was going to happen, or when it was going to happen, and feeling helpless and confused about what to do in the meantime. "Many people," she said, "say that this part was worse than the loss itself. They often speak of an enormous relief when it's over."

I doubted that would be the case. Mama Jo wasn't just my mother. She was now my best friend, my ideal roommate, and, most of all, the child I had so longed for. I remembered Charlotte's words of grief when Julie passed: "I've lost my job." Mama Jo was that, too.

I felt like my life was ending as well.

Offsetting these heart-wrenching moments were the comedic ones Annie brought with her on every visit. A hard-core Tar Heels fan, she was fuming over the *News-Record*'s constant coverage of Duke's star basketball player J. J. Redick and even scrawled mean remarks over his photo. One morning she marched in, called the newspaper, and asked whoever answered to connect her to "the person that keeps writin' these dad-blamed stories about Redick." She yelled at the man who took her call: "I just wanna know one thing! Are you his *significant other?*"

We laughed again when Annie complained about a woman who was envious of her when she was taking care of her husband. "He was eighty-six, blind, diabetic, and broke. Now, who would want him?"

She still loved to pick on my fancy New York ways. When the hospice nurse asked me what my mother ate, Annie didn't hesitate to complain about my cooking. "She gave me this chicken soup that had so much lemon in it I couldn't eat it! I tried everything to fix it. Salt, pepper, waterin' it down . . ."

"Annie," I said, bemused, "it's called Greek *lemon* chicken soup. You're supposed to taste the lemon."

"Well, you can have it. And what was that thing you cooked the other day? Looked like a white carrot."

"Parsnips."

"Parsnips! Ever hear of such a thing? And the worst of all is the *goat* cheese. Now who on earth eats that?"

"People who shop at *Wal-Mart*, where I found it."

"Go on! I ain't never seen it there!"

The nurse directed her attention back to me. "So what does your mother like to eat?"

I ran down a list of things, and when I said grilled cheese sandwiches her head popped up. "With goat cheese?" she asked, clearly appalled.

"No! Cheddar."

What was I going to do when Mama Jo was gone? I still felt like an outsider here, but where else could I go? I was now spoiled by the lower costs and less stressful way of life here—outside of the rabid animals, that is.

Mama Jo was now in a hospital bed because it was closer to the ground, making it easier to get her in and out of it. It could also be adjusted to various positions. Her antique bed had been pushed against the wall where the windows were. I slept in it every night, often waking up and creeping over to her side to make sure she was still breathing. If her soft plastic nasal tube that delivered a constant stream of oxygen to her had fallen out of her little nose, I gently put it back in. If she woke up, I'd turn her so she wouldn't get bedsores. I had to do it in a special way by pulling the large pad that was underneath her since she didn't have the strength to turn on her own.

When everyone was gone, I kept waiting for her to impart some final words of wisdom to me, or one last confession. Nothing came. I told myself she had said everything she needed to say to me, but I still wanted more.

She was lucid most of the time, but occasionally mentioned wanting to go home to see Florence and Granny. I wanted to tell her in a reassuring voice that she'd see them soon, that I was ready to let her go, but I couldn't have uttered the words even if I'd had the courage to say them. More often than not, when I looked at my mother, my throat was closed as tight as a vacuum-sealed lid on a jar.

During the day, Annie would sit with her and watch TV while I worked upstairs. Ever since the beginning of the year, I'd been inundated with voice-over jobs that I forced myself to get through. It was much-needed income and took my mind off what was going on downstairs with Mama Jo.

One day, during a break, I was watching an Animal Planet show with Mama Jo and Annie when a commercial came on pitching an insurance policy that would pay your funeral expenses.

Annie said, "That policy will never cover the funeral I want. Don't ask me why, but I want to be buried in a mausoleum, not stuck in the cold ground. I seen one with a carpeted floor that was *only* nine thousand dollars!"

I saw the chance to bring up a subject I'd avoided discussing with Mama Jo. "I do *not* want to be cremated," I said. "It just gives me the willies to think about being burned up. What about you, Mama Jo?"

She said, "Just do whatever's the cheapest."

I looked at Annie and then back at Mama Jo, and said to my mother, "That means being cremated. Are you sure that's what you want?"

"No. I don't want that."

That night her oxygen tube was out again, and I became angry with her for removing it. Then I was sobbing. "You have to keep it in or you'll die! I don't want you to die! I love you so much! Don't you know how much this upsets me? I love you!"

She was leaning over to the left, as she was prone to do, and said quietly, "Now you know how I feel about you."

I told myself to stop thinking of my pain, to think of hers. My tears could only be making her feel worse. When I calmed down, she said, "I want to say a prayer to Florence."

All I could do was respond with a sniffle as I dabbed at my eyes.

"I want her to be proud that I'm her daughter."

"Of course she's proud of you," I said softly.

"Most of my family is in heaven now. I have a good family."

"And we all love you very much."

"I love you, my beautiful daughter."

I'm sobbing again. Why do I react this way? I'm like a little girl who's lost her mother in a department store. Maybe I was the kid all along, not Mama Jo. How wrong I was to think I was the one more competent and in control. I had no memory of ever seeing my mother cry. The most I'd ever witnessed were her eyes turning bloodshot and moist, as they were now. Even her sadness was delicate, an inward doll-like cry.

Later, I read a story in the paper about a local woman who transformed Barbie dolls, or her clones, to look like their owner. Many brides-to-be hired her to make one wearing a miniature version of their wedding gowns. At first the madness of it made me groan, and then I succumbed to it.

I sent her photos of myself in my "Rock and Roll Madame" DJ days and Mama Jo in her Alaska fringed-leather-jacket period. I was sure the dolls would delight my mother. I also found it ironic that the last dolls I would add to the collection were not just Barbies, a doll I used to hate, but that we were merging our identities with hers.

Mama Jo's reaction to our very own Mini-Me's was a heart-melting smile and "I'll be darned." But her interest was fleeting. Between that and her turning down my fresh-baked cookies, I knew this was really the end.

My mother, late 1920s, on her horse that flew across the backyard

30

The Utmost Grace

I met with a funeral home director, and we put together a slide show of Mama Jo's life that would be shown at her memorial service. I feared I'd be far too distraught to do this when she actually passed. The fact that he was a laid-back Jimmy Buffet fan who proudly referred to himself as a Parrothead made it much easier to get through.

The song I chose to accompany her life in photographs was "His Eye Is on the Sparrow," sung by Carmen McRae. After I completed this project, *The Hour of Power* offered a small jewelry box that played this very song. Of course I now own it.

For Valentine's Day I showed Mama Jo the slide show of her life, telling her it was a gift of love that I'd made for her. I wasn't sure if it was maudlin and might even upset her, but concluded that I'd enjoy seeing something like that, or at least I imagined I would, if I were in her place. I really didn't know if it was the right thing to do. "That was nice," she said with a smile when it was over. "I wish I had something for you."

"Mama Jo, you've given me three wonderful years with you. That's the best present of all." I listed the many things we did together and all the fun we had. She just smiled, especially when I mentioned, "watching you dance with a He-bee She-bee."

When I drove in her car and thought about her never sitting next to me again while singing along to the big-band station or bopping her beret-covered head to a pop hit, I'd lose it. I thought of how calm she seemed in the face of death. If I could go out of this world with one-tenth of her grace, I'd be happy.

A hospice worker told me that people with a strong faith usually have a peaceful passing. It was those who had not reached a resolution about their lives and beliefs who become agitated at the end. Though I was more religious than when I arrived here, I was sure that the cause of my demise would be human error or a technical malfunction, like a pacemaker being put in upside down. My last statement would probably be "Dammit!" or "I smell f#&k up."

Ginny came for a quick visit, and so did Akasha Diamonds, sans drag. He brought Mama Jo a fiber-optic angel that changed colors and added the perfect magical touch to her bedroom.

Mike kept saying he would make it down, but one thing after another prevented him, from unexpected houseguests to a case of hives he said he'd had only one other time in his life—when he put his wife in a nursing home. A part of me was sad, for I was sure she'd go before he arrived. Then I'd think it was for the best. Mama Jo was undoubtedly crossing over to the other side. She could only eat with a plastic spoon now. Metal utensils tasted funny to her.

My confusion was relentless. I didn't know what to ask, what not to ask. What she wanted to hear, or didn't want to hear. If I did screw up the courage to say something like "Mike is going to come see you," she stared at me with a half-smile and said nothing.

A hospice worker confirmed what I had heard about a dying person hanging on until they saw a particular individual they loved. I hoped my telling Mama Jo he was coming would keep her alive a little longer.

He finally made it. His visit was short and predictably heartbreaking for him and me, but my mother handled it beautifully and smiled throughout it and after. And she wasn't on morphine or any painkiller, either.

A few days later, as a new pair of bluebirds nested in the box outside the kitchen window, and there were enough tulips in bloom in the yard to make a nice bouquet, Mama Jo was still in a state of utmost grace and humor. When the hospice nurse asked her that morning how she felt, she quipped, "With my hands."

She was barely eating. We managed to get a few spoonfuls of yogurt in her and a couple of sips of an Ensure shake, but as the day drew to a close I could tell something was very wrong. She was slumped over even more to the left, her skin tone was changing color, and she could only take short, shallow breaths as her teddy bear lay on the pillow behind her, one arm outstretched and touching her back. Her eyes were open and moving back and forth. She looked at me as though she wanted to speak, wanted to be alive, but she just couldn't do it anymore. Or was she talking to Florence and Granny? Was she oblivious of me?

I called the hospice nurse on duty. She said she'd be right over. I popped an Ativan. I may have taken two. I'm told the family gathered, but I don't remember much.

I'm holding Mama Jo's small hand. I'm telling myself, *Think of all you were lucky enough to share. She's tired. She's lived a full life. Let her go.*

I can't.

The nurse is on the other side of the bed. Her hand is on my mother's tiny wrist monitoring her pulse. She says, "It won't be much longer."

Before I can ask if that means minutes or hours, she gently says, "She's gone."

My mother and father on a rare trip together, London, 1966

31

Giving Up Dreams

Life has a way of rushing back in when it's been taken off the hold button. The chest-exploding missing–Mama Jo moments I had braced myself for weren't nearly as frequent as I had expected. It wasn't just from having a lot of work and postmortem tediocity to occupy my thoughts; I also felt released from the burden of worrying about her. I had been doing it for most of my life. That's not to say I didn't miss her. I did, and will, for every day that I'm alive.

I said to close friends who inquired as to how I was doing, "It's like I've been on a long, beautiful hike up a mountain. I had no idea how heavy my backpack was until I took it off." Of course, a few said, "I can't imagine *you* hiking."

Bob Dylan was right:

What looks large from a distance,
Close up ain't never that big.

There's nothing like a crisis to pull people together. There's nothing like a crisis to pull them apart. No doubt part of the success of our outcome came from the unusual circumstances that led my mother and me to give up our former lives and create a new one together. Zoloft, Aricept, and Ativan were indispensable. Despite my initial cynicism, keeping the faith in a higher power was key. And the fact that my mother's condition wasn't nearly as bad as it could have been until the very end was a tremendous blessing. But what if I'd never taken the chance to find out if it could have worked? I would never have known how wonderful my mother was. I would never have grown in the ways I needed to.

Now it was time to move on, starting with where I would call home.

A brief trip to New York filled me with so much energy, and appreciation for my friends and the octogenarian Charlotte, that I felt a strong pull to move back there. I also felt like I belonged in North Carolina. I even found my own Pilates Mafia. Sometimes I was right back in New York when clients driving Jaguars and Mercedes talked about their trips abroad. Other times the conversations were unlike anything I'd ever heard up north, and I loved it.

Woman 1: We never used hormones on our livestock when I was growing up. Daddy just put a rubber band around their testicles so they wouldn't run around so much, and that fattened 'em up.

Woman 2: And then they'd dry up, fall off, and you'd eat 'em, right? Mountain oysters, we called them.

I found a yoga class, too, but it was held at a gym inside a megachurch. The instructor would say things like, "Next is the Chaturanga Dandasana position" while we listened to Christian rock music.

My local shopping center now had a bistro in the capable hands of a Frenchman who made authentic, delicious croissants. Other businesses there were run by East Indians, Chinese, Mexicans, Koreans, Vietnamese, Italians, and Kazakhstanis. I wasn't in *quite* such "good ole boy" country anymore.

I especially loved my frequent visits with Arthur and his family, and the ways we helped each other out. Each time my brother and I shared a memory from the past, it was like examining a tiny tile from a mosaic that formed a portrait of a unique family that I could now lovingly appreciate. Janet, too. "I never hear these stories from him," she said to me. "They only come out when you two are together."

Unbelievably, I couldn't bring myself to sell the dolls. They were Mama Jo's legacy. I would tap into my IRA, if I had to, before selling those little people staring into space. That, quite simply, is deranged. Go ahead. Call me Norma Bates. I didn't want to sell the house either. It was *our* legacy and filled with wonderful memories.

The only decision I made about my future was to not make any decisions for a year.

When a neighborhood yard sale was announced, I found renewed strength to go through twenty-two trunks in the garage and additional boxes throughout the house. It forced me to reflect on my relationship with material objects. They trapped me and at the same time comforted me. I could easily discard some things, but was unable to let go of items like a ruler that had the name of the secretarial school my mother attended, or an old pay stub of hers. I didn't want to turn into a hoarder like Mama Jo, but it was much harder to let go of things than it had been for me in the past.

There were fleeting moments when I wanted to give the heave-ho to everything. I almost threw out a cardboard box without looking through it, changed my mind, and angrily tore it open. I was not ready for what I found.

My first discovery was a stack of typed letters addressed to my grandmother Florence from the mysterious married oral surgeon. They spanned the time he was stationed in another city in the early 1940s. Ah! He was after Florence, my reticent grandmother who was widowed at age twenty-nine, reportedly never looked at another man, and had the curious habit of not saying good-bye when a phone call was over. She just hung up on the person. With her hair in a tight bun, clunky black shoes, and long, loose, handmade dresses, even in her thirties she looked like a matron in her sixties. Florence had a lover!

He signed each one "Always with deepest love," but that was as mushy as he got. There was a mention here and there of things that they had done together in the past, such as a movie they had seen. Either this was one exquisitely sublimated romance, or he was being smartly discreet. How far had they gone? Had it ended at smoldering glances and tortuous, chaste good-byes? Or one passionate kiss and then her pushing him away? Did it escalate further? Florence with any man was unthinkable, but a married one?

Wait. He mentioned my mother not writing back to him, and he hoped that she wasn't mad at him. He mentioned it again. And again.

It must have been Mama Jo he had fallen for. She worked for him. She was so young, petite, and sweet. How could he not succumb to her charms?

But why did Florence save the letters? Could he have been the only man who ever wrote to her, and she coveted these missives? Did she think one day my mother would want them? Did my mother ask her to save them?

Then I found a carbon copy of my mother's letter to him. It was dated shortly after her twenty-second birthday in 1943 as World War II raged.

As you know, when I first met you, I was very much engrossed in someone back home and had no "serious" eyes for anyone else. Then rather suddenly (or so it seemed to me) that someone gave me the brush off and I couldn't take it. Down I went to the depths of despair, no foolin'. And I got to the point where I didn't care what I did or where I went or what happened to me. Gladly could I just fold up and die, or so I thought. Then you came along—kind, thoughtful, understanding, and comforting, and the type of tall, dark, and handsome fellow that makes so many blonds lose their hearts.

You were something new to me; a kind of person I'd never known before. You had traveled. You had lived and done so many things that to me were just words on a paper. Your gifts to me were of the finest and you made me feel like a queen. You restored my faith in human beings and I am indebted to you for knowledge. There are no more like you and no one can ever take away the part that you have played in my life.

You asked me in your letter if I would have you if you were free. There is only one way that could be accomplished. Having been brought up by a Grandmother with a strict moral code, I must admit I could not marry you because I would feel that I was doing a very great wrong. I don't set myself up as an example of angelic perfection and I don't want to preach, but if you will read the 10th chapter of St. Mark, the 1st and 12th verses, it may help to explain my belief in this matter. I believed this from the first. That's why I tried so hard to put on the brakes when my heart said "let yourself go." Cruel as it may seem, you realize as well as I that not everyone gets to marry the person they love the most.

Everyone's emotions are at a fever pitch nowadays. You want to keep the zest of youth, but can't you realize that life with any one person cannot always be Utopia no matter who they are? Please try to appreciate what you have and give up this dream that is making a mess of your life. It makes me feel wretched to think I am the cause of such unhappiness and I hope you will forgive me. Be man enough to face the truth.

The powers that shape our destinies are bigger than we are, and there must be a purpose for things to happen as they do. That may be Presbyterian predestination but it sounds like pretty good logic to me. We must make the best of our present situations and live for bigger things to come.

After all, when it comes to drawing an exact line between what is right and what is wrong, it is a rather big question for a mere human being to decide. Ask for strength and have faith that you will get it . . . I'll do the same.

May I always be one of your very best friends.

It was the most heartbreaking, eloquent letter I'd ever read. My mother wasn't just an outstanding writer (how I wished she'd written more); she was an incredible human being. Sadly, I had no idea until the very end of her life.

I wondered about the man she had been "engrossed in" back in Kansas City. Was it the Catholic boy she said Florence and Granny didn't approve of? I had tried to find him through the Internet when Mama Jo was still alive. I had thought her mother and grandmother were cruelly narrow-minded. Did he break it off because of them? Did his parents not approve either? Was he simply not in love?

I looked up the Bible passages she referred to on adultery and was struck by the fact that at twenty-two, she refused to break up a marriage. Seven years later, she was married to my father, who was married when they met.

A psychiatrist might say she was drawn to those who were unavailable because her father died when she was a girl. Or was it simply a case of the cliché "the good ones are always taken" being true, and she wasn't going to settle for the young men who took her out on the town? They were her peers. She needed a real man, a smart man like her inventor father had been, someone she could look up to.

Did my father remind her of her forbidden admirer? He, too, had traveled the world. He was older. He was wiser. In his uniform he was dashing, in a tuxedo irresistible. Was her impending thirtieth birthday the catalyst for her not to wait for perfection any longer? How else could she have the daughter she wanted so badly?

With a heavy heart I returned to the box of papers and found a typed letter she had written to my father six months after Arthur was born. The ulcer she'd had in Alaska when I was five had apparently started at least nine years before.

You claim I am childish in stirring up trouble. Maybe it's just an instinctive way of fighting for that which is rightfully mine—a little attention from my husband.

She addressed his concern for his son from his previous marriage, his son's mother, his aging parents, his house, and his work. She felt like "the low man on the totem pole." I could see my father being overwhelmed with all that was on his plate, and was about to take his side as I had always done. Then she said:

Their importance cannot be denied, but I need you, too. And not just the so-called affection you show when you go to bed and my insides are flipping and I'm exhausted and need rest. I need your sympathy and a little understanding now when I'm physically upset and not feeling like myself. After all, did you ever put your arm around my shoulder and say you were kinda glad it happened anyway or that you think it will be sorta nice to have a new inmate at the house? It may be old stuff to you but remember it's a new experience for me and I need a word of encour-

agement now and then, not invitations to leave. You may think your abstract worldly attitude is manly but it puts you on a par with a teenager.

Sizzle now. But then think on these things.—Your wife

I read the letter several times, conjuring up what everyone was feeling at that time, even the infant Arthur. And then I found what I was searching for.

Henrietta—

Your back-scratcher awaits his orders.

—Georgina

It was my father's handwriting. At the bottom was his signature cartoon that depicted his eyes, eyebrows, and several vertical lines for his mustache. Their pet names for each other were derived from his first and middle names. At last a sign of cuckoo love!

There were also letters he had written while on business trips where he outright said he felt sad leaving her, that he missed her "and the BEAST" that I presumed was my toddler brother. And one where he said, "I guess I just love my adenoidal wife." Knowing my mother, she probably found that funny.

A long letter she wrote to Florence from Alaska made me laugh out loud.

Jody's Chatty Cathy [doll] so intrigued her Poppa, he carried it around for a day talking to it.

And again at: *Laundry and K.P. seem to put me in perpetual motion, if you can call the way I move "motion." But who knows, if I'd been dashing around like mad all the time maybe by now I would have high blood pressure or had a heart attack.*

I rolled my eyes as she described scrutinizing her new Peter Playpal, and chuckled when she said I was distressed the dolls were "wardrobe shy." *At $2.98 a dress I wish I could sew and had time.*

I tried to envision her and my father attending the three lectures by the state Department of Fish and Game that she described, especially the part where they showed how to "dress out" a moose. *Either the local orphanage or Native Hospital had some mighty tender meat the next day.*

It was thrilling to find more proof that there was once something special between them, that there was playfulness, a connection, and far more good times than I remembered. I was ecstatic that Mama Jo never threw anything out. I thought I'd never hear myself say that. With all the boxes I still had to go through, I could be finding out new things about her and my family for the rest of my life.

Not all that I unearthed was uplifting. A postcard from my father dated 1966 said: *Had a very interesting scouting expedition re. Fla. homes. Have lots to show & tell.* He signed it with his cartoon. So he thought she was on board with the move to Miami. At what point did he know she wasn't coming? When did she?

I have yet to get to the bottom of the Granny and Pamp story. I found the bill for his Nebraska funeral that had been sent to his daughters, not Granny. The amount was torn out. I spoke to one of Pamp's grandsons who was a genealogy buff. He was extremely curious about him as well, but the trail was cold, other than some vague impression that he may have liked to drink too much. Not a single photo could be found, and his now-deceased mother would never speak about her father.

Pamp was seventeen years older than Granny. I strongly suspect he had another family elsewhere. It would add more ammunition to why Granny was dead set against my mother getting involved with a married man beyond it being wrong in the eyes of God. I have to accept I'll never know the truth and drop it all into a mental folder labeled "Unsolved Mysteries."

It was the Fourth of July weekend following Mama Jo's April funeral. I was standing before my father's "locker" at the Arlington National Cemetery Columbarium. His full military honors funeral with a horse-drawn caisson followed by a marching band and a platoon of crisply turned out soldiers was as vivid in my mind as though it were the day before, not more than two decades earlier. How could I forget the line of young men in uniform firing into the air twenty-one times? Then one went to the caisson and with great pomp retrieved the urn and put it inside its awaiting locker, which was in a wall surrounded by others just like it. I remembered my heart sinking. I was expecting a coffin with six valiant men carrying it on their strong shoulders. This twist seemed an indignant end to an extraordinary life.

But today I felt differently. It didn't matter how he was laid to rest. What counted was who he was when he was alive. True, he had his flaws. I still loved him. I also better understood what my parents saw in each other. They probably found each other very funny, now that I knew my mother's dry wit was every bit as sharp as his. My father was undoubtedly invigorated by my mother's youth and touched by the kindness she bestowed on his son. He probably got off in some nutty way on her childlike qualities, like her obsession with dolls. She saw a handsome, worldly man who understood her sense of humor, was a leader, and had a secure job. Evolutionary biologists, who believe our choices in mates are driven by the desire to procreate up the social food chain, would say she picked a man with the attributes she lacked for her future children's sake. I was glad she did.

I gazed about the expansive, humbling, peaceful Arlington National Cemetery that day and wondered where my final resting place would be. It couldn't be here. I wasn't a veteran. Most likely, I'd be buried in the family plot in Kansas City next to Mama Jo, and, unlike my previous thinking, I was serenely content with that.

While I was in the Washington, D.C., area, I visited two family members I hadn't seen in a very long time. In the course of our chatting I heard a story that, even knowing all that I did about Mama Jo, still shocked me. My relative's wife had once caught my mother and her husband kissing! Mama Jo was forty, he twenty-five. She could laugh about it now, but all I could say was, "I bet the family gatherings were interesting after that."

As I drove back to North Carolina, tuned in to the big-band channel my mother and I loved to listen to, I couldn't get that story out of my mind. What a little minx my mother was! The expression "Still waters run deep" certainly applied to her. She was a housewife during the 1950s and '60s, married to an older man married to his job who didn't light her fire, and she did something about it. She may have been from a completely different generation than I was, but it could be argued she was more liberated for her time.

Perhaps she didn't ask for alimony from my father as an act of defiance and independence rather than her caving in out of weakness and depression. Her new husband had a good job. She didn't need my father's help. Maybe she didn't want her adultery made public. That was highly likely. If my father did step out on my mother, he was in a position to be more discreet about it since he worked far from home and often went on trips for business. She would have a harder time proving it.

My mother's loss of her children was undoubtedly softened by her new younger man who made her feel sexy, was a Mason, accompanied her to Eastern Star activities, and adored her. He gave her what she had ached for throughout her marriage to my father.

Her children had become self-absorbed teens. It was time to let them become who they wanted to be. And at that rebellious age, they needed the firm guidance of their father. Her hands-off approach was not abandonment. She was embroiled in a tortuous struggle of self-realization versus doing what she felt was best for her children, the latter the ultimate act of selfless love.

I wondered if she felt something similar as she was dying. Her frail body was shutting down, and she didn't have the strength to continue. But was she also thinking that I needed to get on with my life? I didn't even have the energy to put a Christmas tree.

Now I could move on, but I wasn't having too much success in that mission. For one, I had zero desire to date. I told myself I was still grieving and to give it time. I also heard a voice in me that sounded a lot like Annie's saying: "You're over fifty, have an unpredictable cash flow, and a room full of dolls. Now, who would want you?"

I finally pulled into my driveway on that languid summer night, glad to be home—until I saw that my garage door was wide open. I drowned out the whirring cicadas with a deep groan and a "NOW WHAT?"

It turned out that while I was in D.C., lightning had struck a nearby tree, skipped over, and blew out the garage door opener. That was the only damage: a tree and the garage. Of course, I would have to call Forrest and Kyle to rectify the situation. Now what were the odds of that happening?!

About the same as the I'm-never-getting-married-again-because-no-woman-has-everything-I'm-looking-for tree man, Forrest, sporting a gold wedding band when he appeared. His explanation was: "Somethin' dropped on my haid."

As for Kyle. Oh, Kyle. Wonderful, lanky Kyle with his sweet, smooth Andy Griffith voice and style. He showed up immediately and gave me the kind of embrace that made me recall with powerful precision what I had seen in him in the first place. Making him look even better was the fact that he had known Mama Jo. He'd given her many hugs. He'd held her hand, helped her into the car, and buckled her seatbelt. He'd laughed at many of her jokes. He understood my loss.

"I'm so sorry," he said soothingly. We kept holding each other. "She was wonderful."

As I fought back tears, I could swear I heard her in heaven saying, "Kick it, dammit!"

Am I still stuck at age fourteen? Well, I'll never stop listening to hit radio. And I do love the reality show *The Bachelor/Bachelorette* (my friends claim it's my only major flaw). Other than that, I've moved into my fifties with a clear conscience, my rough edges smoothed, a wardrobe that isn't all black, and many great years still to come. Every doomed relationship and setback in my past, even not marrying and having children when I wanted to so much, I'm certain were leading me to my extraordinary, irreplaceable Mama Jo—and to my new vibrant life in the South. Had my prayers been answered then, I would have been too tied down to have had this experience, and I don't think I would have been happy. I strongly suspect if you're not right with your mama, you're not going to be right with anyone.

I still adore, and often see, my Yankee friends, who want me to move back permanently. I haven't ruled it out, especially if Charlotte should need me, but I did just switch to using pine needles for mulch. I'm also part of a bunco group that meets every month. Basically, it's a socially acceptable way for women to drink and gamble.

Mama Jo would say I've become geographically bilingual.

But most of all, I think of her. Constantly. When I enter the doll room. When I sleep in the bed where she was conceived. And especially when I pore over the endless photos she took when I was a child. It's as though I can feel what she felt when she snapped the shutter and captured a fleeting moment of innocence that I was oblivious to.

I can still see her tiny frame and how it shook with her silent laugh. I see her wide, happy smile. I remember her soft hand and how it felt in mine. I feel her steadfast love that was so sweet and pure at the end of her life. I expect I'll feel it even more at the end of mine.

"I have a good family," she said when she knew she was dying.

I have a good family, too. And it was there all along.

Me, my father and brother, 1960.

Shout Outs

Though they're unfortunately no longer here to read this, I'd like to thank my father, who instilled in me the love of storytelling, whether it was one of his own tales or a classic he read to me while doing the voices of all the characters, and my mother, whose eye for detail I never fully appreciated until I became a writer.

A heartfelt thank-you to my loyal volunteer test readers: Jill Brooke, Meg Busch, Anna Ladd, Jean Nayar, Tara Owen, Michele van Grondelle, and the "pros" Richard Goodman, John Paine, and Charles Salzberg. Also, the incomparable and linguistically "particularest" Peter Brunette; my outstanding agent, Kevan Lyon; everyone I've worked with at Da Capo; and, above all, Renée "Hoo Boss" Sedliar, who took this book to a whole other level. Ron Rinaldi, Terry Gilbert, and Doug Rice/Allure Photography: thank you for your photographic expertise. A "bonjour y'all" to Julien and his crew for delicious sustenance, and just enough caffeine, to get me through this. Jerome, you've been an indestructible source of wisdom and humor, and I can't leave out that scoundrel Stan Pottinger who "outed" me as a writer.

My deepest gratitude goes to my family and extended family, my mother's aides, and "Mike," "Ginny," and "Kyle." I sincerely hope that you don't clam up around me from now on. I would also like to thank the vivacious Janet. If you hadn't married my brother, and opened up your heart to Mama Jo and me as well, there'd be no story to tell.

Excellent elder-care resources are: the Jane Gross *New York Times* blog "The New Old Age" (*www.nytimes.com*), the AARP (*www.aarp.org*), and the National Family Caregivers Association (*www.thefamilycaregiver.org*). To enlighten all ages on what it feels like to grow old, take part in a Macklin Intergenerational Institute "Xtreme Aging" workshop (*www.mackliniginstitute.org*). You can also go to my Web site for info and links, and to soak up more of the inimitable Mama Jo: *www.jomaeder.com*.

And finally, I'd like to give encouragement to anyone caring for an elderly loved one. Whether in-home or not, it's never easy. If you're merely a bystander in such a case, offer your help in any way that you can. All gestures, no matter how small, are appreciated. A world that embraces compassionate care of their elderly is a better world in general.